W9-AOK-354

SUPERMAN

VOL. 1 THE UNITY SAGA: PHANTOM EARTH

SUPERMAN

VOL. 1 THE UNITY SAGA: PHANTOM EARTH

BRIAN MICHAEL BENDIS
writer

IVAN REIS
penciller

JOE PRADO
OCLAIR ALBERT
inkers

ALEX SINCLAIR
colorist

JOSH REED
letterer

IVAN REIS, JOE PRADO & ALEX SINCLAIR
collection cover artists

SUPERMAN created by **JERRY SIEGEL** and **JOE SHUSTER**
SUPERBOY created by **JERRY SIEGEL**
By special arrangement with the Jerry Siegel family

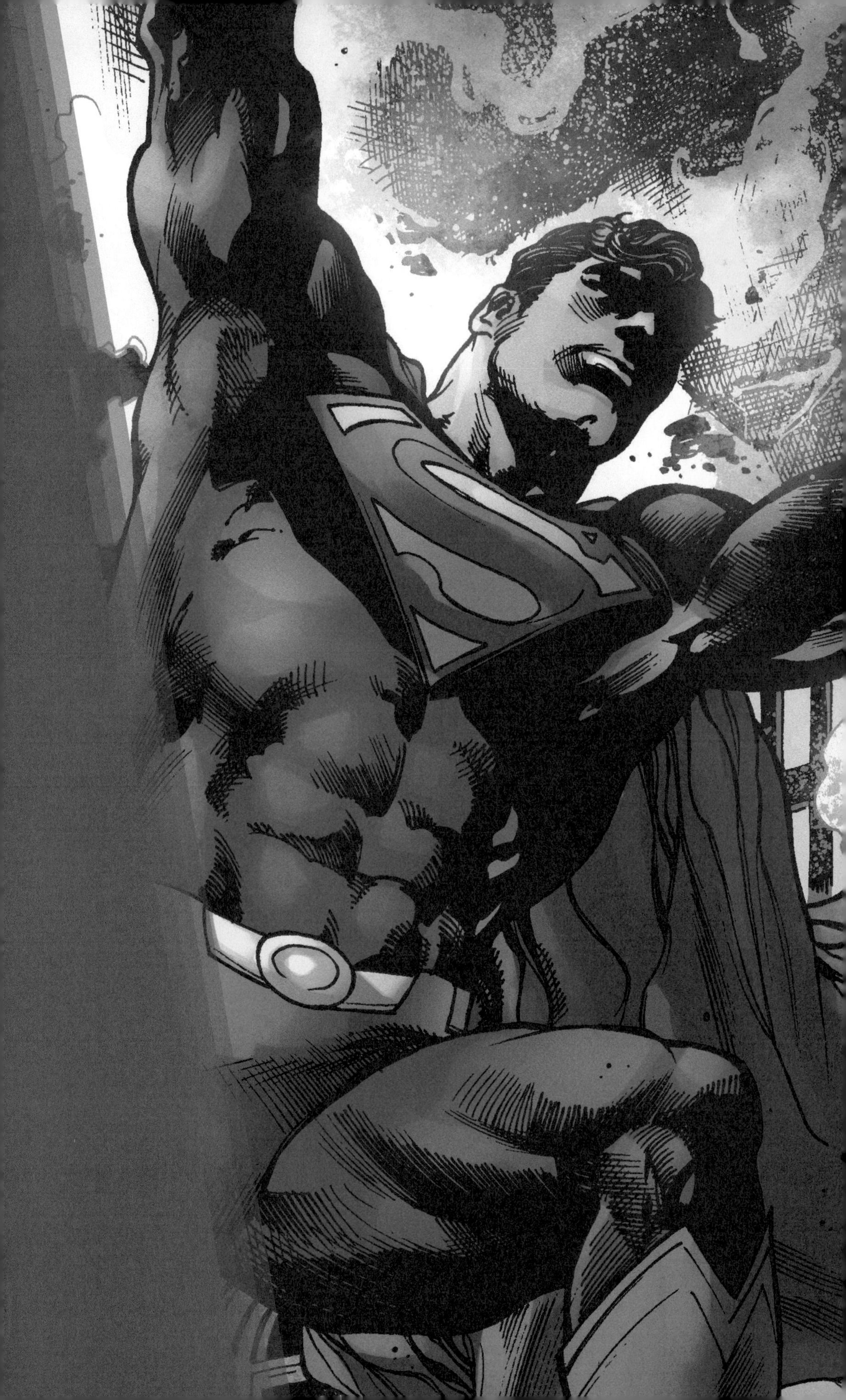

MIKE COTTON Editor – Original Series
JESSICA CHEN Associate Editor – Original Series
JEB WOODARD Group Editor – Collected Editions
ROBIN WILDMAN Editor – Collected Edition
STEVE COOK Design Director – Books
MONIQUE NARBONETA Publication Design
DANIELLE DIGRADO Publication Production

BOB HARRAS Senior VP – Editor-in-Chief, DC Comics
PAT McCALLUM Executive Editor, DC Comics

DAN DiDIO Publisher
JIM LEE Publisher & Chief Creative Officer
BOBBIE CHASE VP – New Publishing Initiatives & Talent Development
DON FALLETTI VP – Manufacturing Operations & Workflow Management
LAWRENCE GANEM VP – Talent Services
ALISON GILL Senior VP – Manufacturing & Operations
HANK KANALZ Senior VP – Publishing Strategy & Support Services
DAN MIRON VP – Publishing Operations
NICK J. NAPOLITANO VP – Manufacturing Administration & Design
NANCY SPEARS VP – Sales
MICHELE R. WELLS VP & Executive Editor, Young Reader

SUPERMAN VOL. 1: THE UNITY SAGA: PHANTOM EARTH

Published by DC Comics. Compilation and all new material Copyright © 2019 DC Comics. All Rights Reserved.
Originally published in single magazine form in SUPERMAN 1-6. Copyright © 2018 DC Comics. All Rights
Reserved. All characters, their distinctive likenesses and related elements featured in this publication are
trademarks of DC Comics. The stories, characters and incidents featured in this publication are entirely
fictional. DC Comics does not read or accept unsolicited submissions of ideas, stories or artwork.
DC – a WarnerMedia Company.

DC Comics, 2900 West Alameda Ave., Burbank, CA 91505
Printed by LSC Communications, Owensville, MO, USA. 8/30/19. First Printing.
ISBN: 978-1-4012-9438-0

Library of Congress Cataloging-in-Publication Data is available.

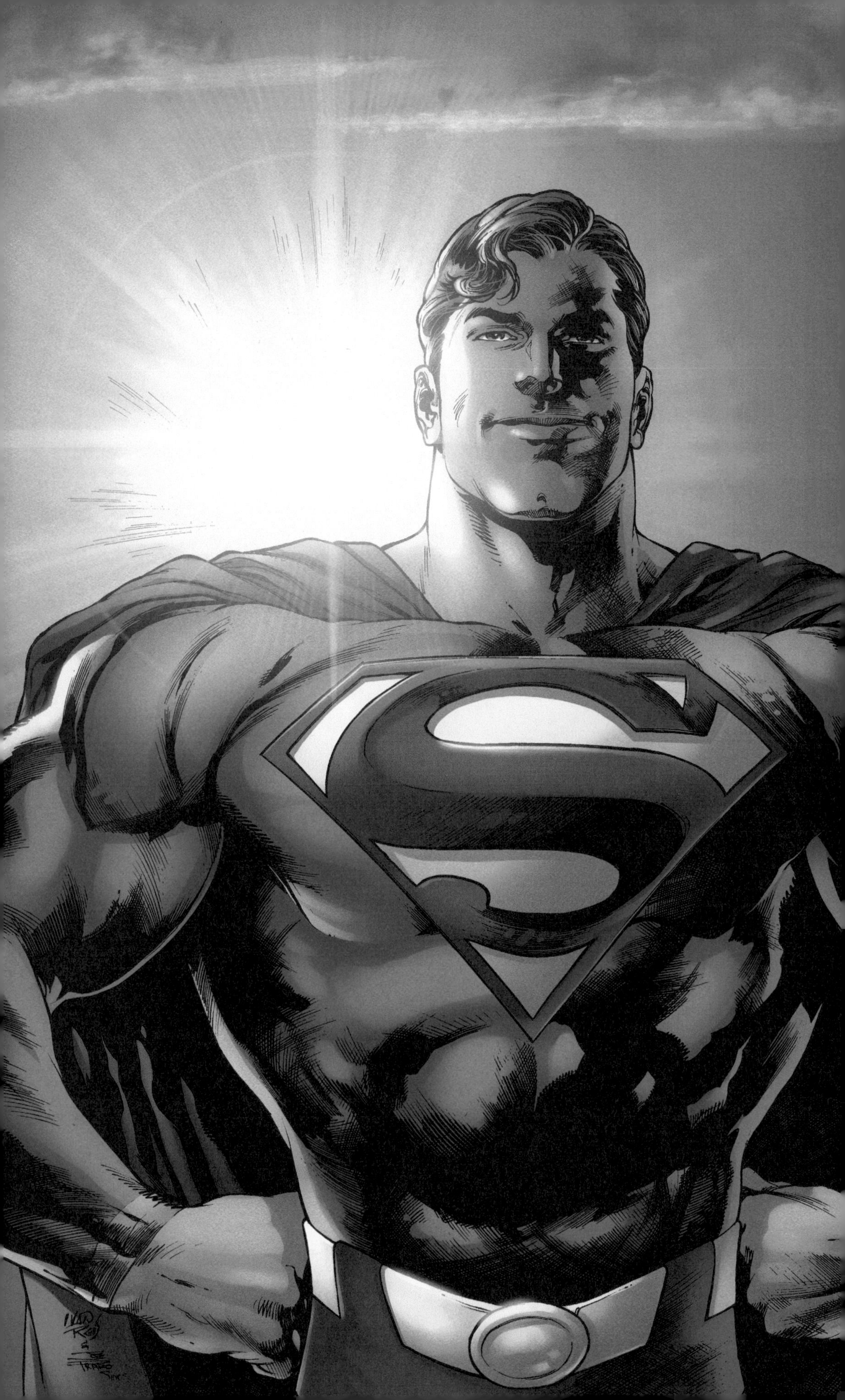

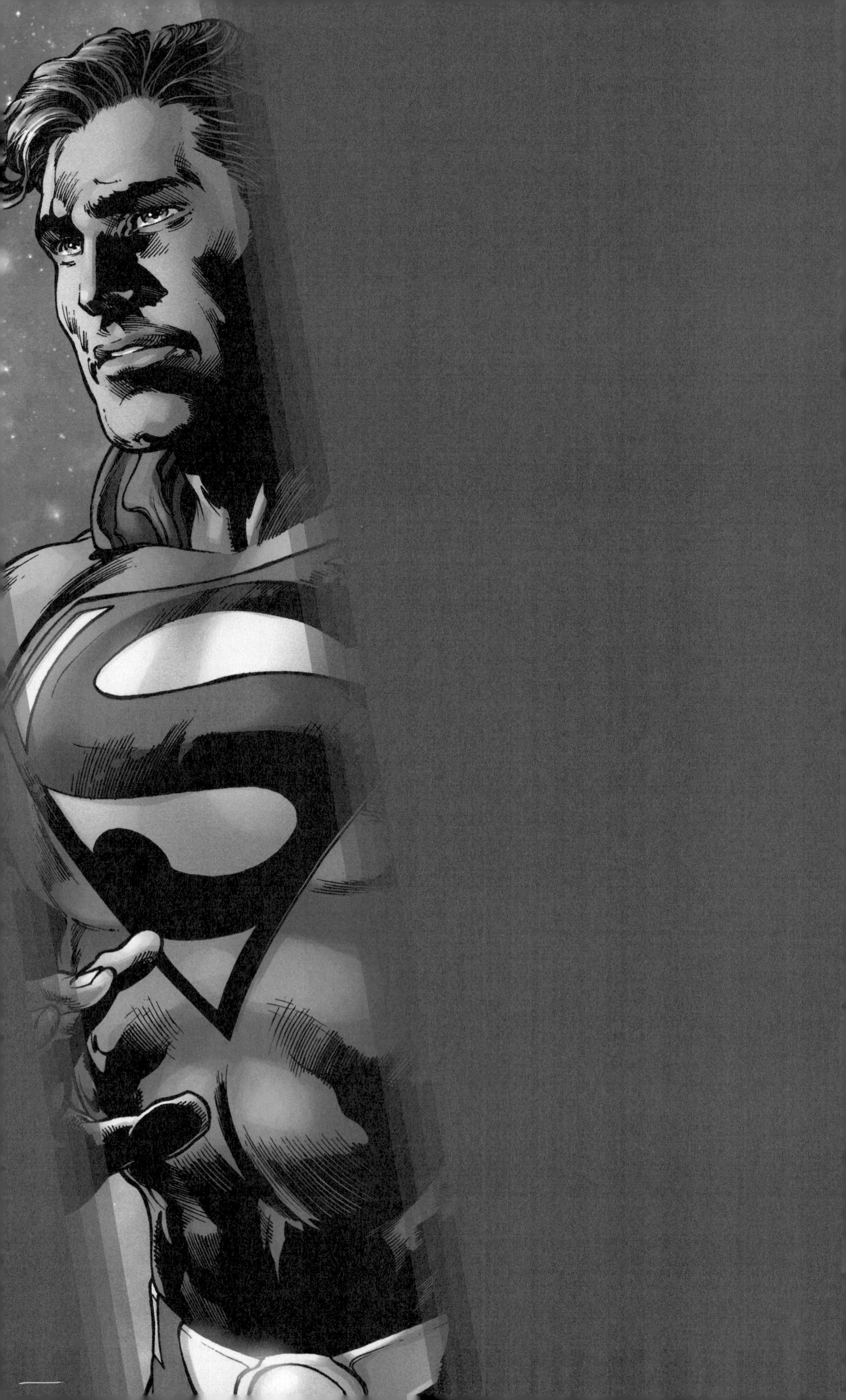

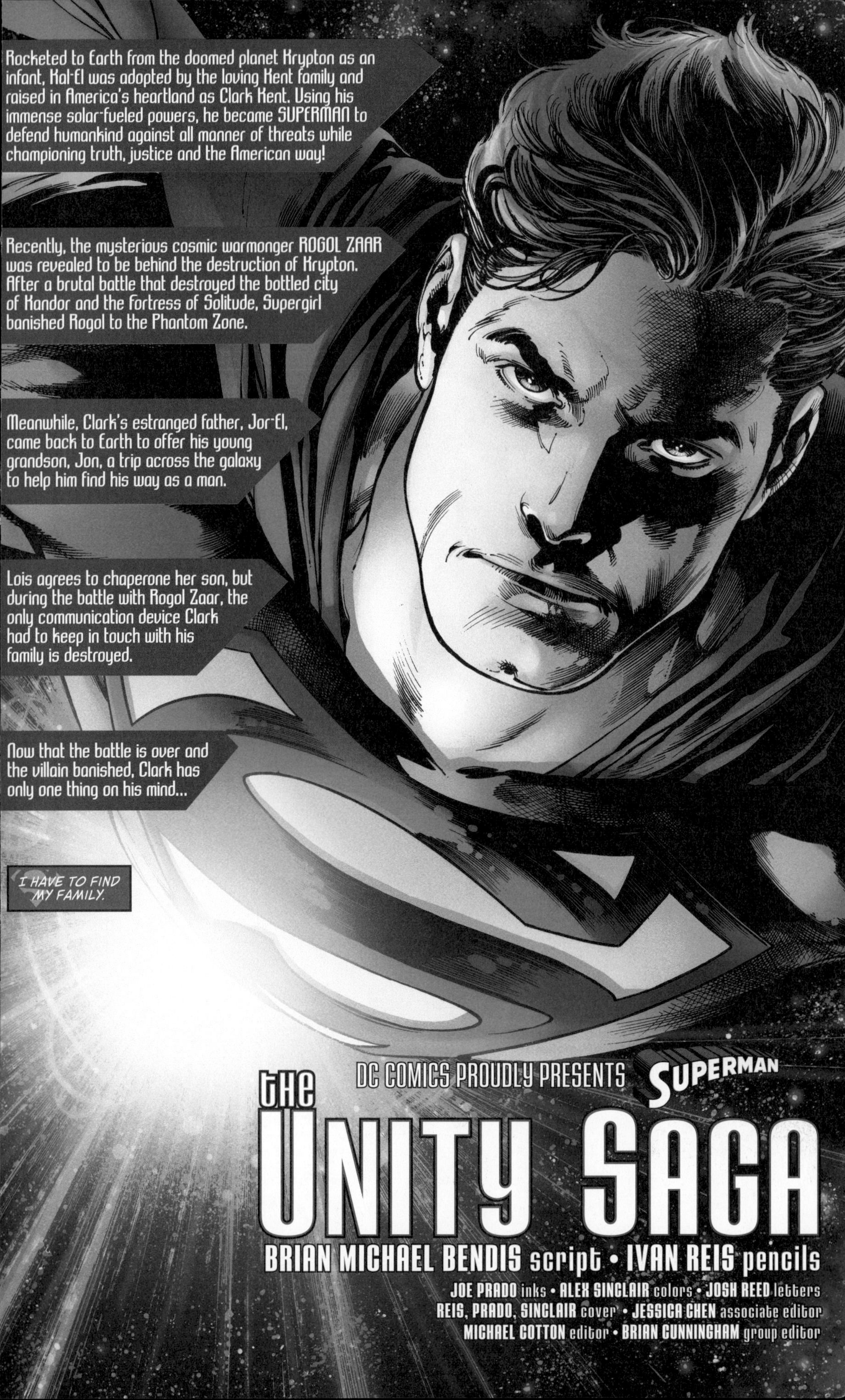
Rocketed to Earth from the doomed planet Krypton as an infant, Kal-El was adopted by the loving Kent family and raised in America's heartland as Clark Kent. Using his immense solar-fueled powers, he became SUPERMAN to defend humankind against all manner of threats while championing truth, justice and the American way!
Recently, the mysterious cosmic warmonger ROGOL ZAAR was revealed to be behind the destruction of Krypton. After a brutal battle that destroyed the bottled city of Kandor and the Fortress of Solitude, Supergirl banished Rogol to the Phantom Zone.
Meanwhile, Clark's estranged father, Jor-El, came back to Earth to offer his young grandson, Jon, a trip across the galaxy to help him find his way as a man.
Lois agrees to chaperone her son, but during the battle with Rogol Zaar, the only communication device Clark had to keep in touch with his family is destroyed.
Now that the battle is over and the villain banished, Clark has only one thing on his mind...
I HAVE TO FIND MY FAMILY.
DC COMICS PROUDLY PRESENTS SUPERMAN
THE UNITY SAGA
BRIAN MICHAEL BENDIS script • IVAN REIS pencils
JOE PRADO inks • ALEX SINCLAIR colors • JOSH REED letters
REIS, PRADO, SINCLAIR cover • JESSICA CHEN associate editor
MICHAEL COTTON editor • BRIAN CUNNINGHAM group editor

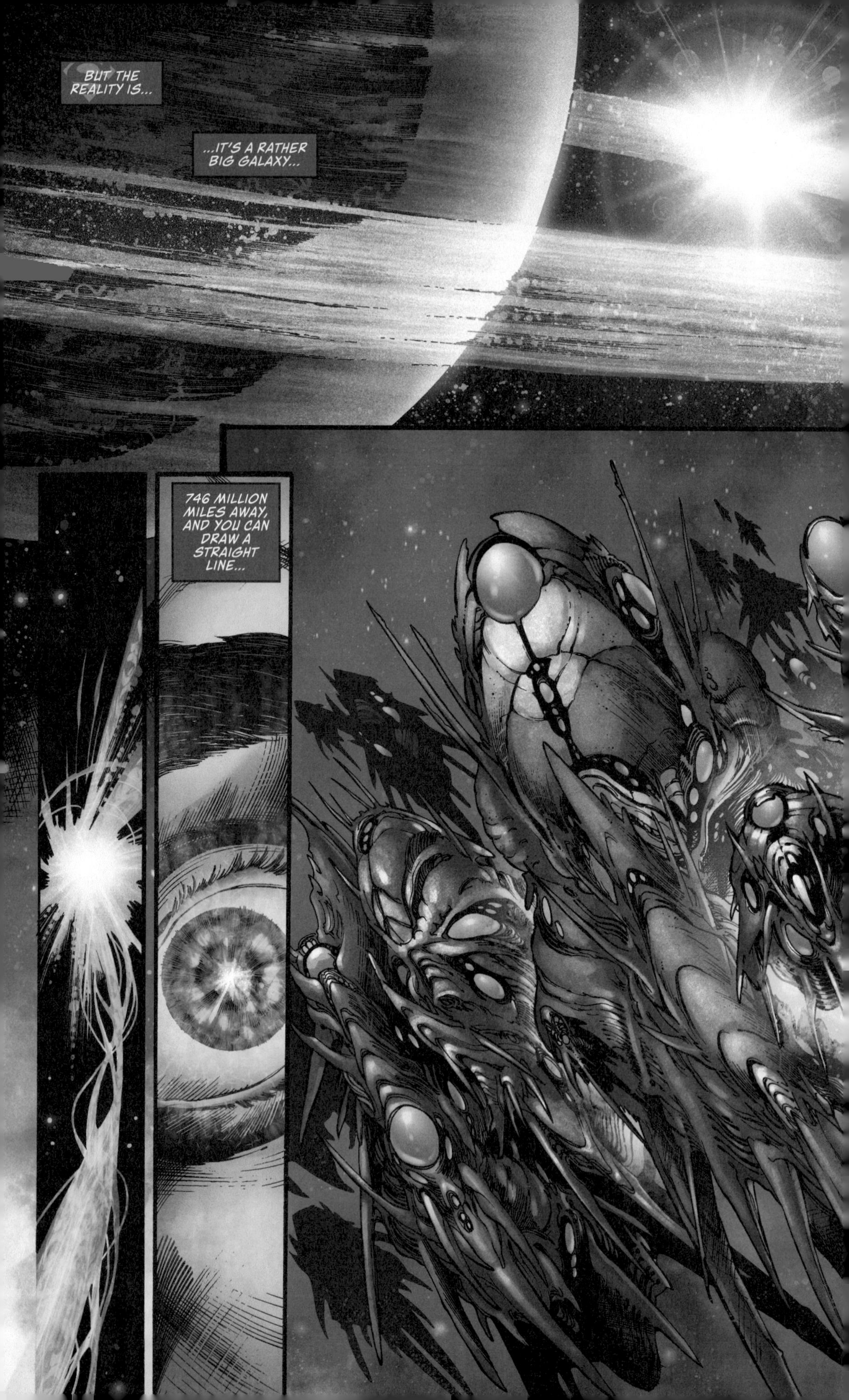
BUT THE REALITY IS...
...IT'S A RATHER BIG GALAXY...
746 MILLION MILES AWAY, AND YOU CAN DRAW A STRAIGHT LINE...

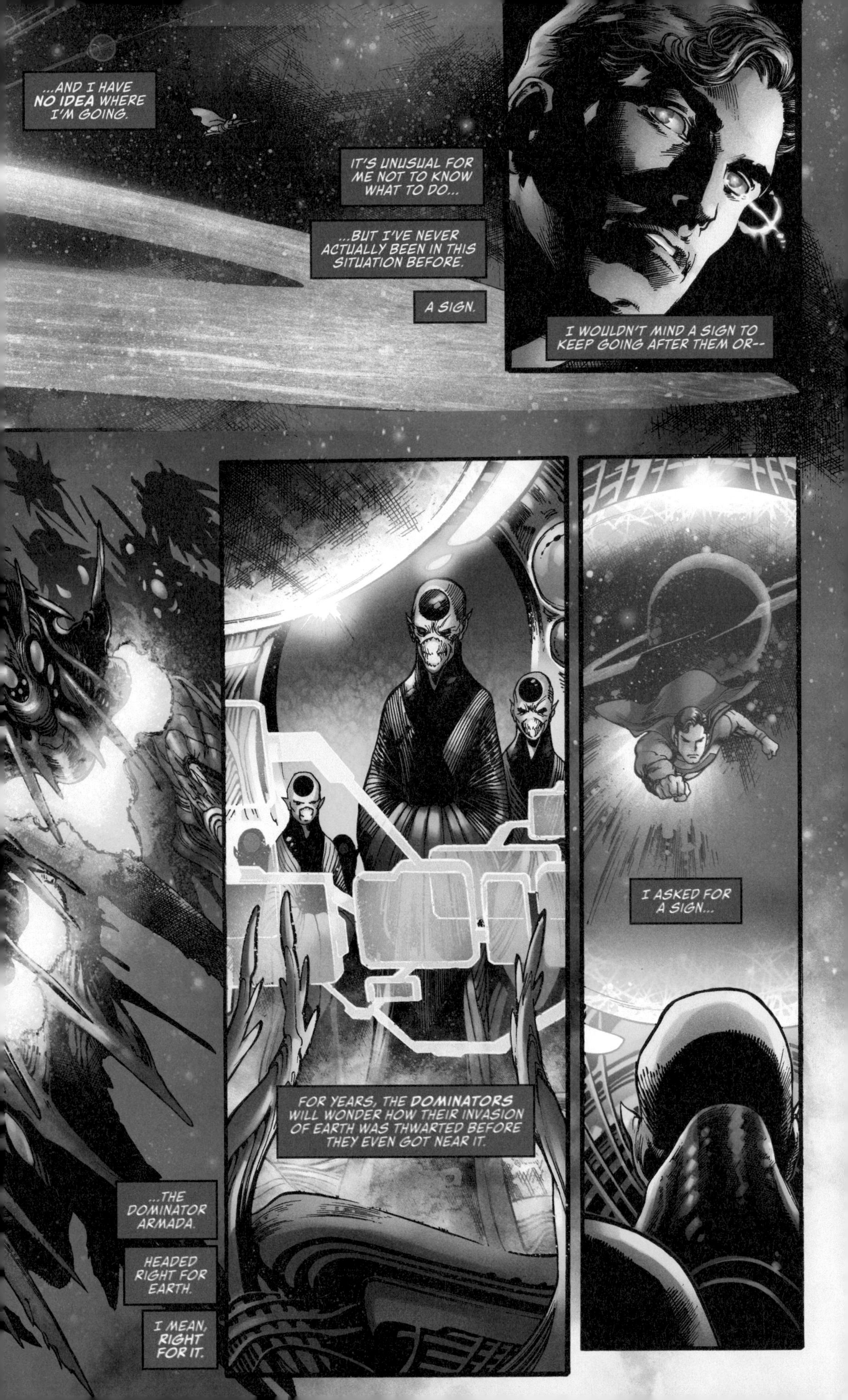

...AND I HAVE NO IDEA WHERE I'M GOING.
IT'S UNUSUAL FOR ME NOT TO KNOW WHAT TO DO...
...BUT I'VE NEVER ACTUALLY BEEN IN THIS SITUATION BEFORE.
A SIGN.
I WOULDN'T MIND A SIGN TO KEEP GOING AFTER THEM OR--
...THE DOMINATOR ARMADA.
HEADED RIGHT FOR EARTH.
I MEAN, RIGHT FOR IT.
FOR YEARS, THE DOMINATORS WILL WONDER HOW THEIR INVASION OF EARTH WAS THWARTED BEFORE THEY EVEN GOT NEAR IT.
I ASKED FOR A SIGN...

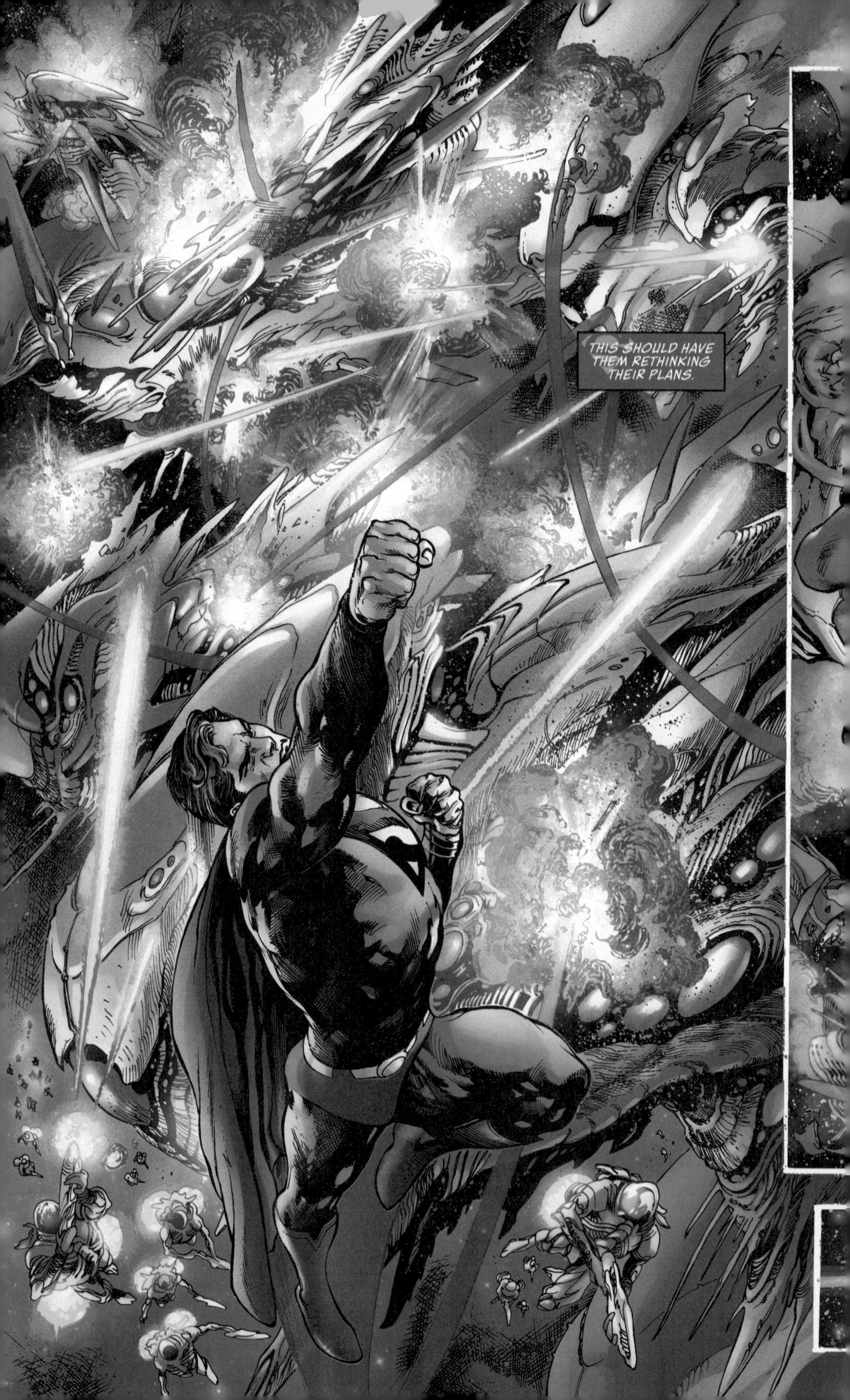
THIS SHOULD HAVE THEM RETHINKING THEIR PLANS.

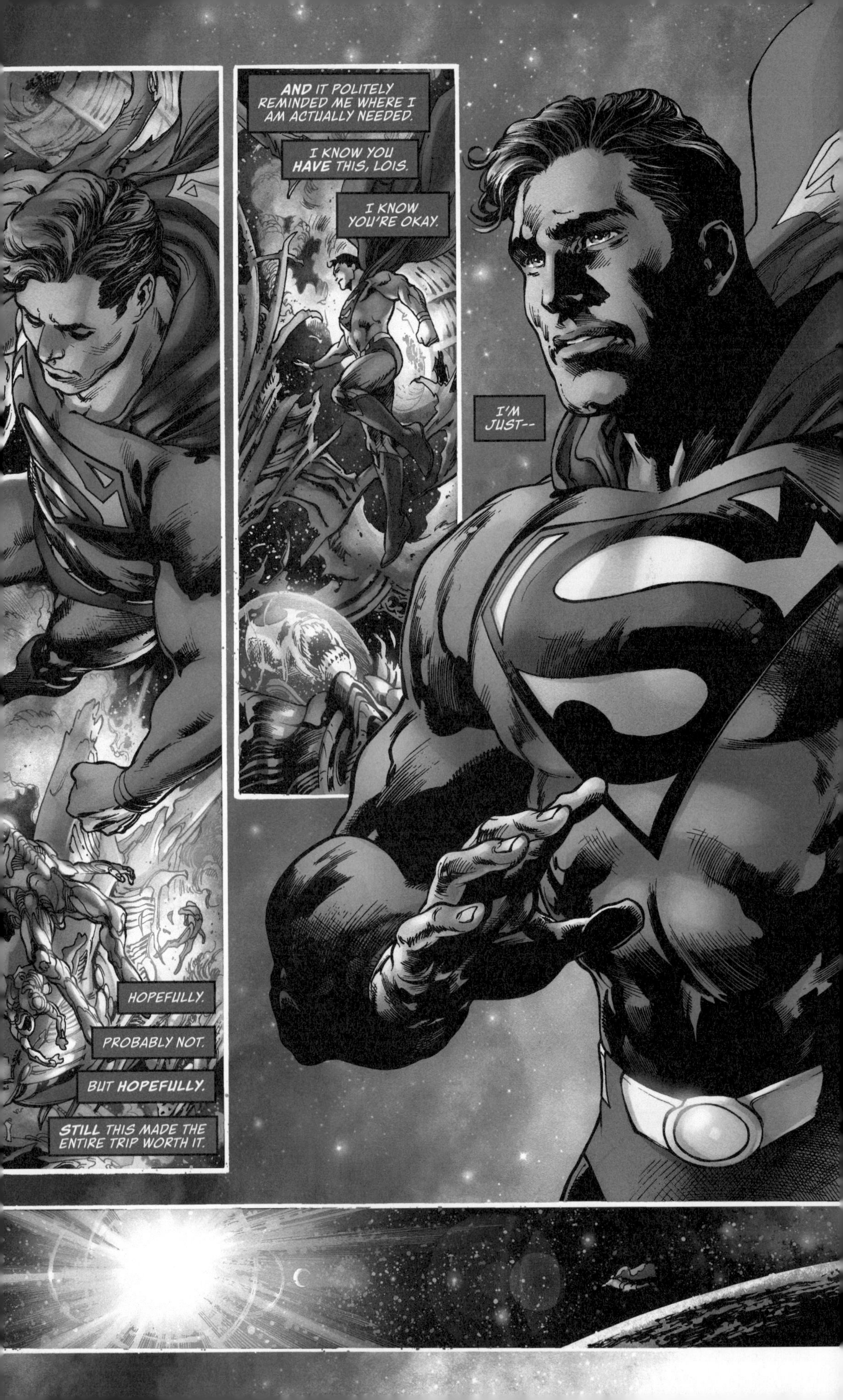

AND IT POLITELY REMINDED ME WHERE I AM ACTUALLY NEEDED.
I KNOW YOU HAVE THIS, LOIS.
I KNOW YOU'RE OKAY.
HOPEFULLY.
PROBABLY NOT.
BUT HOPEFULLY.
STILL THIS MADE THE ENTIRE TRIP WORTH IT.
I'M JUST--

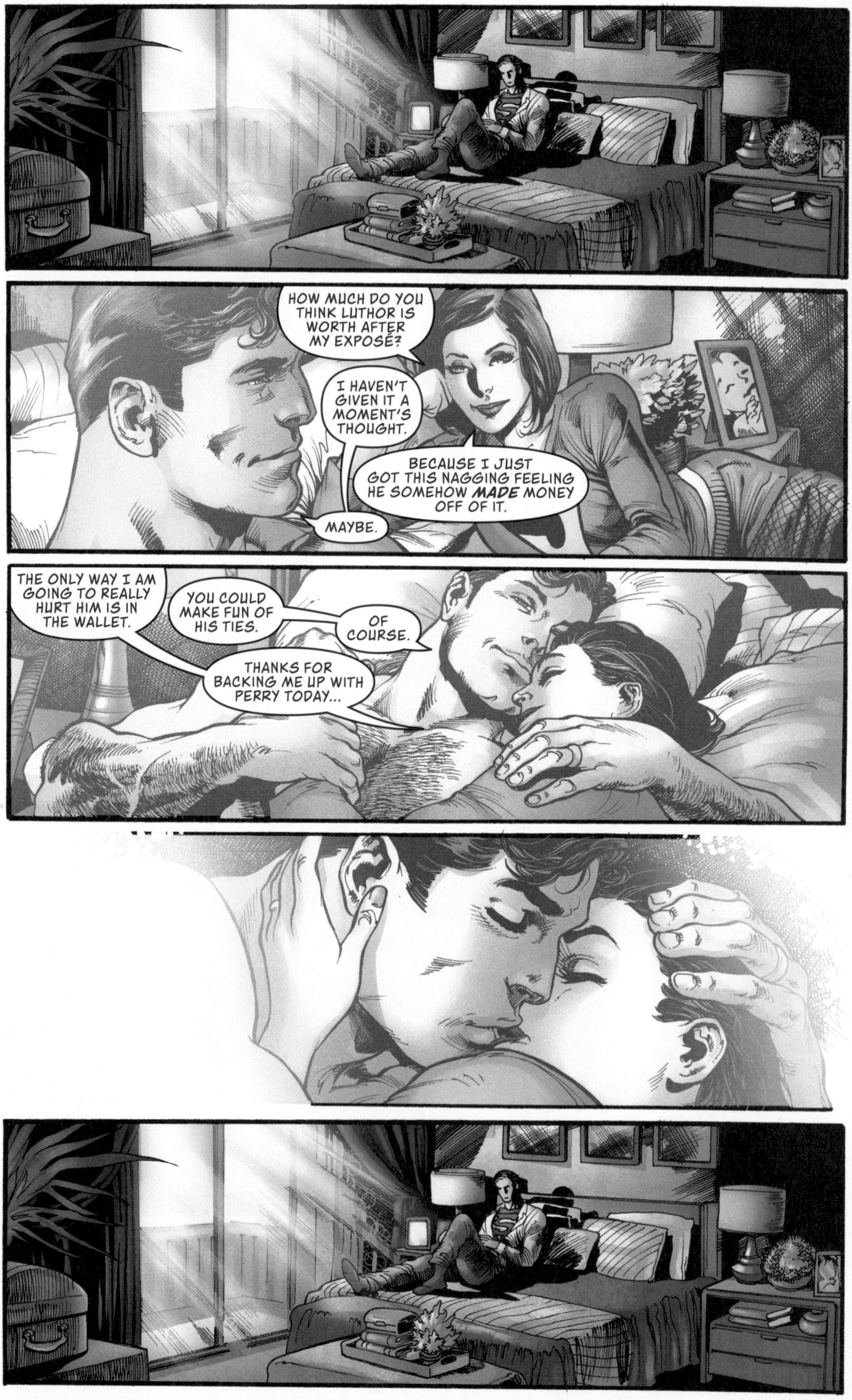
HOW MUCH DO YOU THINK LUTHOR IS WORTH AFTER MY EXPOSÉ?
I HAVEN'T GIVEN IT A MOMENT'S THOUGHT.
BECAUSE I JUST GOT THIS NAGGING FEELING HE SOMEHOW *MADE* MONEY OFF OF IT.
MAYBE.
THE ONLY WAY I AM GOING TO REALLY HURT HIM IS IN THE WALLET.
YOU COULD MAKE FUN OF HIS TIES.
OF COURSE.
THANKS FOR BACKING ME UP WITH PERRY TODAY...

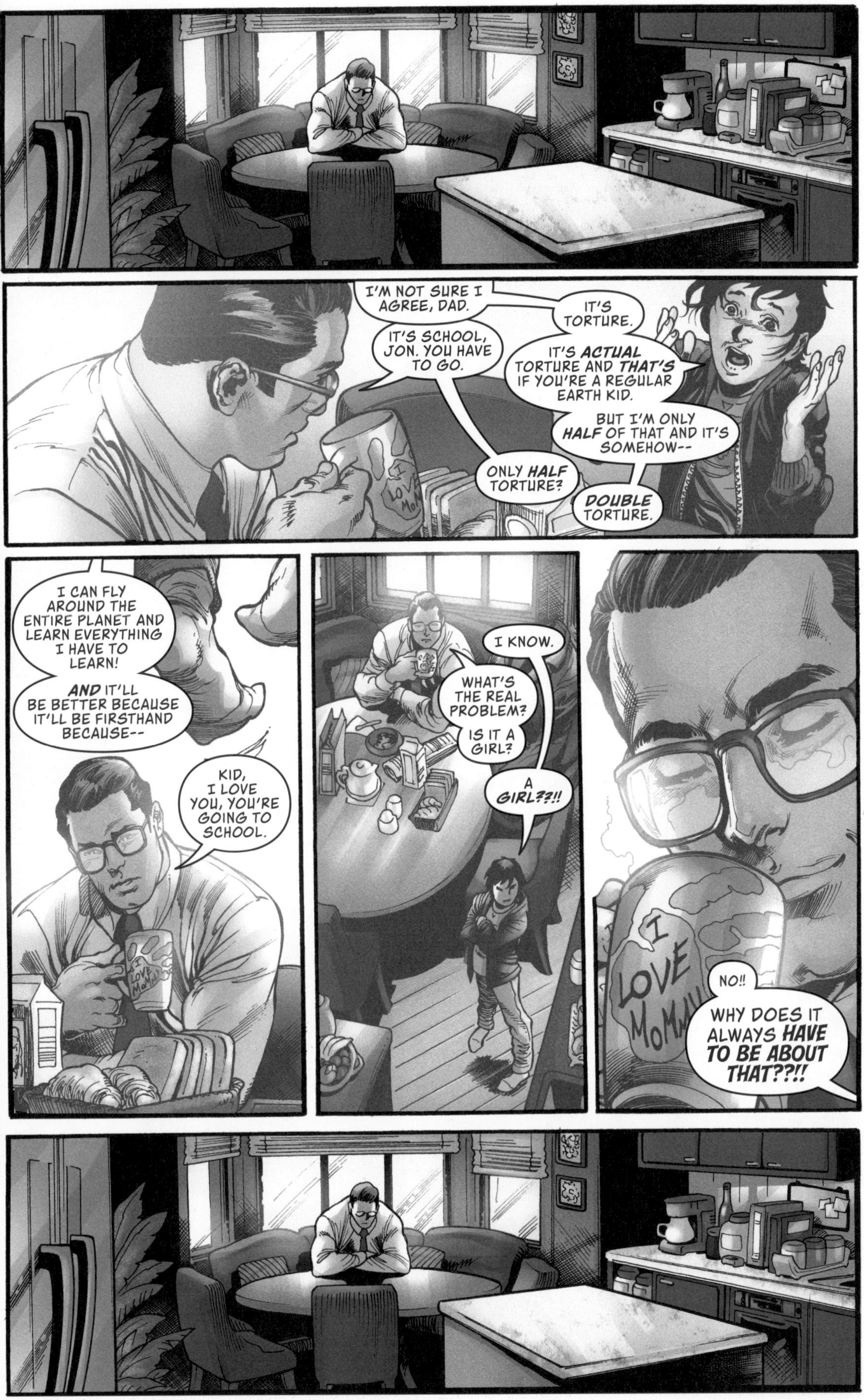
I'M NOT SURE I AGREE, DAD.
IT'S TORTURE.
IT'S SCHOOL, JON. YOU HAVE TO GO.
IT'S ACTUAL TORTURE AND THAT'S IF YOU'RE A REGULAR EARTH KID.
BUT I'M ONLY HALF OF THAT AND IT'S SOMEHOW--
ONLY HALF TORTURE?
DOUBLE TORTURE.
I LOVE MOMMY
I CAN FLY AROUND THE ENTIRE PLANET AND LEARN EVERYTHING I HAVE TO LEARN!
AND IT'LL BE BETTER BECAUSE IT'LL BE FIRSTHAND BECAUSE--
KID, I LOVE YOU, YOU'RE GOING TO SCHOOL.
I KNOW.
WHAT'S THE REAL PROBLEM?
IS IT A GIRL?
A GIRL??!!
I LOVE MOMMY
NO!!
WHY DOES IT ALWAYS HAVE TO BE ABOUT THAT??!!

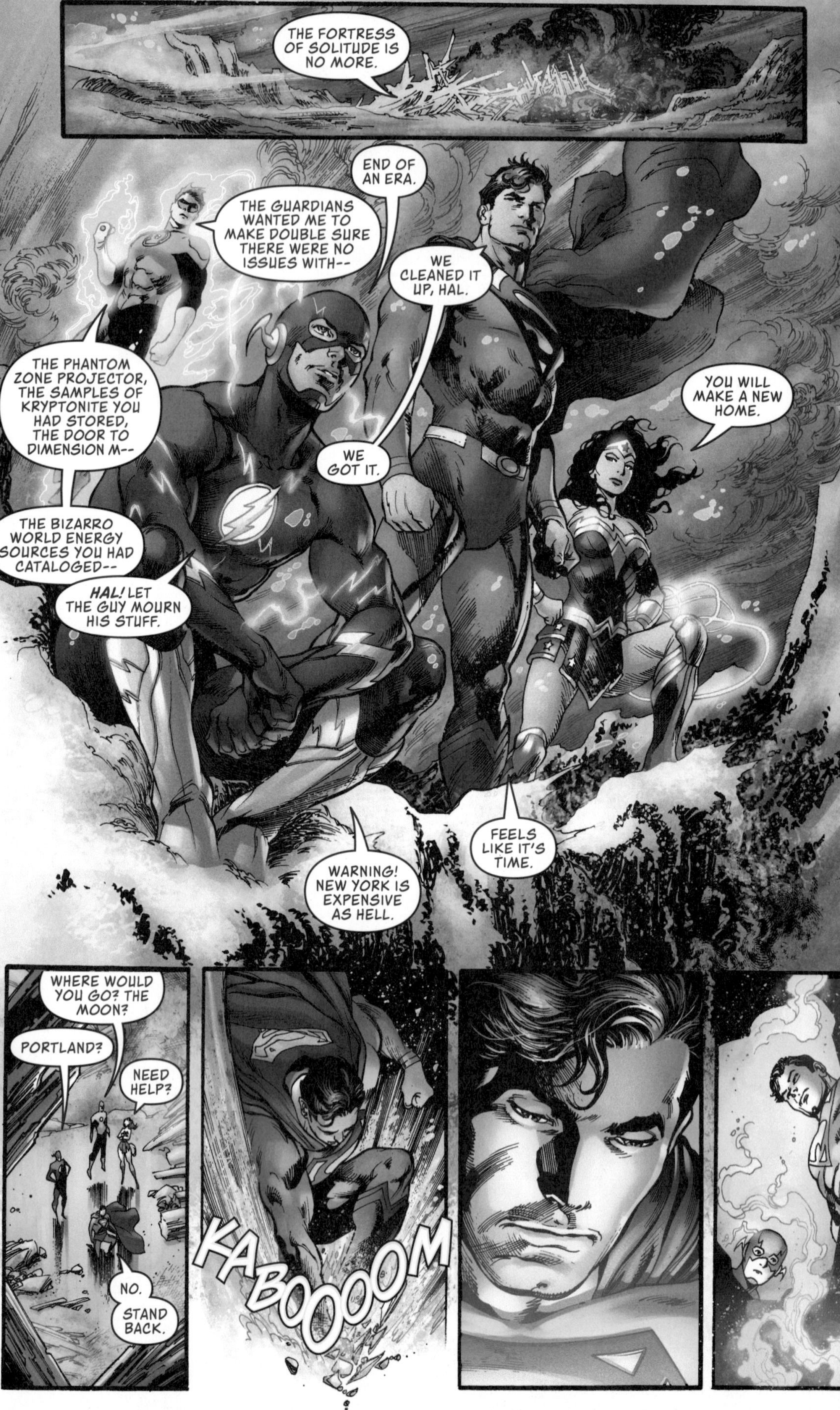
THE FORTRESS OF SOLITUDE IS NO MORE.
END OF AN ERA.
THE GUARDIANS WANTED ME TO MAKE DOUBLE SURE THERE WERE NO ISSUES WITH--
WE CLEANED IT UP, HAL.
THE PHANTOM ZONE PROJECTOR, THE SAMPLES OF KRYPTONITE YOU HAD STORED, THE DOOR TO DIMENSION M--
WE GOT IT.
YOU WILL MAKE A NEW HOME.
THE BIZARRO WORLD ENERGY SOURCES YOU HAD CATALOGED--
HAL! LET THE GUY MOURN HIS STUFF.
FEELS LIKE IT'S TIME.
WARNING! NEW YORK IS EXPENSIVE AS HELL.
WHERE WOULD YOU GO? THE MOON?
PORTLAND?
NEED HELP?
NO.
STAND BACK.
KABOOOOOM

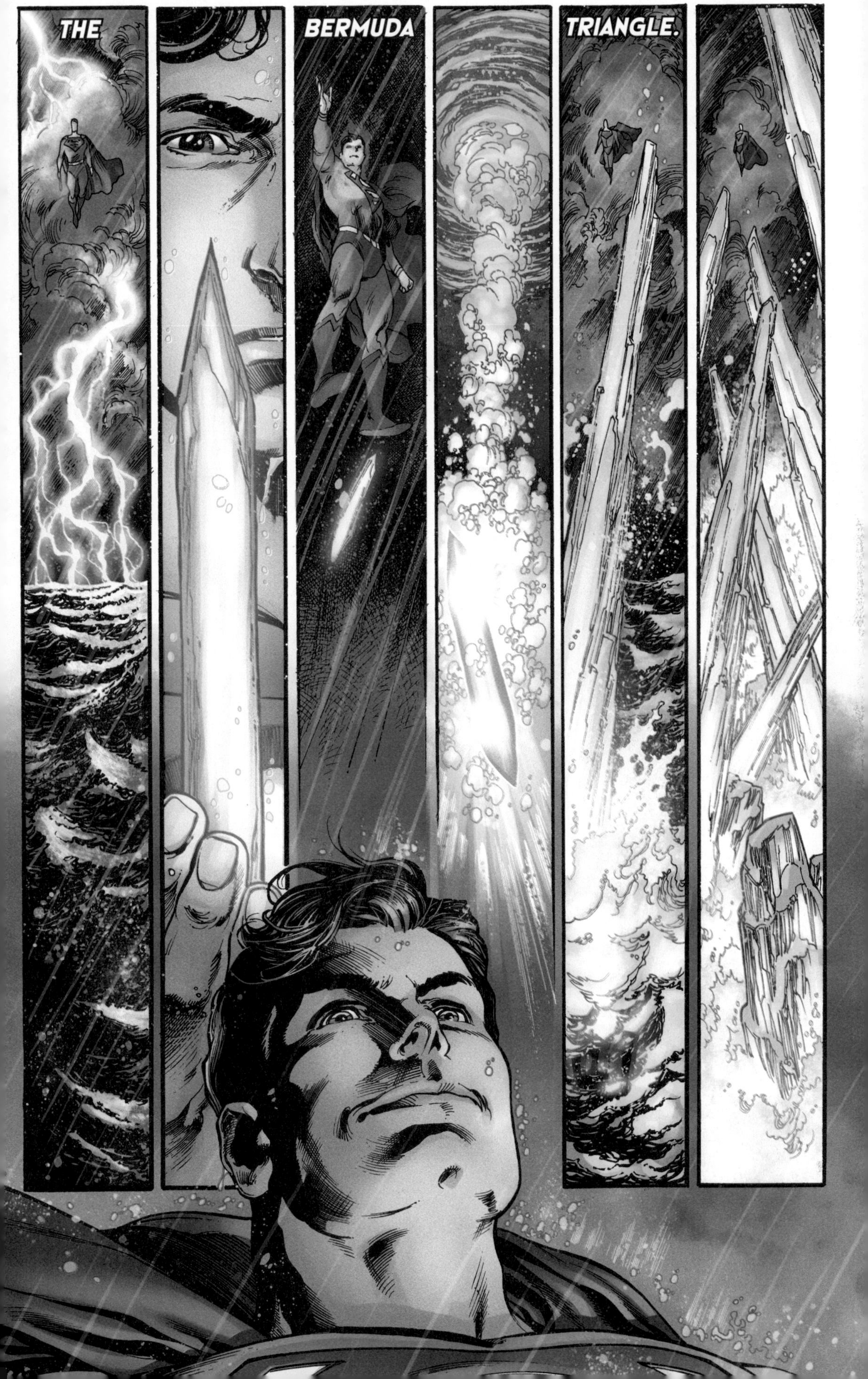
THE
BERMUDA
TRIANGLE.

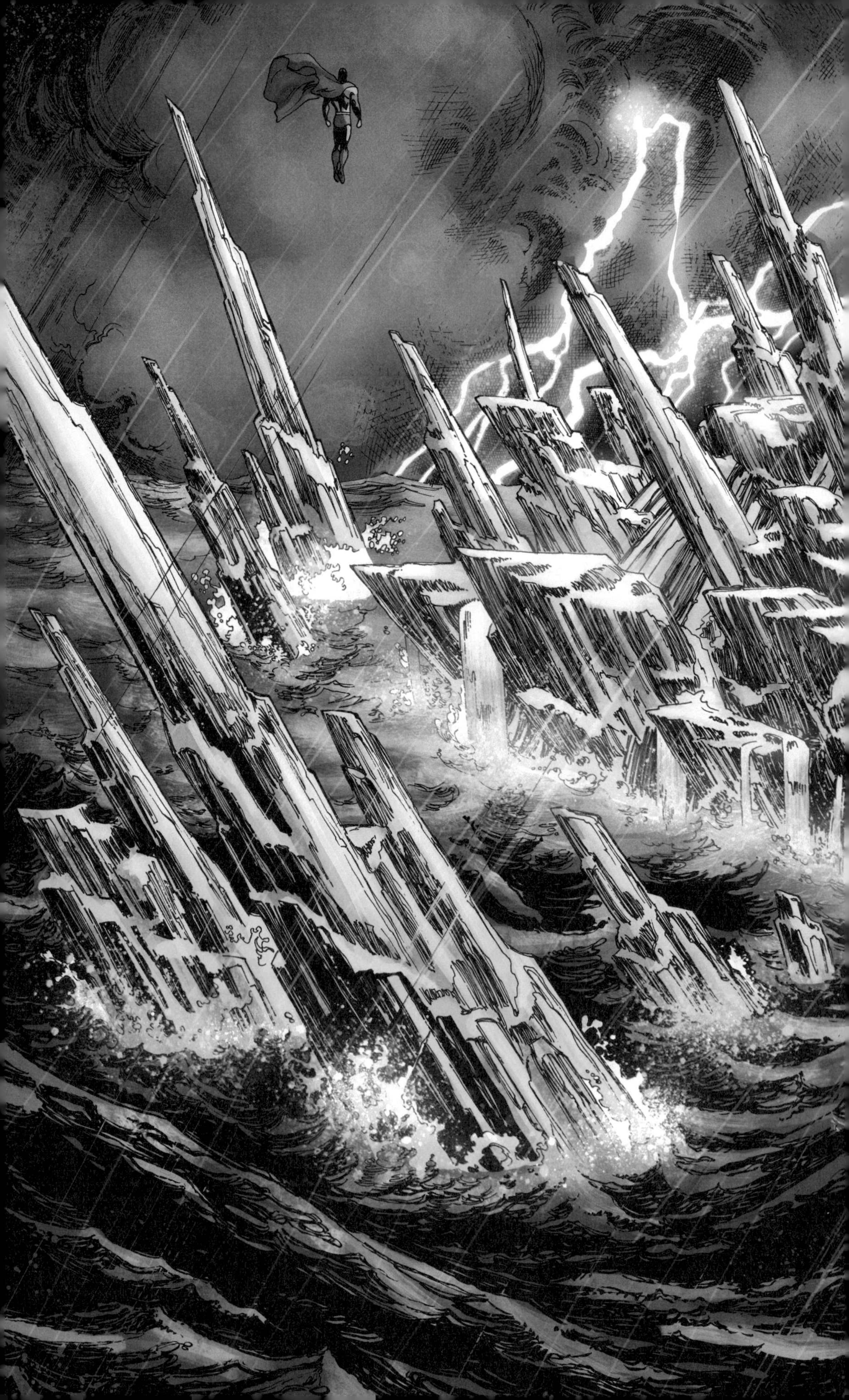

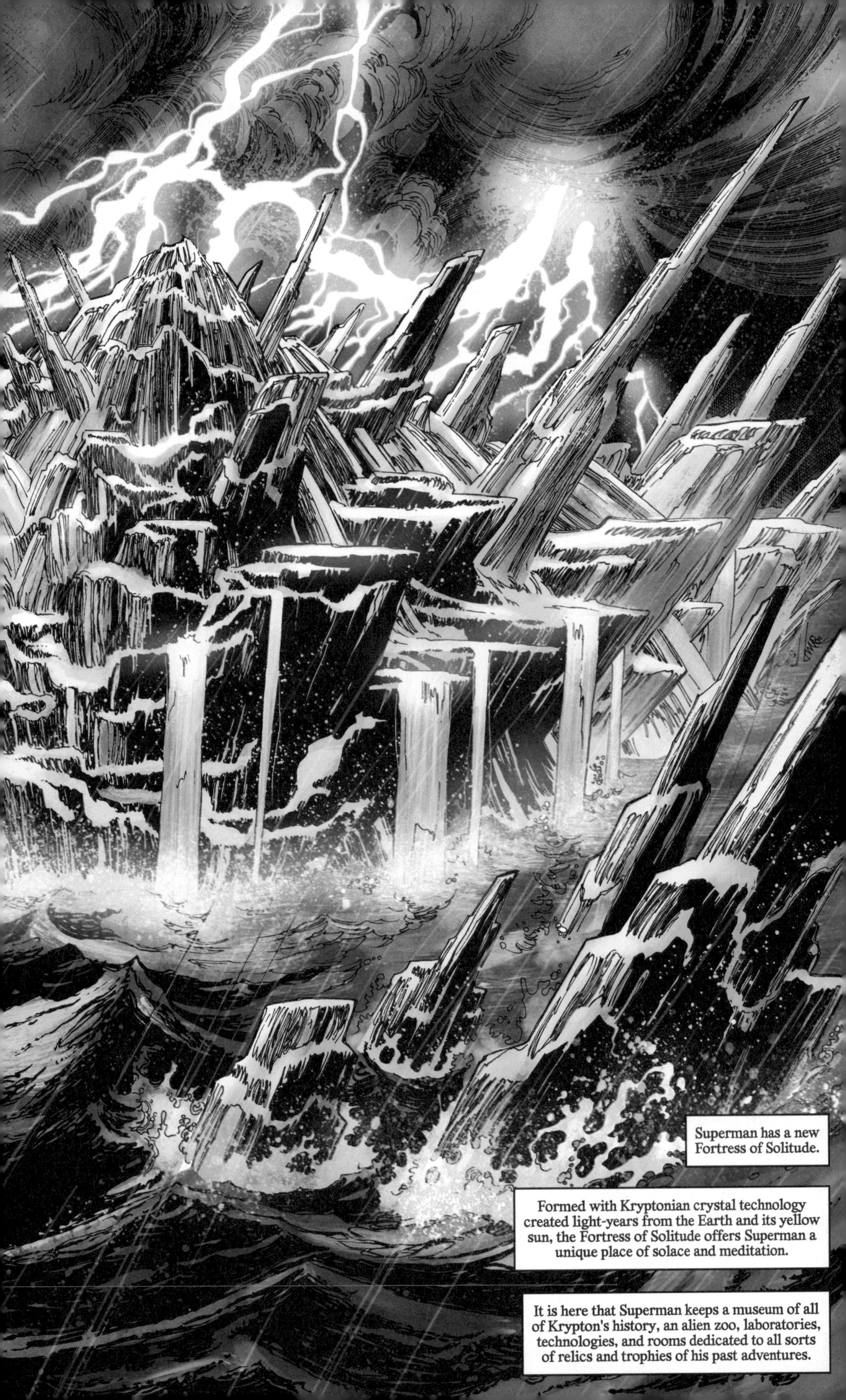
Superman has a new Fortress of Solitude.
Formed with Kryptonian crystal technology created light-years from the Earth and its yellow sun, the Fortress of Solitude offers Superman a unique place of solace and meditation.
It is here that Superman keeps a museum of all of Krypton's history, an alien zoo, laboratories, technologies, and rooms dedicated to all sorts of relics and trophies of his past adventures.

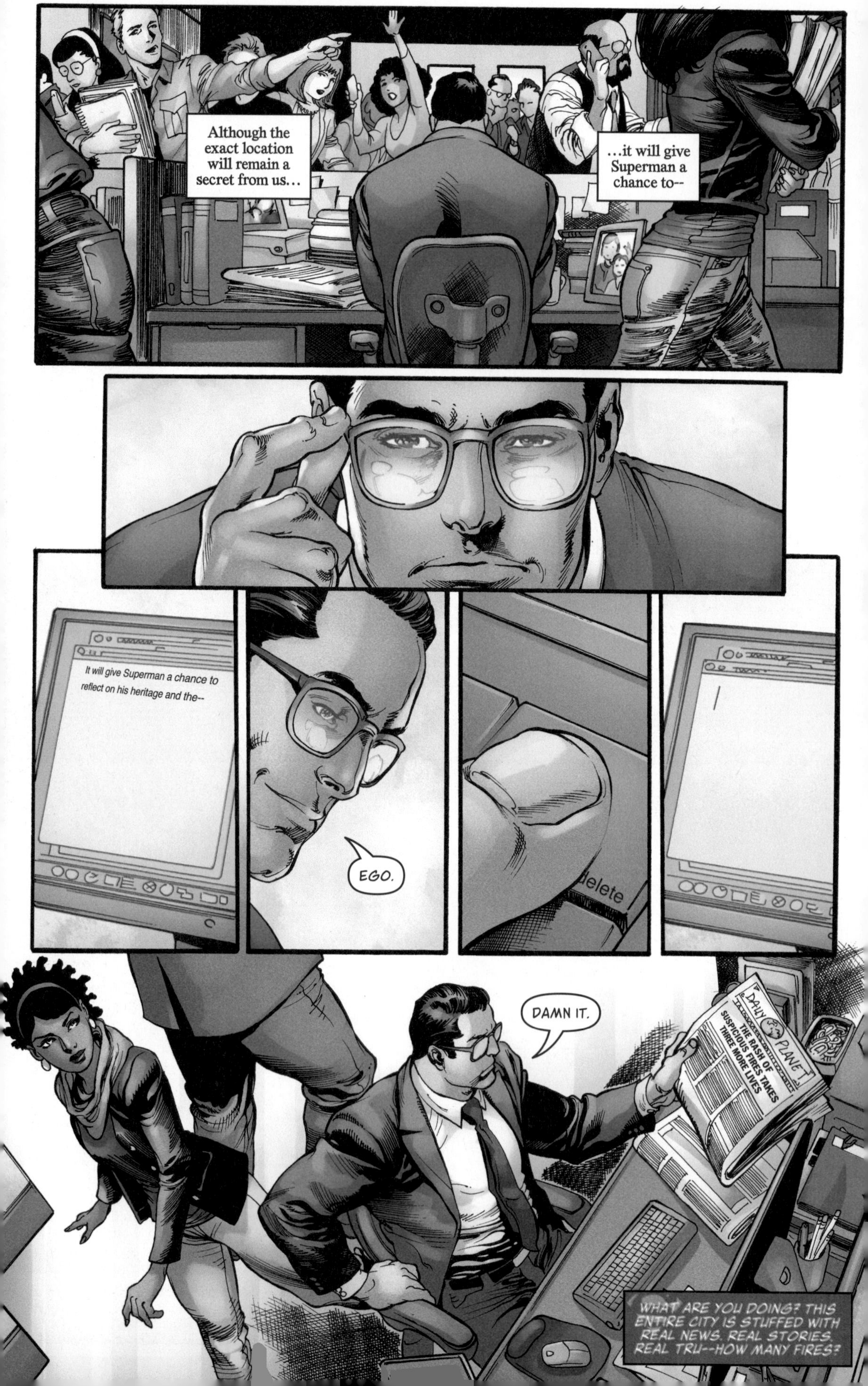

Although the exact location will remain a secret from us...
...it will give Superman a chance to--
It will give Superman a chance to reflect on his heritage and the--
EGO.
delete
DAMN IT.
DAILY PLANET
THE RASH OF SUSPICIOUS FIRES TAKES THREE MORE LIVES
WHAT ARE YOU DOING? THIS ENTIRE CITY IS STUFFED WITH REAL NEWS. REAL STORIES. REAL TRU--HOW MANY FIRES?

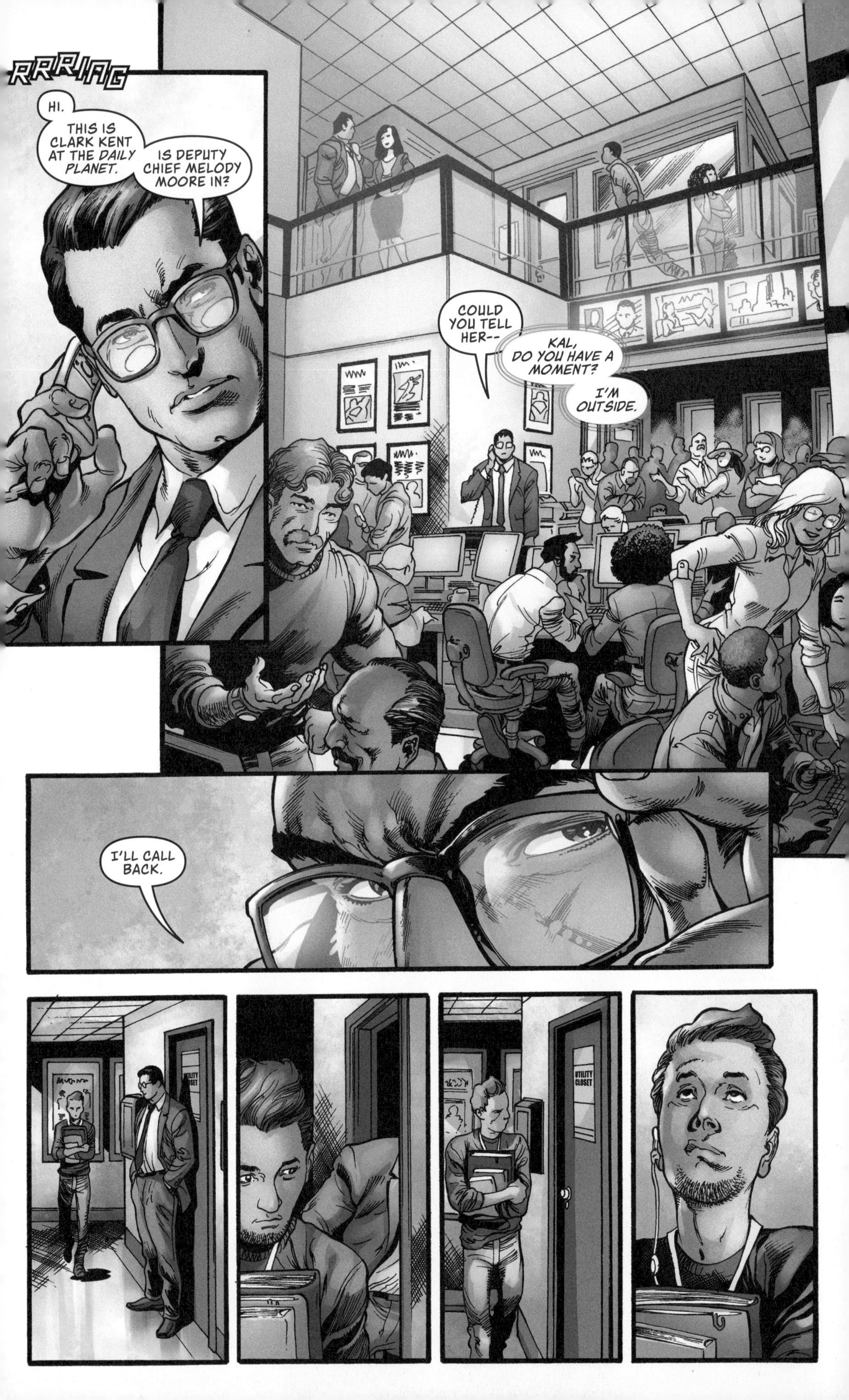
RRRING
HI.
THIS IS CLARK KENT AT THE *DAILY PLANET.*
IS DEPUTY CHIEF MELODY MOORE IN?
COULD YOU TELL HER--
KAL, DO YOU HAVE A MOMENT?
I'M OUTSIDE.
I'LL CALL BACK.
UTILITY CLOSET
UTILITY CLOSET

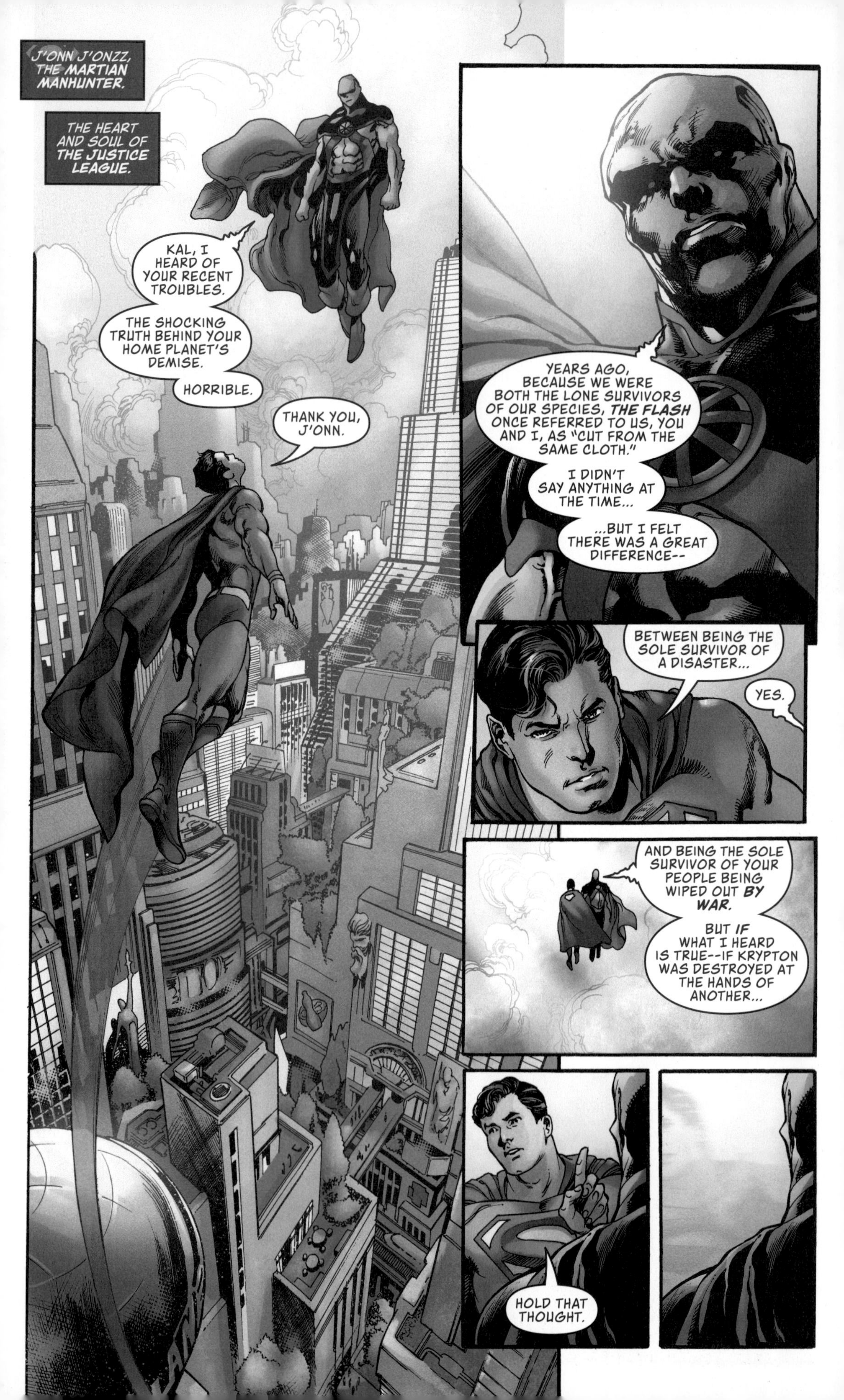
J'ONN J'ONZZ, THE MARTIAN MANHUNTER.
THE HEART AND SOUL OF THE JUSTICE LEAGUE.
KAL, I HEARD OF YOUR RECENT TROUBLES.
THE SHOCKING TRUTH BEHIND YOUR HOME PLANET'S DEMISE.
HORRIBLE.
THANK YOU, J'ONN.
YEARS AGO, BECAUSE WE WERE BOTH THE LONE SURVIVORS OF OUR SPECIES, THE FLASH ONCE REFERRED TO US, YOU AND I, AS "CUT FROM THE SAME CLOTH."
I DIDN'T SAY ANYTHING AT THE TIME...
...BUT I FELT THERE WAS A GREAT DIFFERENCE--
BETWEEN BEING THE SOLE SURVIVOR OF A DISASTER...
YES.
AND BEING THE SOLE SURVIVOR OF YOUR PEOPLE BEING WIPED OUT BY WAR.
BUT IF WHAT I HEARD IS TRUE--IF KRYPTON WAS DESTROYED AT THE HANDS OF ANOTHER...
HOLD THAT THOUGHT.

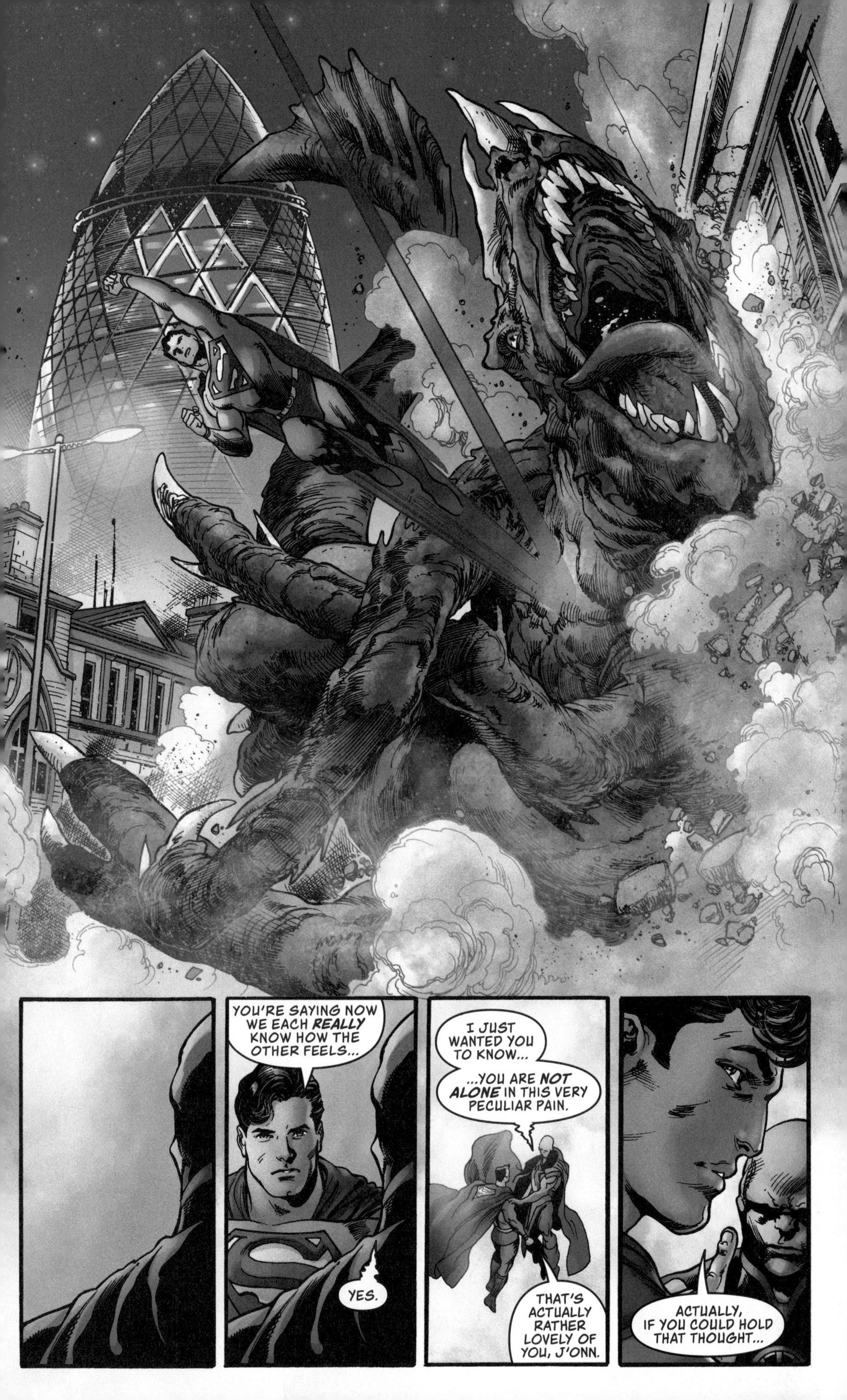

YOU'RE SAYING NOW WE EACH **REALLY** KNOW HOW THE OTHER FEELS...
YES.
I JUST WANTED YOU TO KNOW...
...YOU ARE **NOT ALONE** IN THIS VERY PECULIAR PAIN.
THAT'S ACTUALLY RATHER LOVELY OF YOU, J'ONN.
ACTUALLY, IF YOU COULD HOLD THAT THOUGHT...

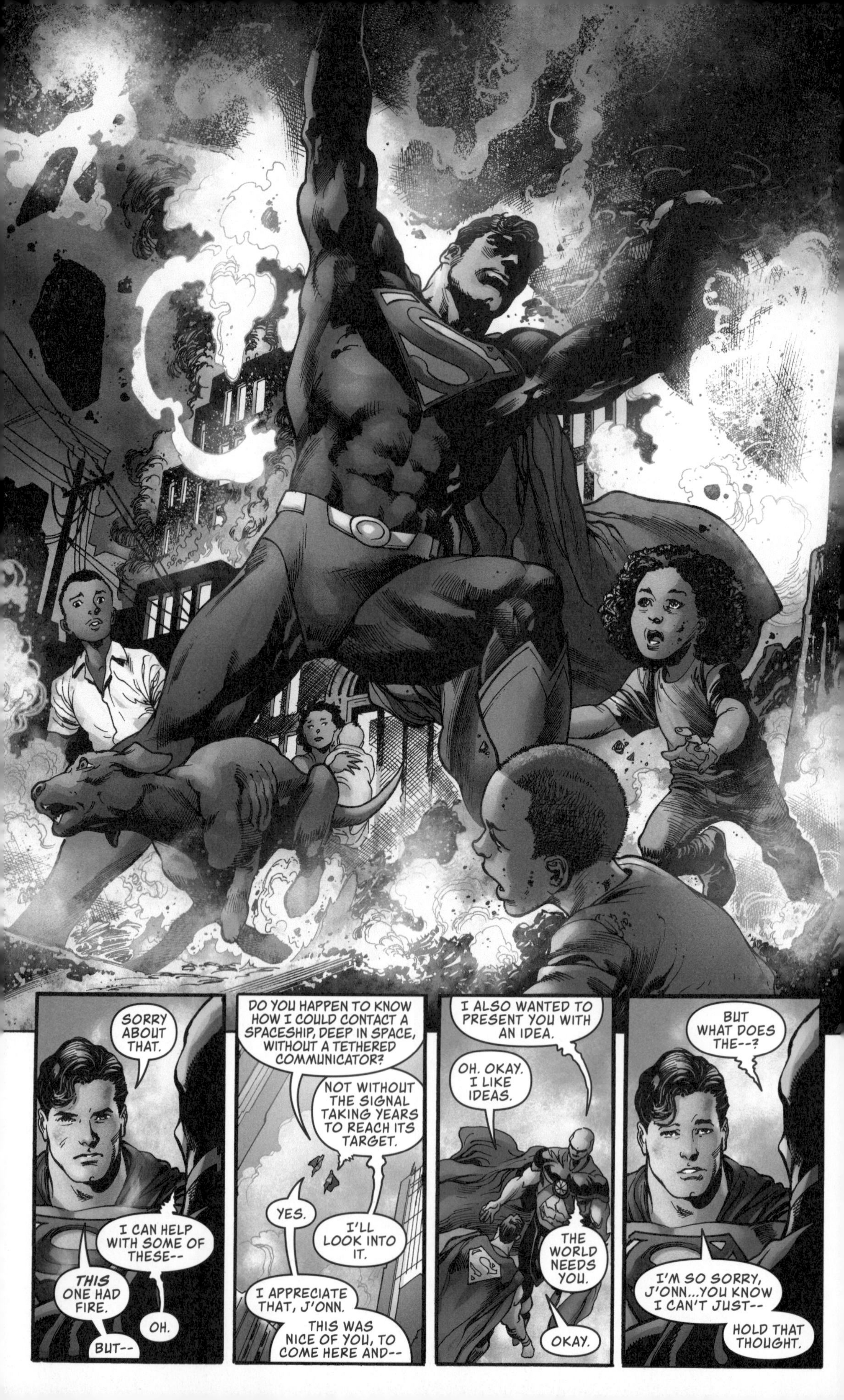
SORRY ABOUT THAT.
I CAN HELP WITH SOME OF THESE--
THIS ONE HAD FIRE.
OH.
BUT--
DO YOU HAPPEN TO KNOW HOW I COULD CONTACT A SPACESHIP, DEEP IN SPACE, WITHOUT A TETHERED COMMUNICATOR?
NOT WITHOUT THE SIGNAL TAKING YEARS TO REACH ITS TARGET.
YES.
I'LL LOOK INTO IT.
I APPRECIATE THAT, J'ONN.
THIS WAS NICE OF YOU, TO COME HERE AND--
I ALSO WANTED TO PRESENT YOU WITH AN IDEA.
OH. OKAY. I LIKE IDEAS.
THE WORLD NEEDS YOU.
OKAY.
BUT WHAT DOES THE--?
I'M SO SORRY, J'ONN...YOU KNOW I CAN'T JUST--
HOLD THAT THOUGHT.

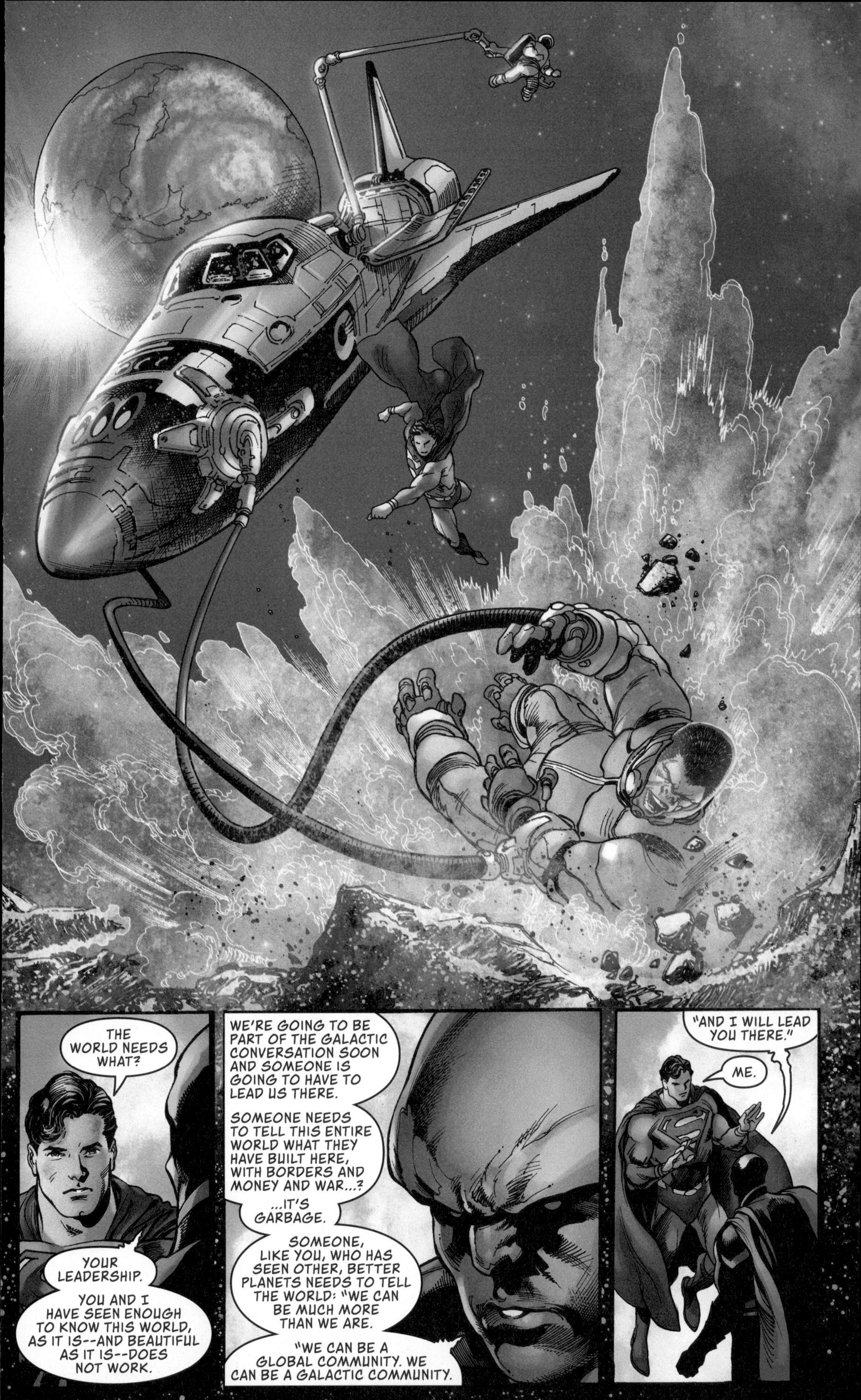
THE WORLD NEEDS WHAT?
YOUR LEADERSHIP.
YOU AND I HAVE SEEN ENOUGH TO KNOW THIS WORLD, AS IT IS--AND BEAUTIFUL AS IT IS--DOES NOT WORK.
WE'RE GOING TO BE PART OF THE GALACTIC CONVERSATION SOON AND SOMEONE IS GOING TO HAVE TO LEAD US THERE.
SOMEONE NEEDS TO TELL THIS ENTIRE WORLD WHAT THEY HAVE BUILT HERE, WITH BORDERS AND MONEY AND WAR...?
...IT'S GARBAGE.
SOMEONE, LIKE YOU, WHO HAS SEEN OTHER, BETTER PLANETS NEEDS TO TELL THE WORLD: "WE CAN BE MUCH MORE THAN WE ARE.
"WE CAN BE A GLOBAL COMMUNITY. WE CAN BE A GALACTIC COMMUNITY.
"AND I WILL LEAD YOU THERE."
ME.

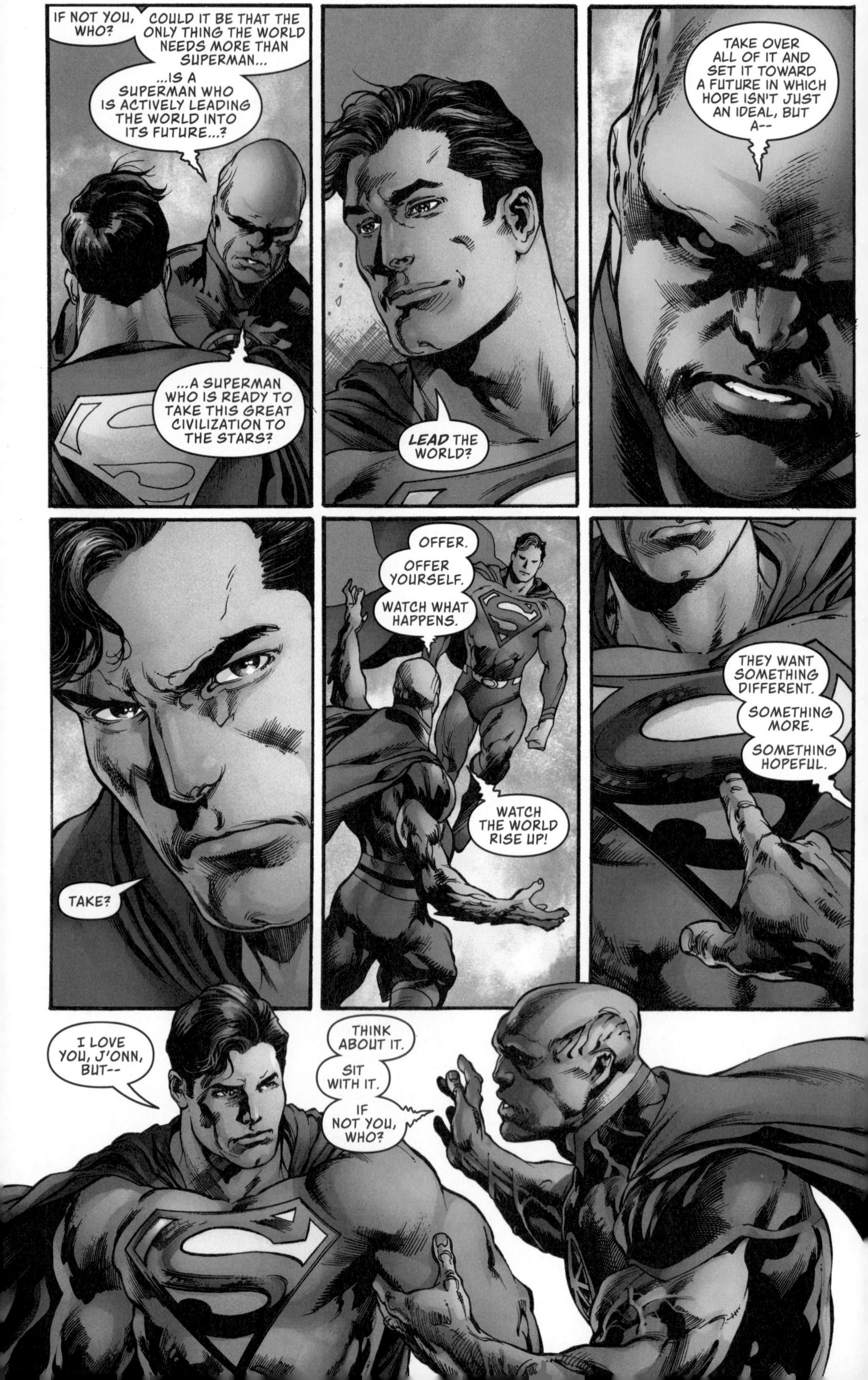
IF NOT YOU, WHO?
COULD IT BE THAT THE ONLY THING THE WORLD NEEDS MORE THAN SUPERMAN...
...IS A SUPERMAN WHO IS ACTIVELY LEADING THE WORLD INTO ITS FUTURE...?
...A SUPERMAN WHO IS READY TO TAKE THIS GREAT CIVILIZATION TO THE STARS?
LEAD THE WORLD?
TAKE OVER ALL OF IT AND SET IT TOWARD A FUTURE IN WHICH HOPE ISN'T JUST AN IDEAL, BUT A--
TAKE?
OFFER.
OFFER YOURSELF.
WATCH WHAT HAPPENS.
WATCH THE WORLD RISE UP!
THEY WANT SOMETHING DIFFERENT.
SOMETHING MORE.
SOMETHING HOPEFUL.
I LOVE YOU, J'ONN, BUT--
THINK ABOUT IT.
SIT WITH IT.
IF NOT YOU, WHO?

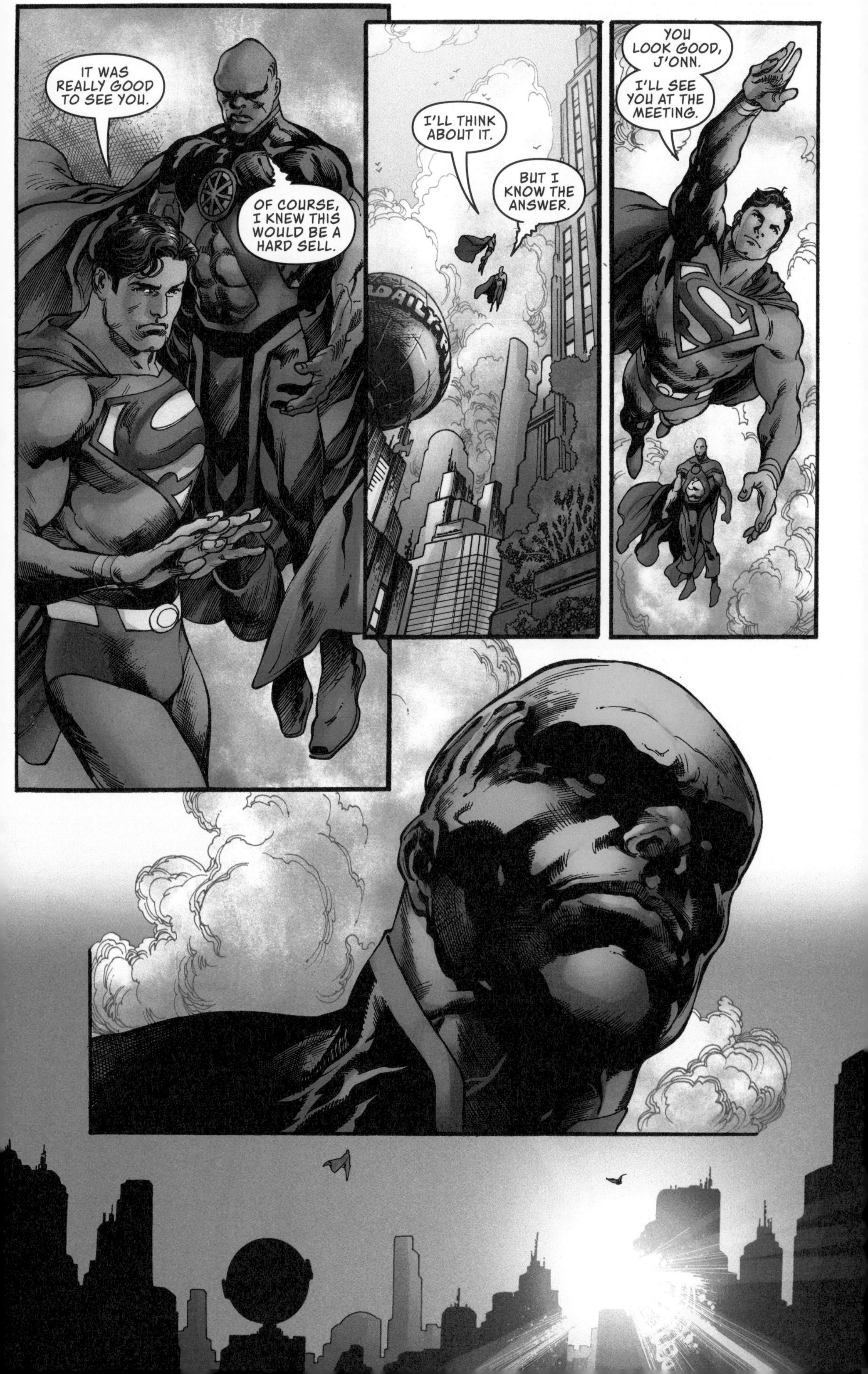
IT WAS REALLY GOOD TO SEE YOU.
OF COURSE, I KNEW THIS WOULD BE A HARD SELL.
I'LL THINK ABOUT IT.
BUT I KNOW THE ANSWER.
YOU LOOK GOOD, J'ONN.
I'LL SEE YOU AT THE MEETING.

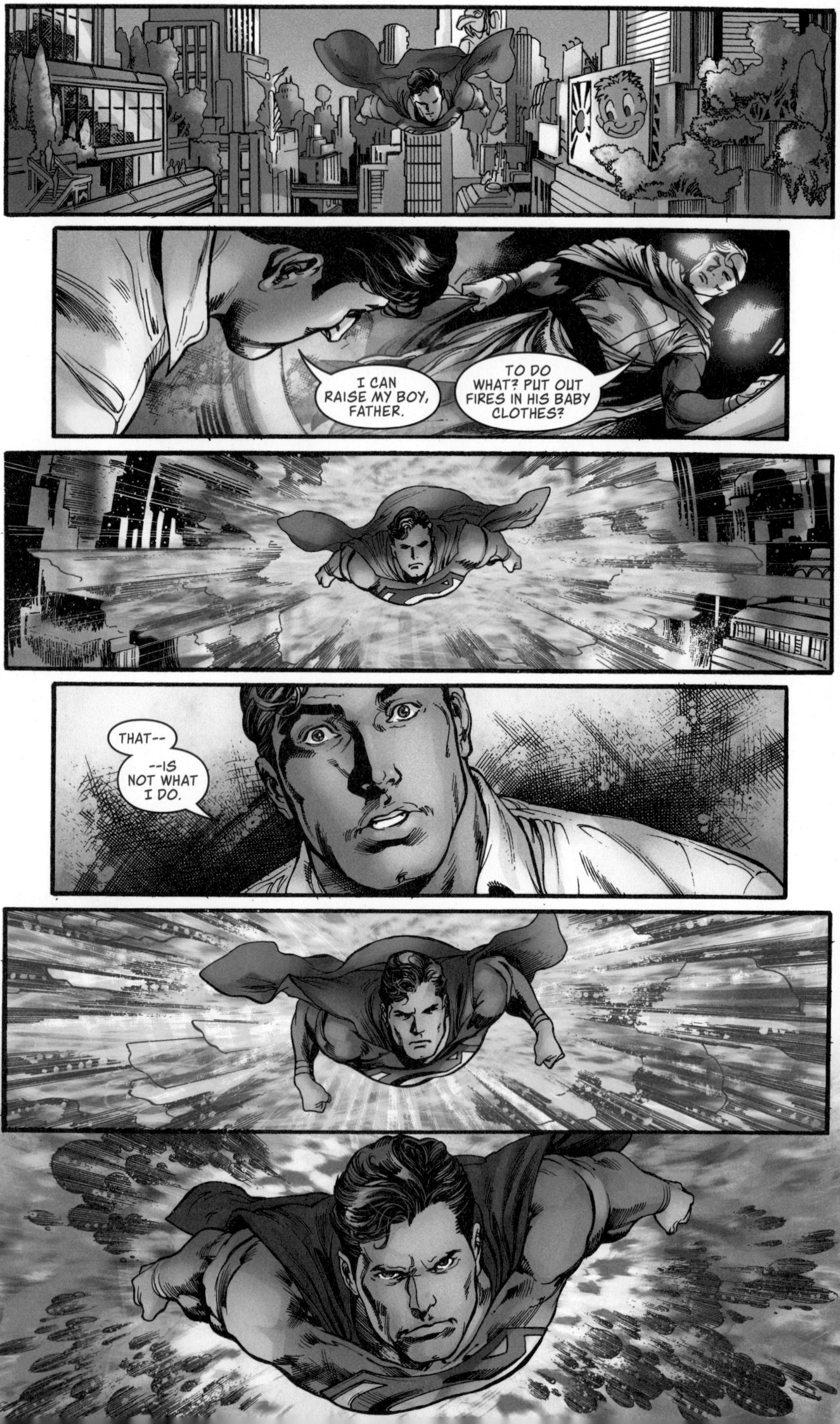
I CAN RAISE MY BOY, FATHER.
TO DO WHAT? PUT OUT FIRES IN HIS BABY CLOTHES?
THAT--
--IS NOT WHAT I DO.

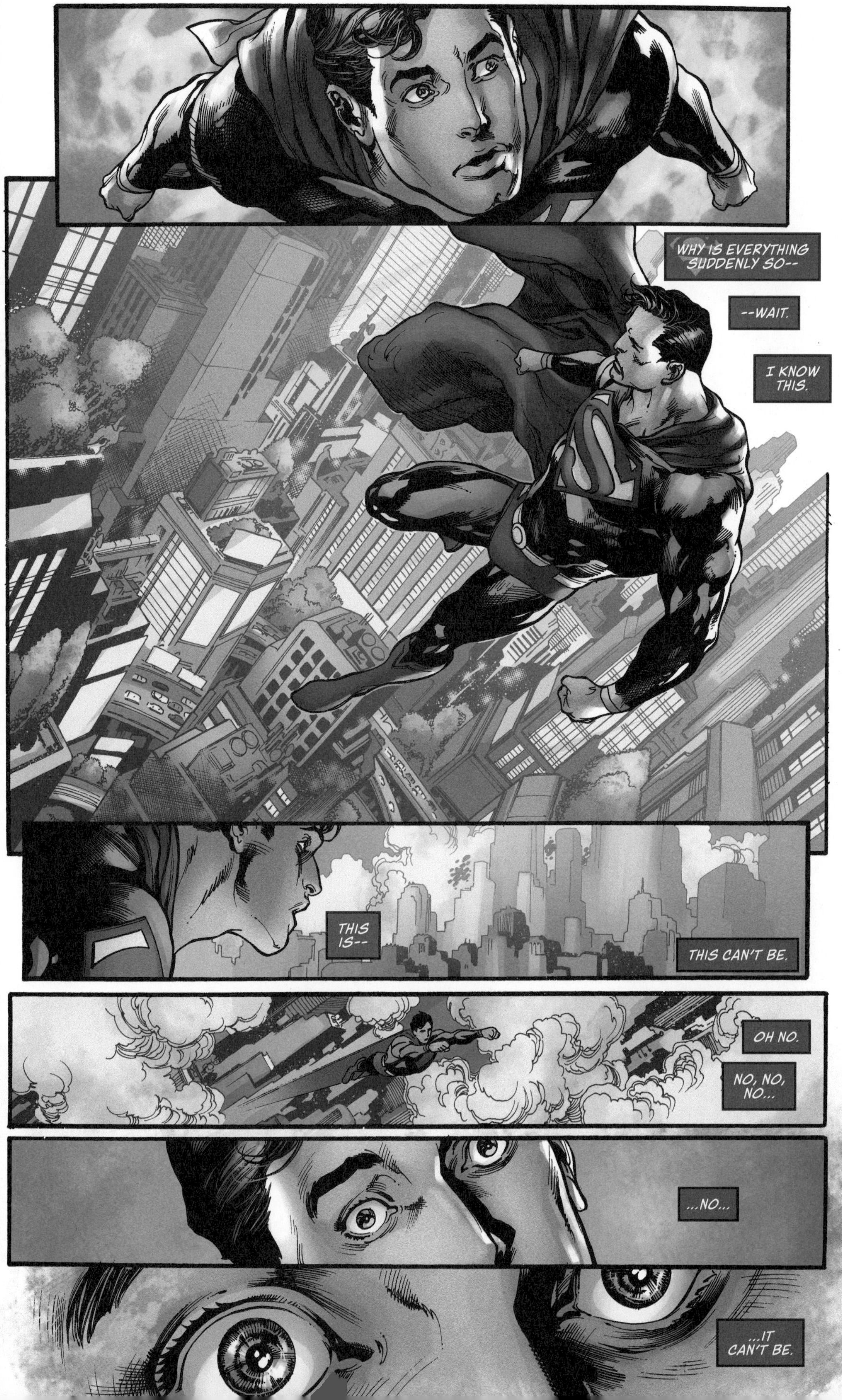
WHY IS EVERYTHING SUDDENLY SO--
--WAIT.
I KNOW THIS.
THIS IS--
THIS CAN'T BE.
OH NO.
NO, NO, NO...
...NO...
...IT CAN'T BE.

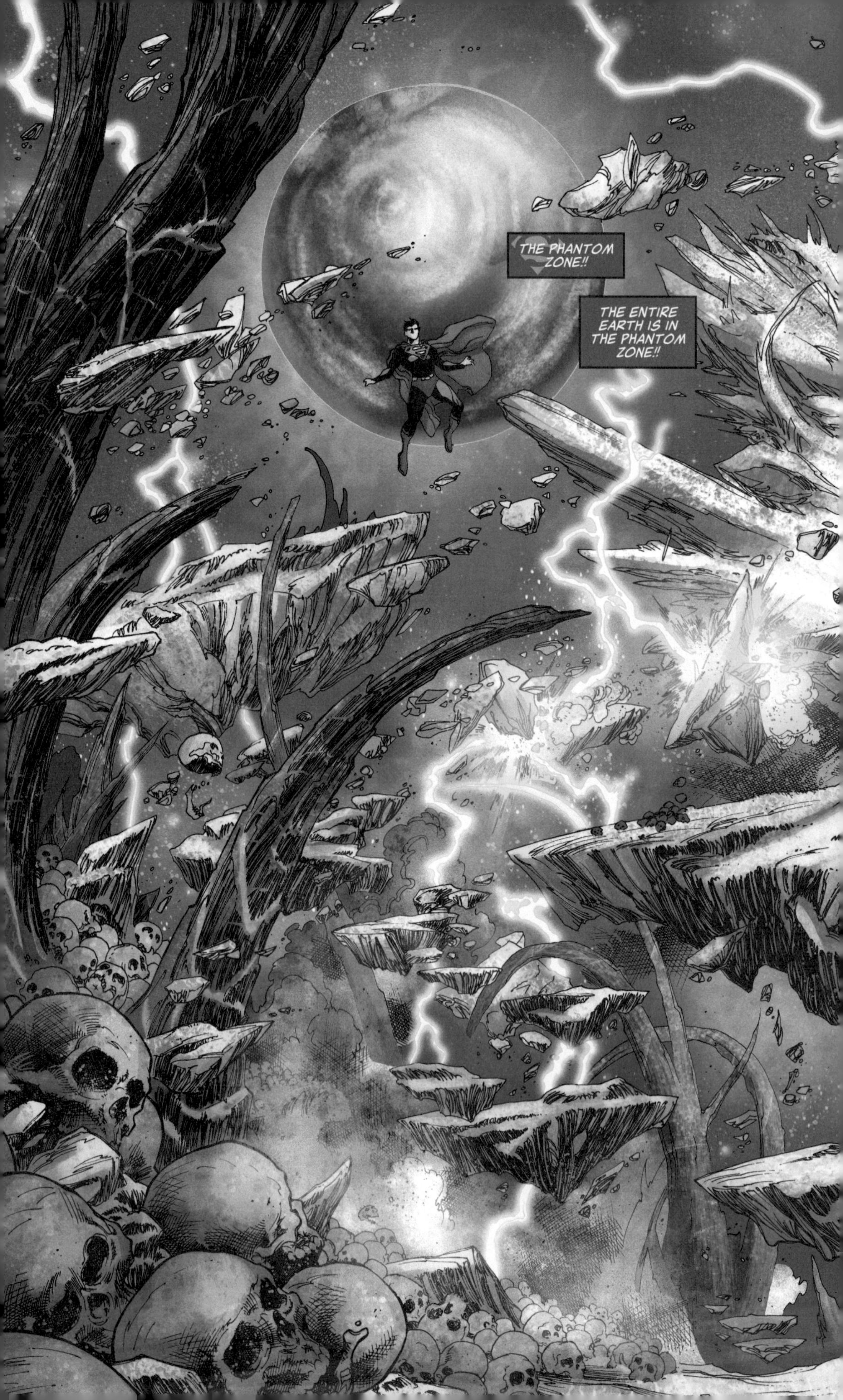
THE PHANTOM ZONE!!
THE ENTIRE EARTH IS IN THE PHANTOM ZONE!!

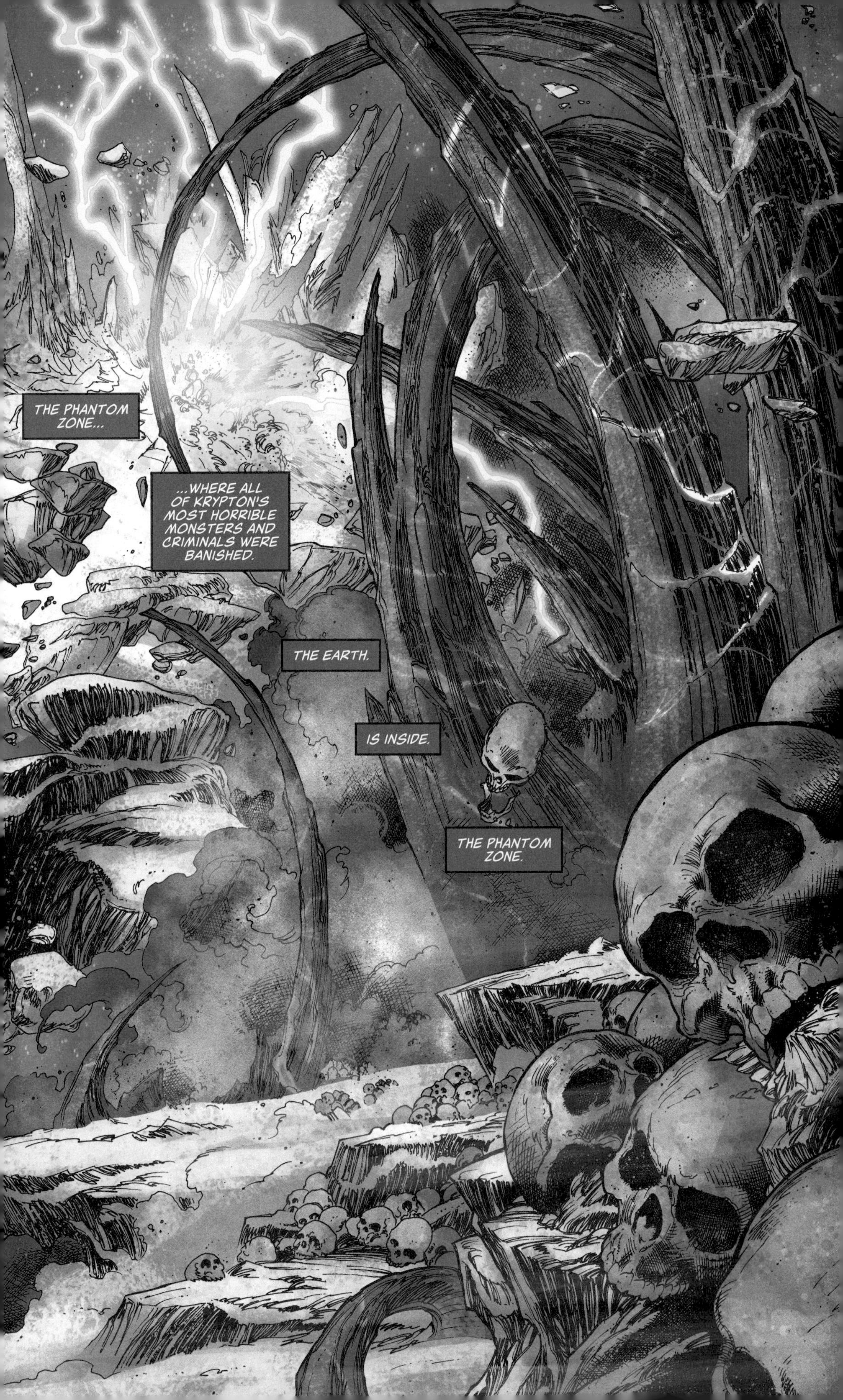
THE PHANTOM ZONE...
...WHERE ALL OF KRYPTON'S MOST HORRIBLE MONSTERS AND CRIMINALS WERE BANISHED.
THE EARTH.
IS INSIDE.
THE PHANTOM ZONE.

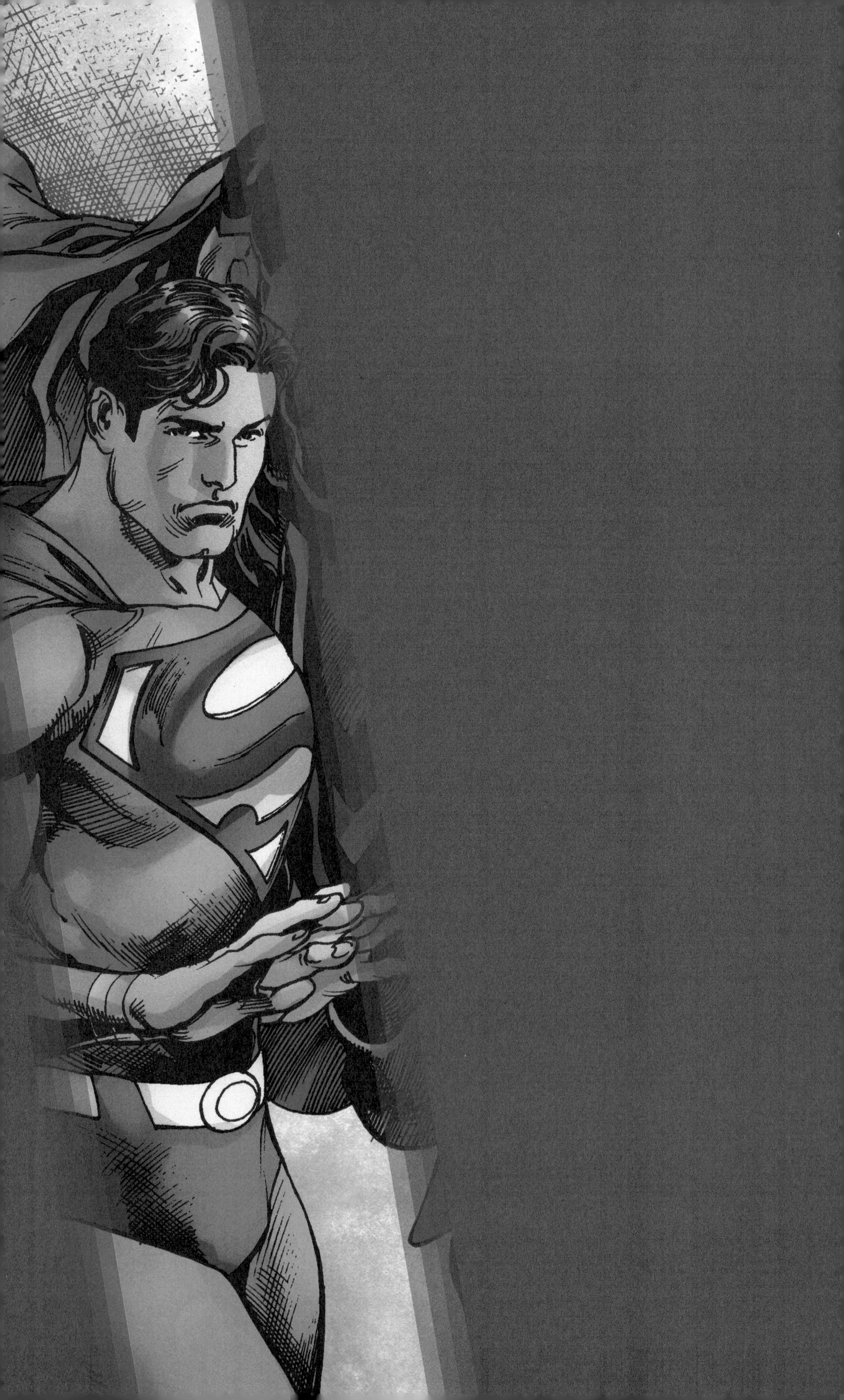

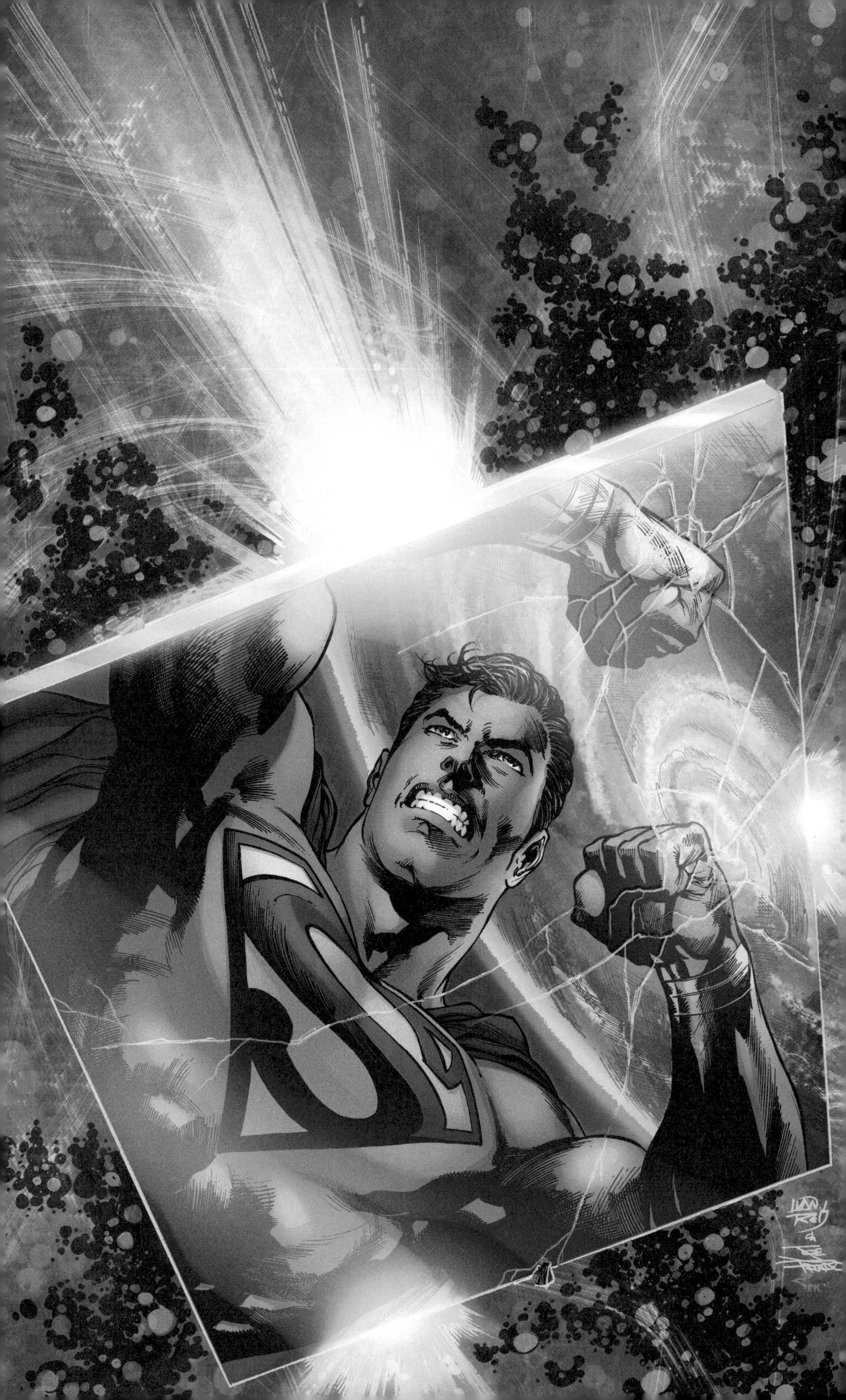

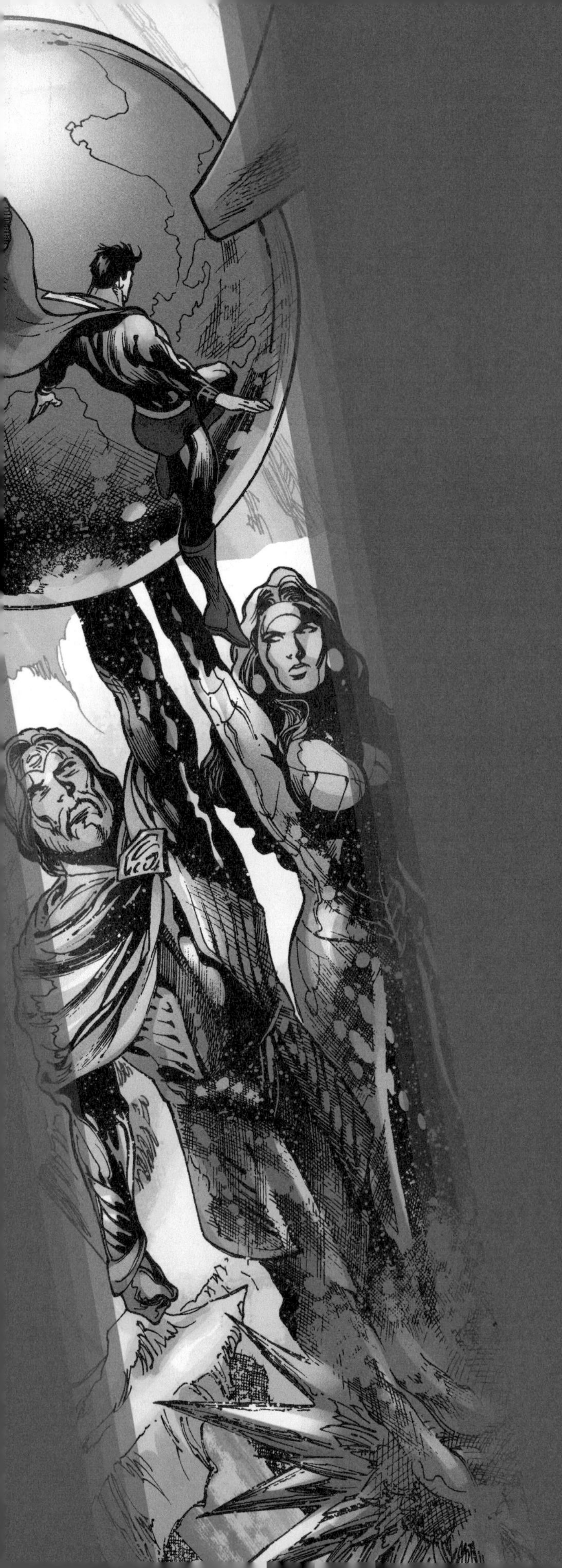

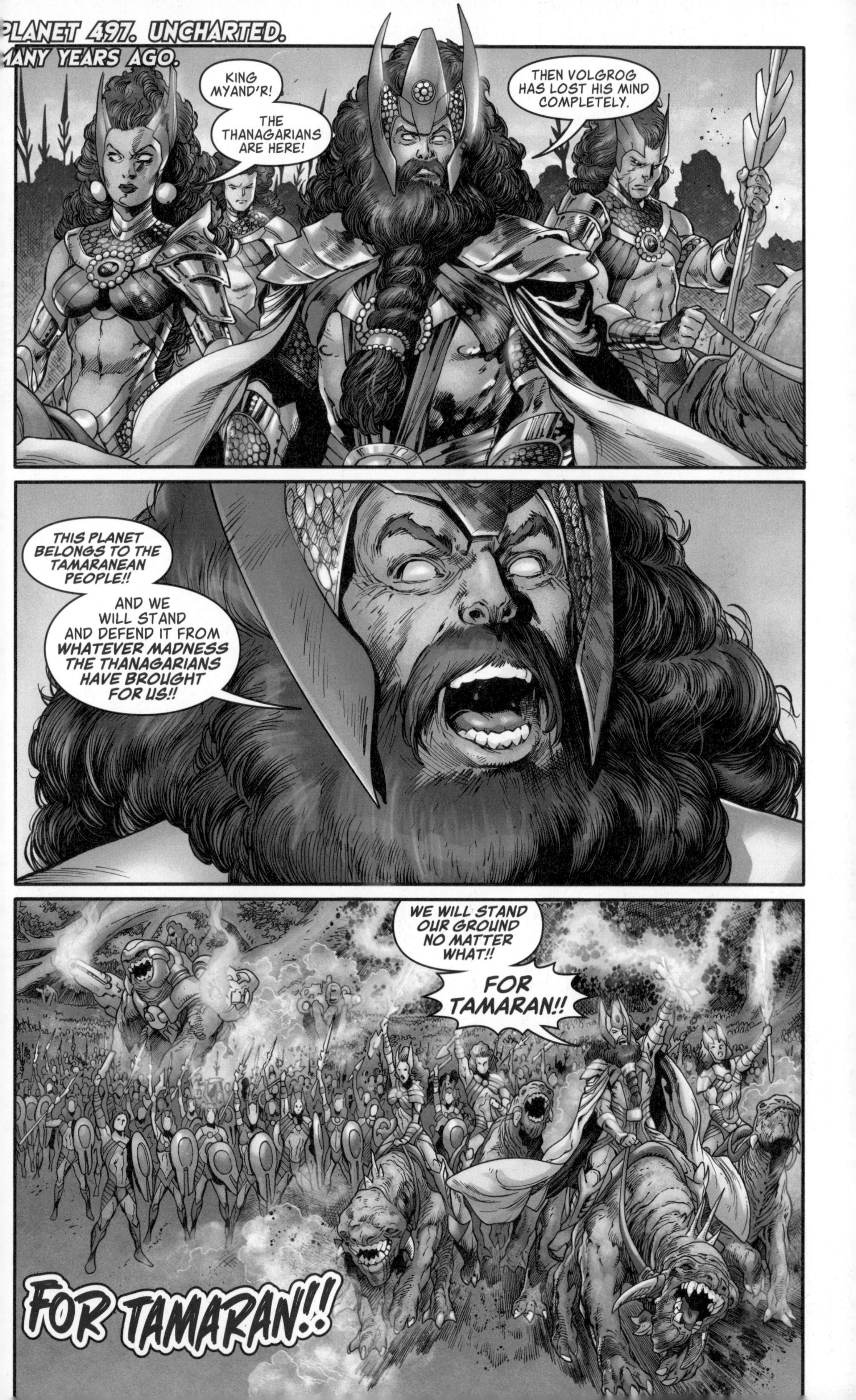
PLANET 497. UNCHARTED.
MANY YEARS AGO.
KING MYAND'R!
THE THANAGARIANS ARE HERE!
THEN VOLGROG HAS LOST HIS MIND COMPLETELY.
THIS PLANET BELONGS TO THE TAMARANEAN PEOPLE!!
AND WE WILL STAND AND DEFEND IT FROM WHATEVER MADNESS THE THANAGARIANS HAVE BROUGHT FOR US!!
WE WILL STAND OUR GROUND NO MATTER WHAT!!
FOR TAMARAN!!
FOR TAMARAN!!

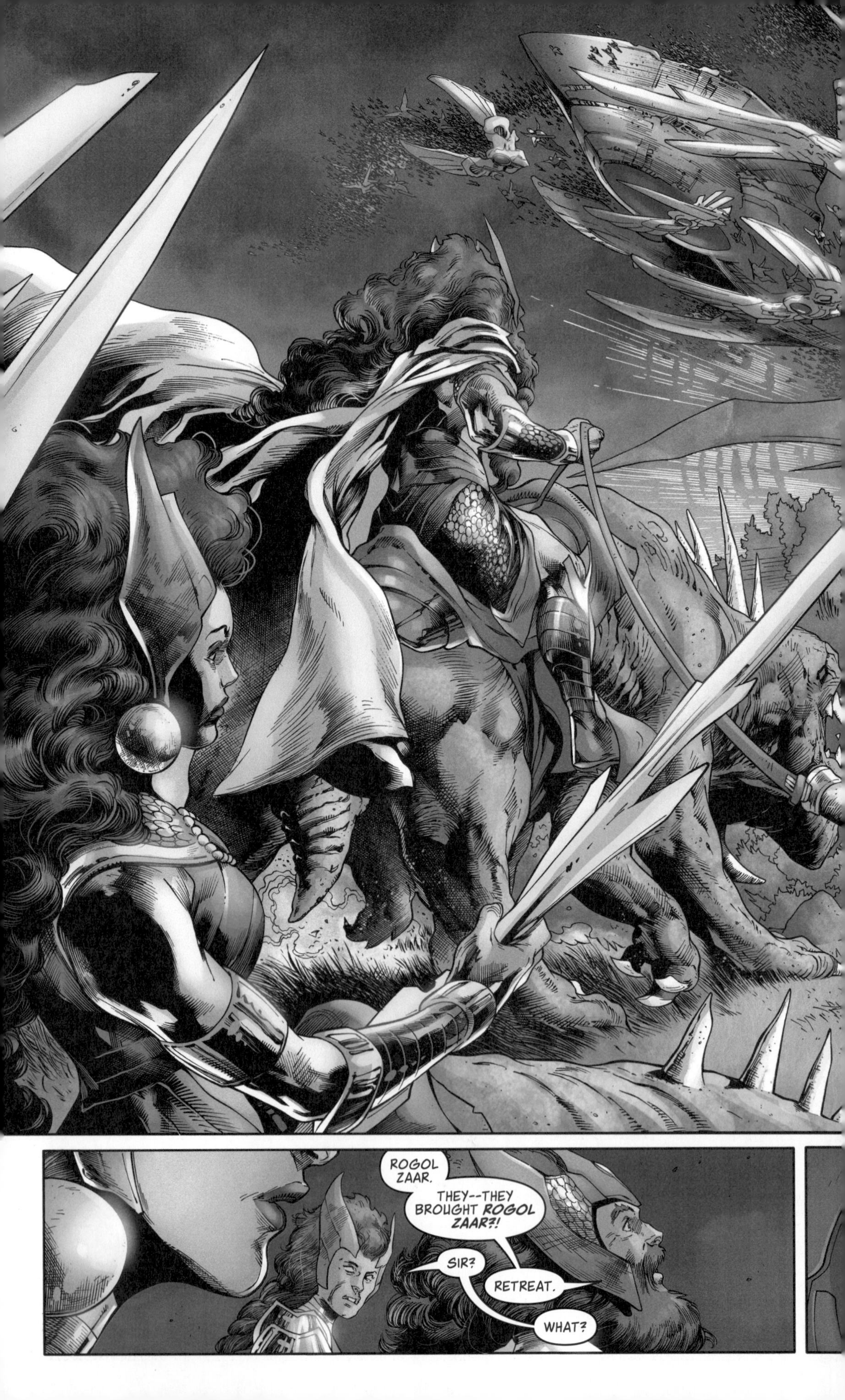
ROGOL ZAAR.
THEY--THEY BROUGHT ROGOL ZAAR?!
SIR?
RETREAT.
WHAT?

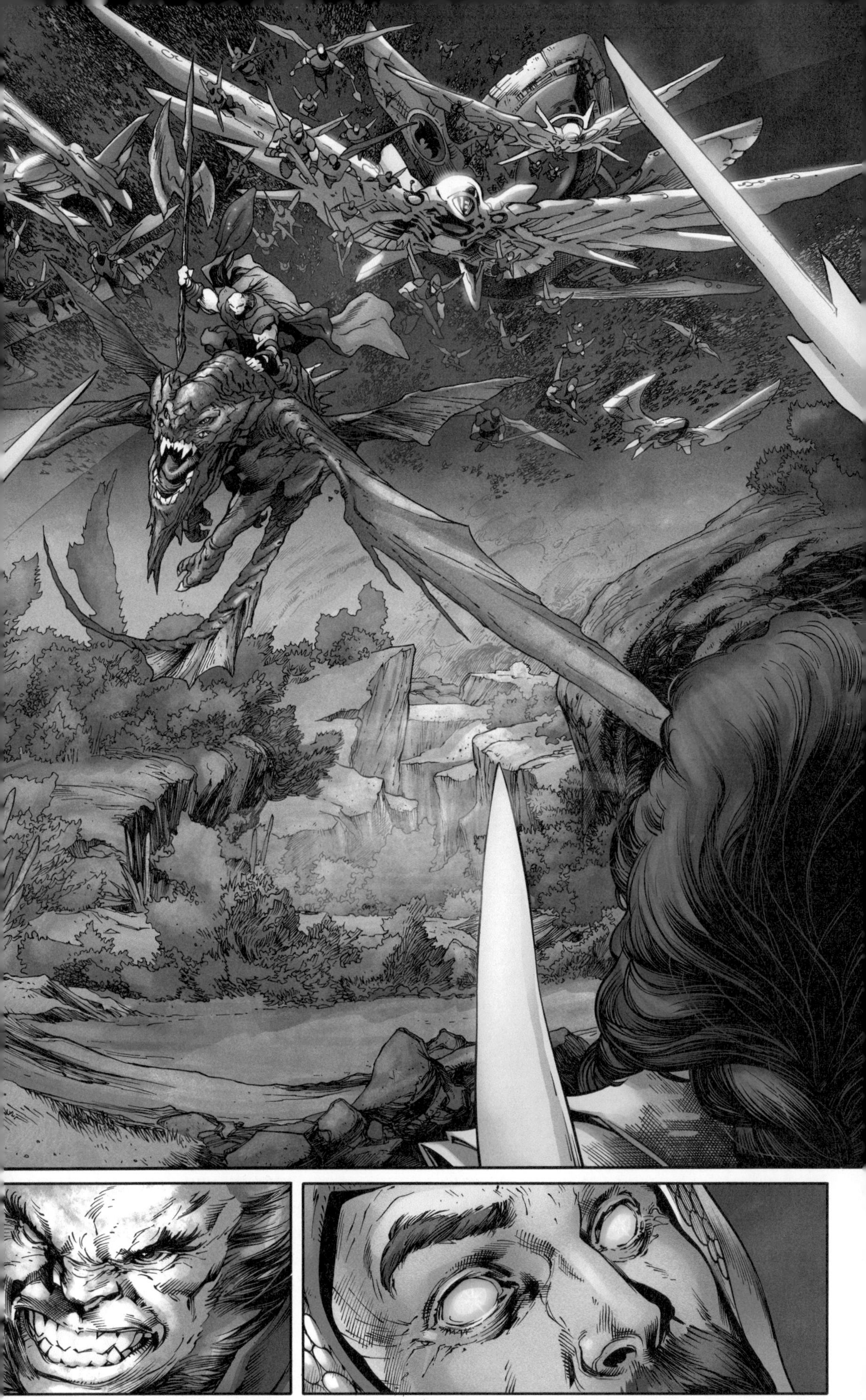

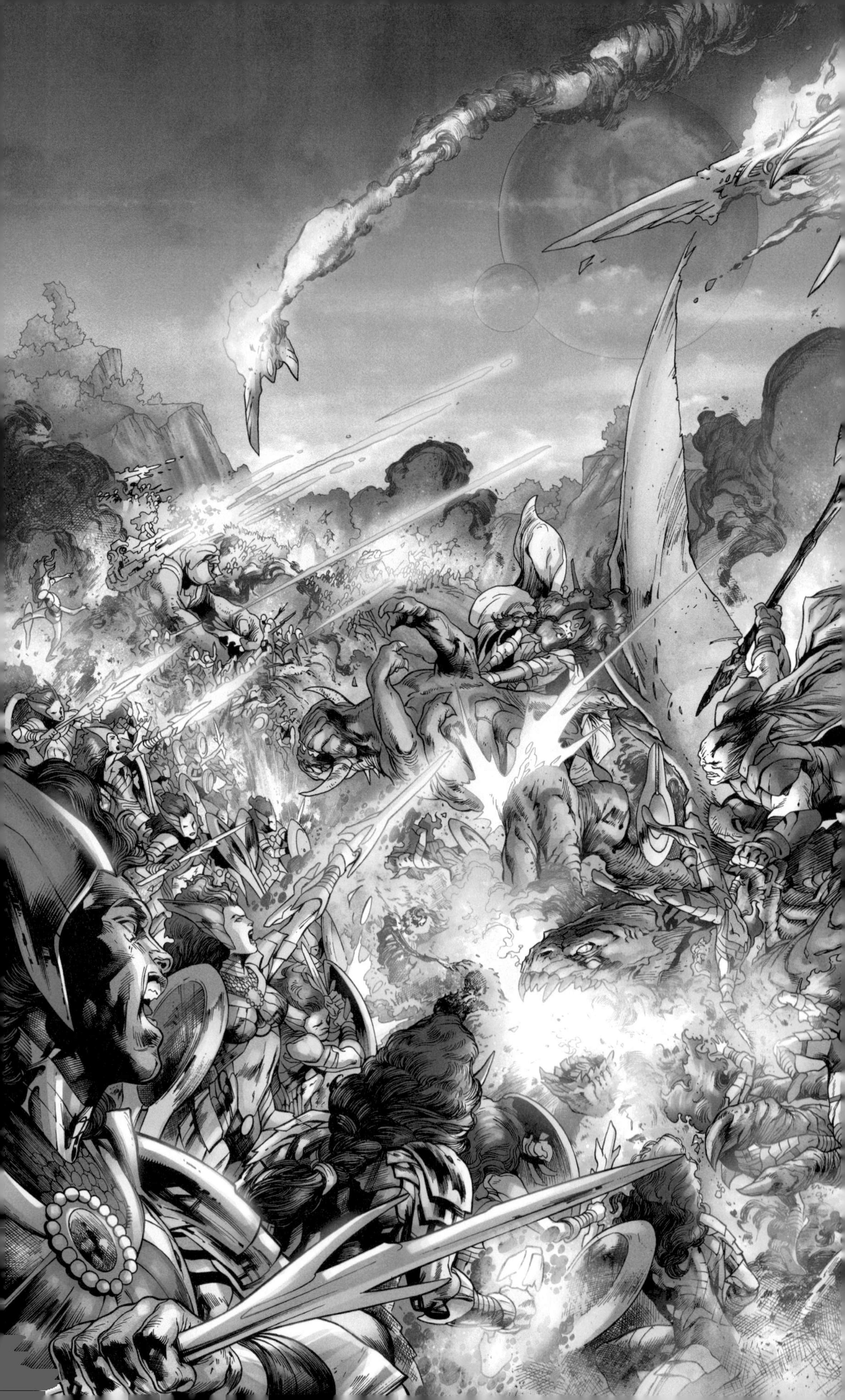

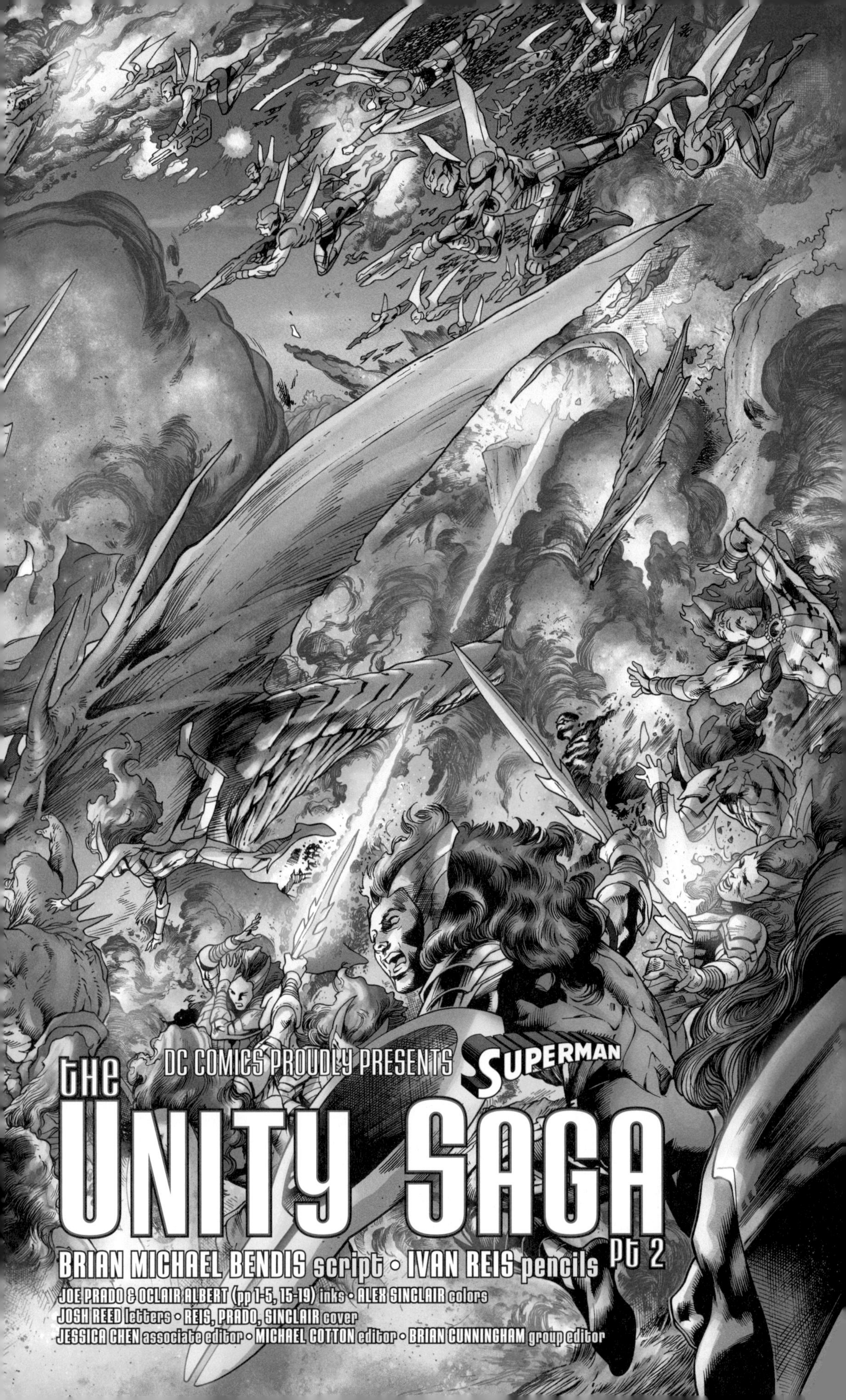
DC COMICS PROUDLY PRESENTS SUPERMAN
THE UNITY SAGA pt 2
BRIAN MICHAEL BENDIS script • IVAN REIS pencils
JOE PRADO & OCLAIR ALBERT (pp 1-5, 15-19) inks • ALEX SINCLAIR colors
JOSH REED letters • REIS, PRADO, SINCLAIR cover
JESSICA CHEN associate editor • MICHAEL COTTON editor • BRIAN CUNNINGHAM group editor

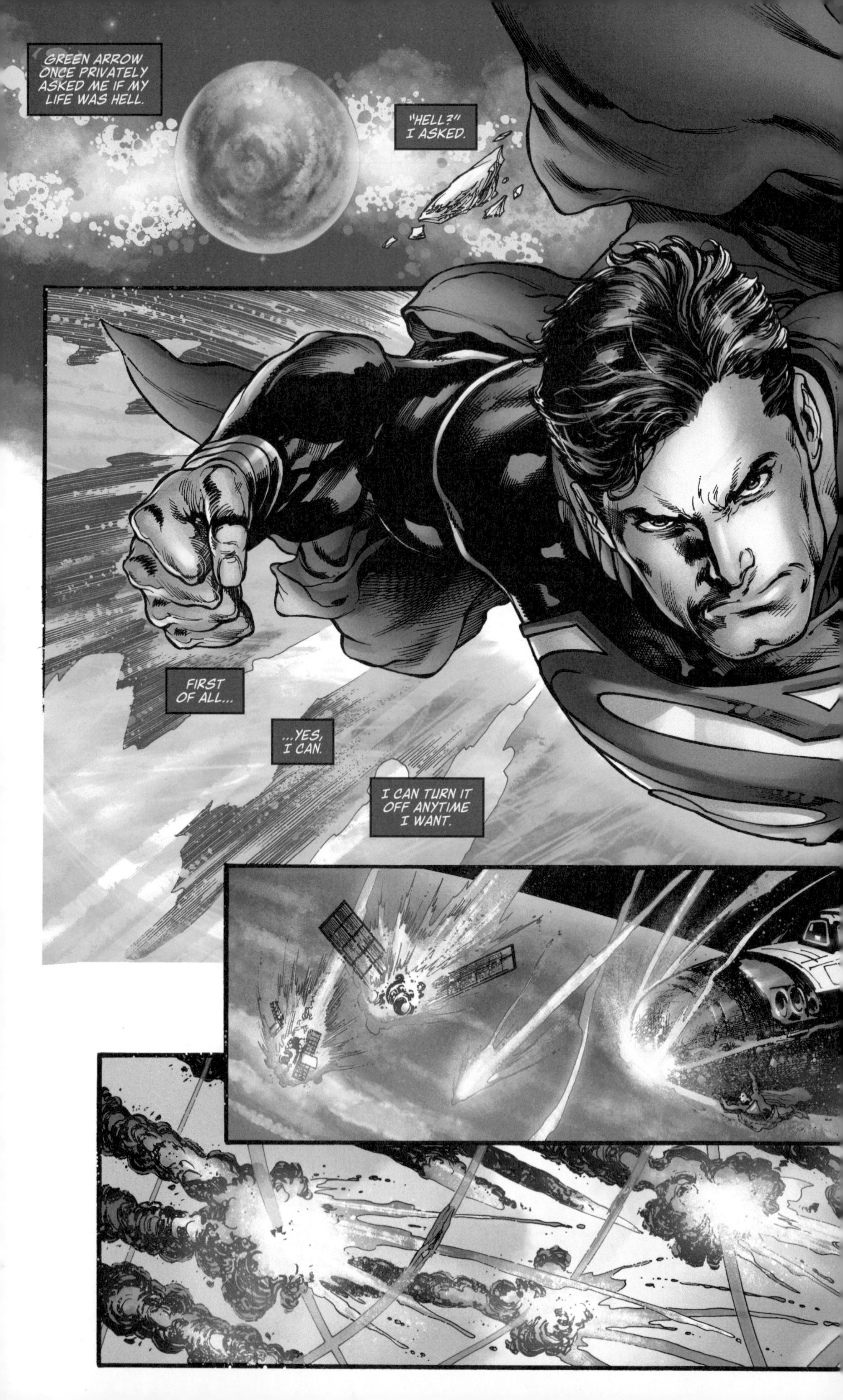
GREEN ARROW ONCE PRIVATELY ASKED ME IF MY LIFE WAS HELL.
"HELL?" I ASKED.
FIRST OF ALL...
...YES, I CAN.
I CAN TURN IT OFF ANYTIME I WANT.

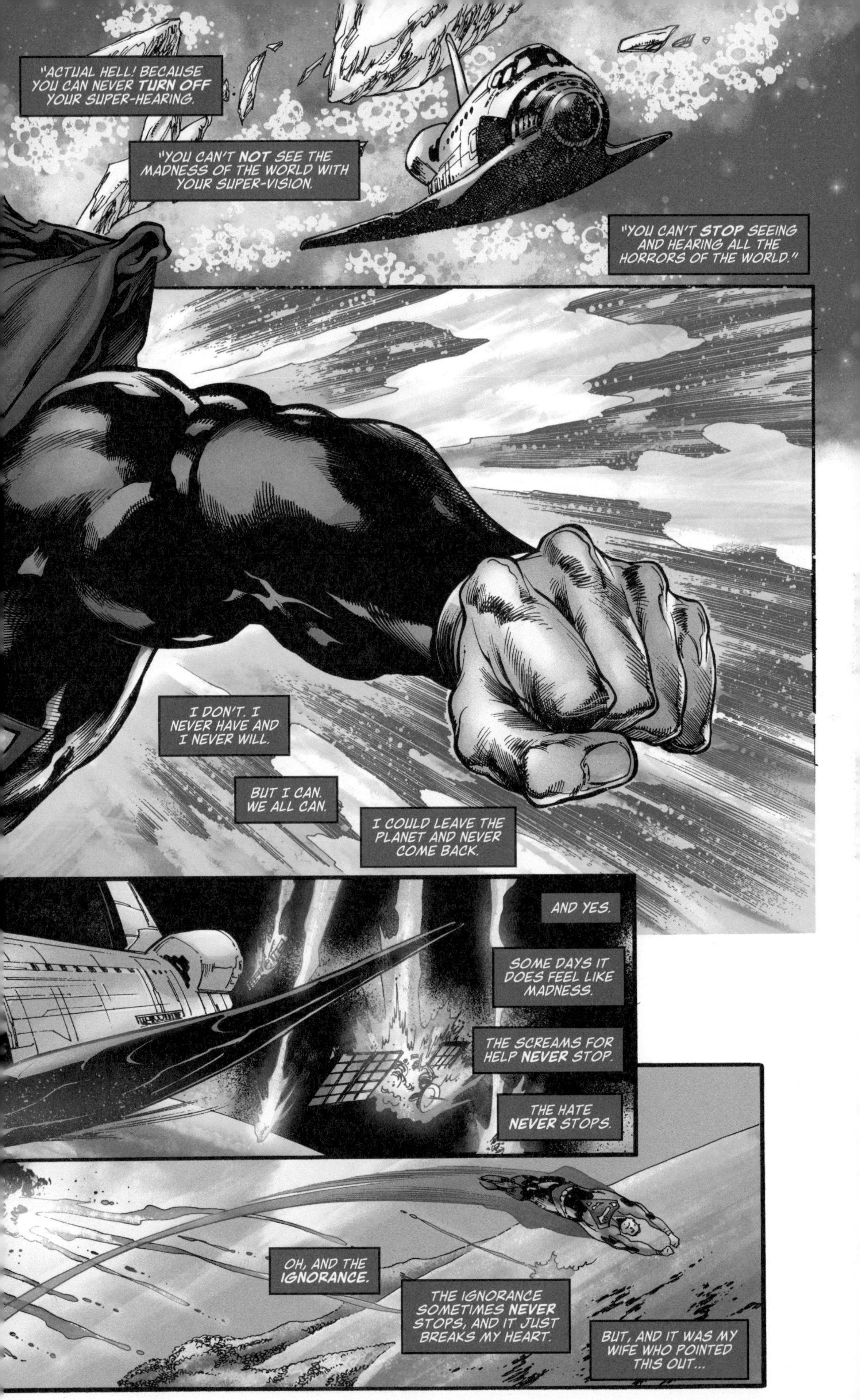

"ACTUAL HELL! BECAUSE YOU CAN NEVER TURN OFF YOUR SUPER-HEARING.
"YOU CAN'T NOT SEE THE MADNESS OF THE WORLD WITH YOUR SUPER-VISION.
"YOU CAN'T STOP SEEING AND HEARING ALL THE HORRORS OF THE WORLD."
I DON'T. I NEVER HAVE AND I NEVER WILL.
BUT I CAN. WE ALL CAN.
I COULD LEAVE THE PLANET AND NEVER COME BACK.
AND YES.
SOME DAYS IT DOES FEEL LIKE MADNESS.
THE SCREAMS FOR HELP NEVER STOP.
THE HATE NEVER STOPS.
OH, AND THE IGNORANCE.
THE IGNORANCE SOMETIMES NEVER STOPS, AND IT JUST BREAKS MY HEART.
BUT, AND IT WAS MY WIFE WHO POINTED THIS OUT...

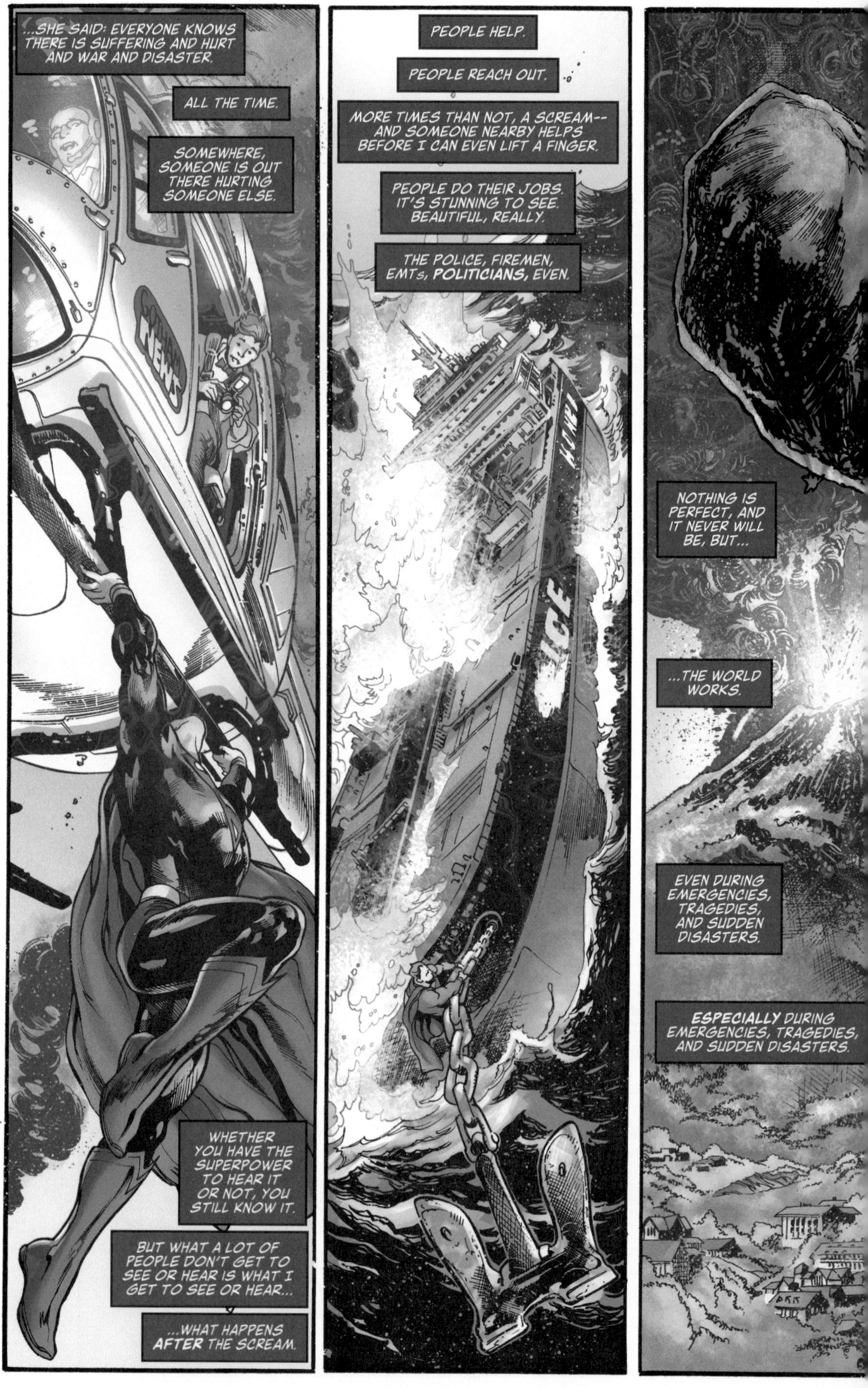
...SHE SAID: EVERYONE KNOWS THERE IS SUFFERING AND HURT AND WAR AND DISASTER.
ALL THE TIME.
SOMEWHERE, SOMEONE IS OUT THERE HURTING SOMEONE ELSE.
WHETHER YOU HAVE THE SUPERPOWER TO HEAR IT OR NOT, YOU STILL KNOW IT.
BUT WHAT A LOT OF PEOPLE DON'T GET TO SEE OR HEAR IS WHAT I GET TO SEE OR HEAR...
...WHAT HAPPENS AFTER THE SCREAM.
PEOPLE HELP.
PEOPLE REACH OUT.
MORE TIMES THAN NOT, A SCREAM-- AND SOMEONE NEARBY HELPS BEFORE I CAN EVEN LIFT A FINGER.
PEOPLE DO THEIR JOBS. IT'S STUNNING TO SEE. BEAUTIFUL, REALLY.
THE POLICE, FIREMEN, EMTs, POLITICIANS, EVEN.
NOTHING IS PERFECT, AND IT NEVER WILL BE, BUT...
...THE WORLD WORKS.
EVEN DURING EMERGENCIES, TRAGEDIES, AND SUDDEN DISASTERS.
ESPECIALLY DURING EMERGENCIES, TRAGEDIES, AND SUDDEN DISASTERS.

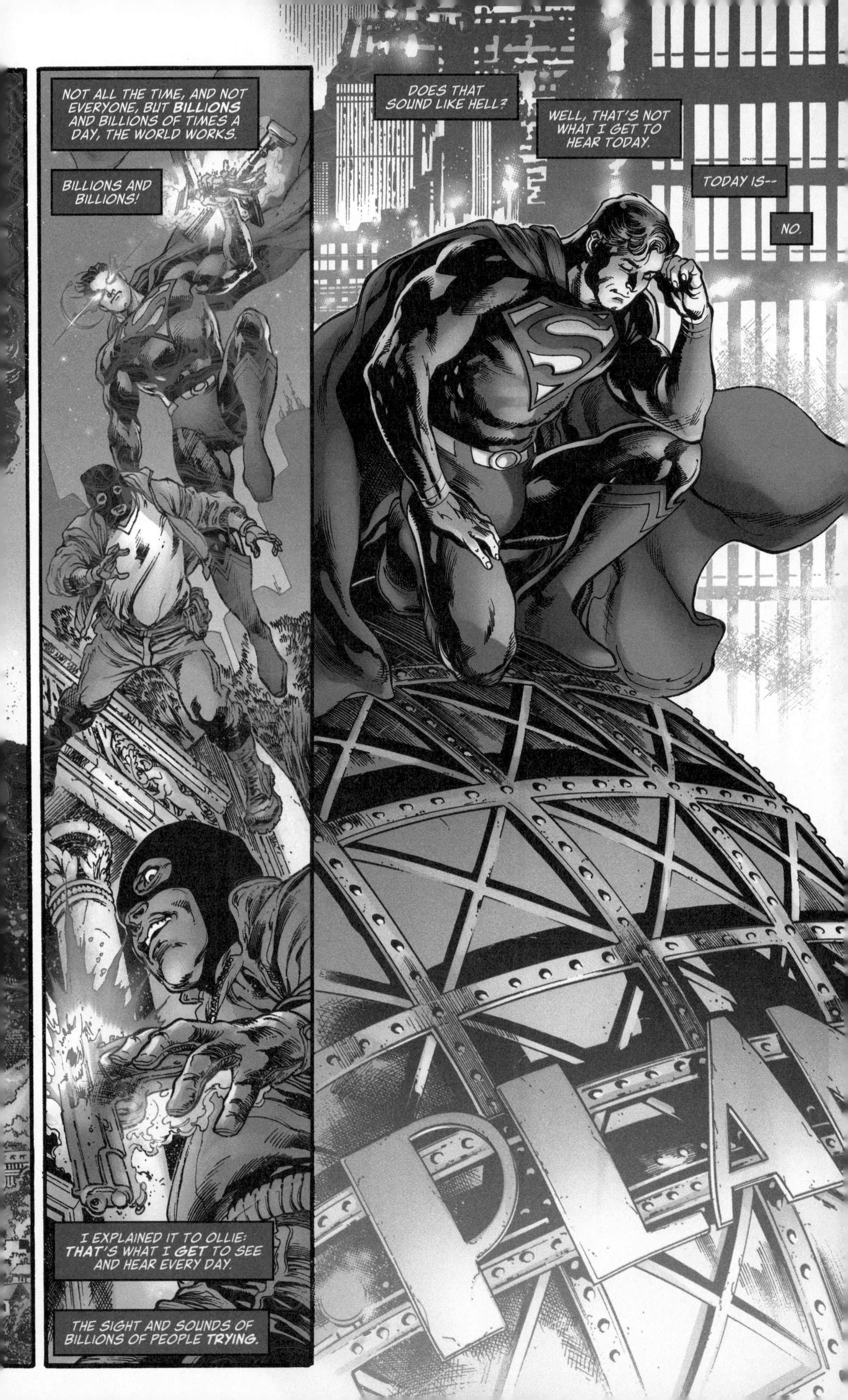
NOT ALL THE TIME, AND NOT EVERYONE, BUT **BILLIONS** AND BILLIONS OF TIMES A DAY, THE WORLD WORKS.
BILLIONS AND BILLIONS!
I EXPLAINED IT TO OLLIE: **THAT**'S WHAT I **GET** TO SEE AND HEAR EVERY DAY.
THE SIGHT AND SOUNDS OF BILLIONS OF PEOPLE **TRYING**.
DOES THAT SOUND LIKE HELL?
WELL, THAT'S NOT WHAT I GET TO HEAR TODAY.
TODAY IS--
NO.

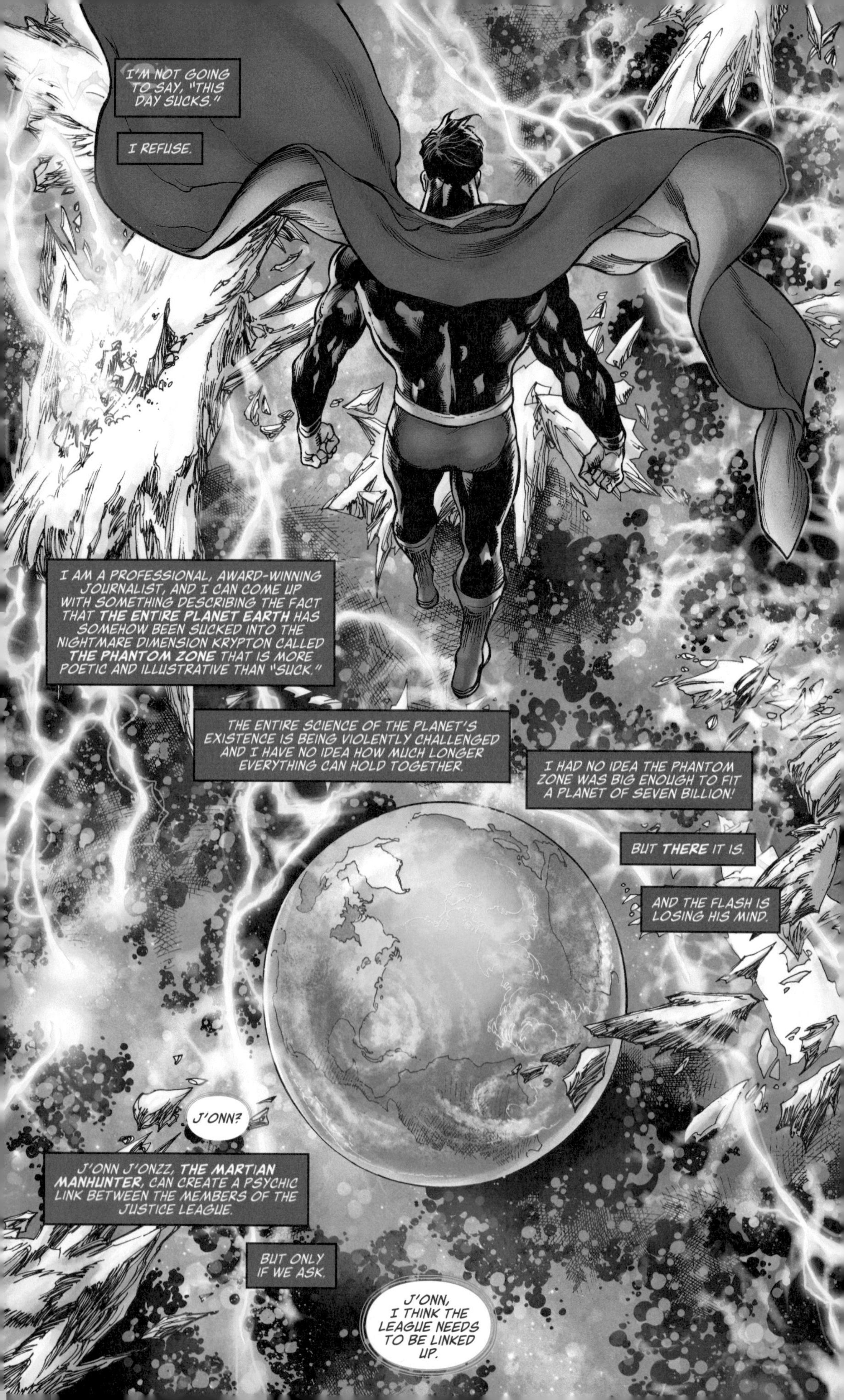
I'M NOT GOING TO SAY, "THIS DAY SUCKS."
I REFUSE.
I AM A PROFESSIONAL, AWARD-WINNING JOURNALIST, AND I CAN COME UP WITH SOMETHING DESCRIBING THE FACT THAT THE ENTIRE PLANET EARTH HAS SOMEHOW BEEN SUCKED INTO THE NIGHTMARE DIMENSION KRYPTON CALLED THE PHANTOM ZONE THAT IS MORE POETIC AND ILLUSTRATIVE THAN "SUCK."
THE ENTIRE SCIENCE OF THE PLANET'S EXISTENCE IS BEING VIOLENTLY CHALLENGED AND I HAVE NO IDEA HOW MUCH LONGER EVERYTHING CAN HOLD TOGETHER.
I HAD NO IDEA THE PHANTOM ZONE WAS BIG ENOUGH TO FIT A PLANET OF SEVEN BILLION!
BUT THERE IT IS.
AND THE FLASH IS LOSING HIS MIND.
J'ONN?
J'ONN J'ONZZ, THE MARTIAN MANHUNTER, CAN CREATE A PSYCHIC LINK BETWEEN THE MEMBERS OF THE JUSTICE LEAGUE.
BUT ONLY IF WE ASK.
J'ONN, I THINK THE LEAGUE NEEDS TO BE LINKED UP.

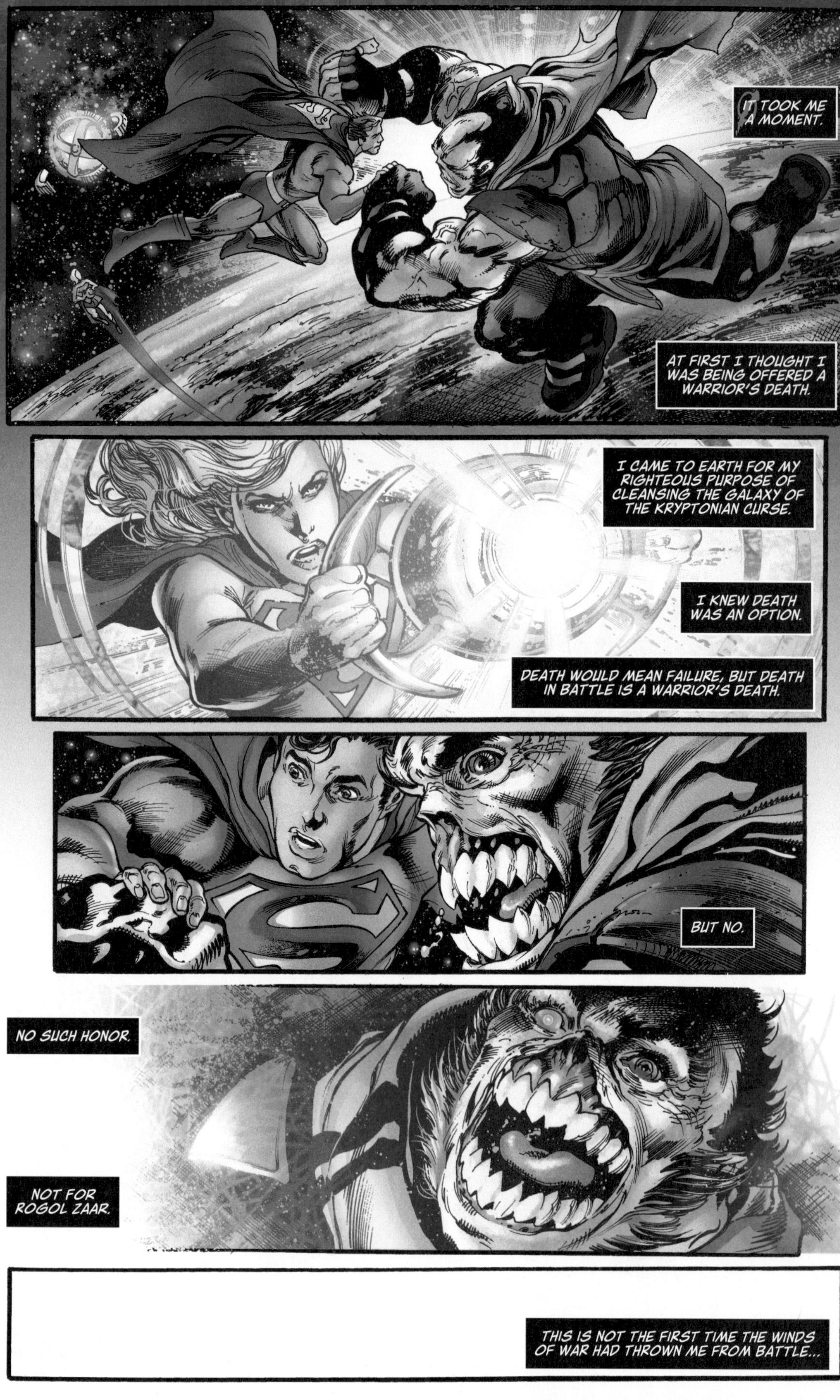
IT TOOK ME A MOMENT.
AT FIRST I THOUGHT I WAS BEING OFFERED A WARRIOR'S DEATH.
I CAME TO EARTH FOR MY RIGHTEOUS PURPOSE OF CLEANSING THE GALAXY OF THE KRYPTONIAN CURSE.
I KNEW DEATH WAS AN OPTION.
DEATH WOULD MEAN FAILURE, BUT DEATH IN BATTLE IS A WARRIOR'S DEATH.
BUT NO.
NO SUCH HONOR.
NOT FOR ROGOL ZAAR.
THIS IS NOT THE FIRST TIME THE WINDS OF WAR HAD THROWN ME FROM BATTLE...

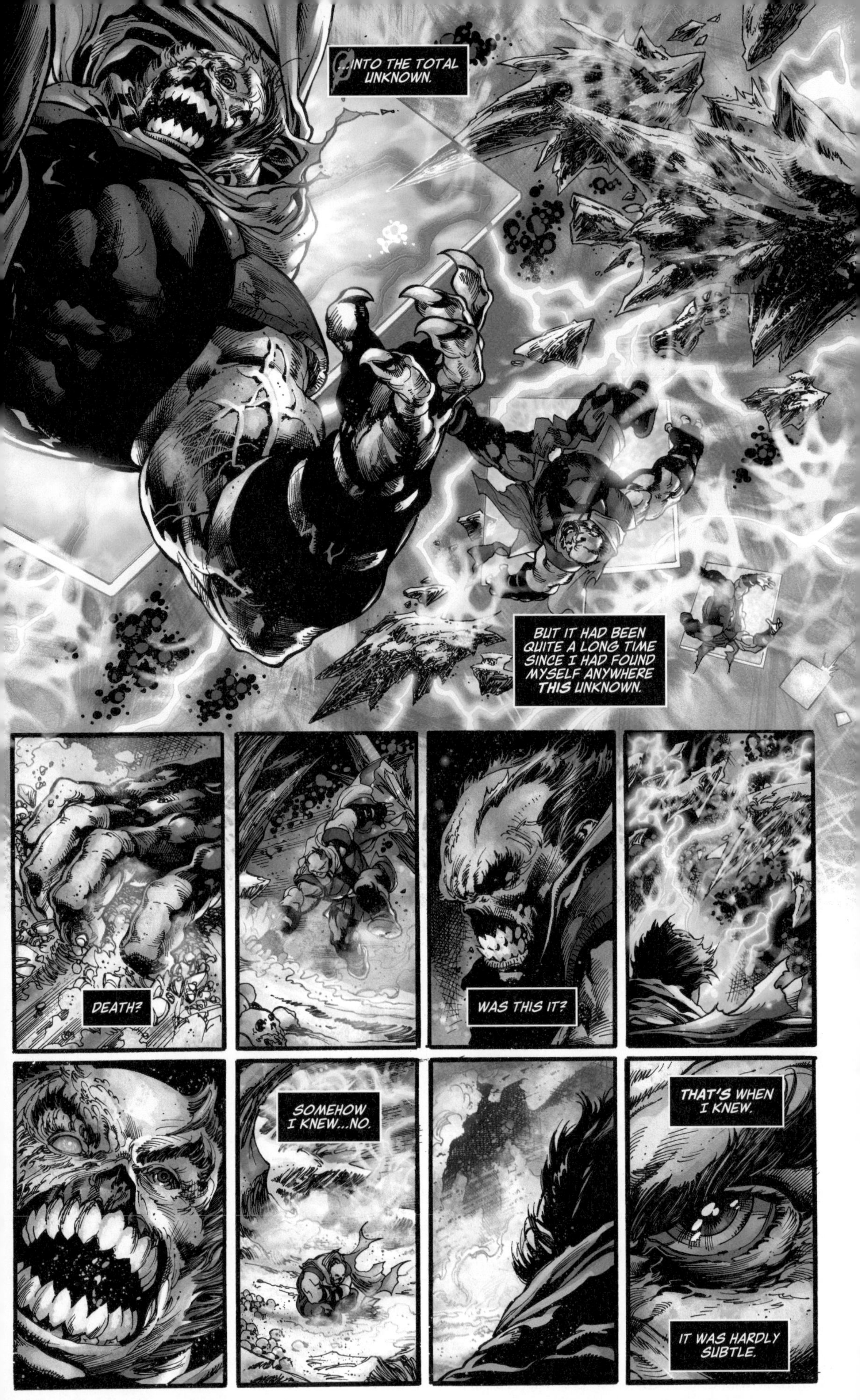
...INTO THE TOTAL UNKNOWN.
BUT IT HAD BEEN QUITE A LONG TIME SINCE I HAD FOUND MYSELF ANYWHERE THIS UNKNOWN.
DEATH?
WAS THIS IT?
SOMEHOW I KNEW...NO.
THAT'S WHEN I KNEW.
IT WAS HARDLY SUBTLE.

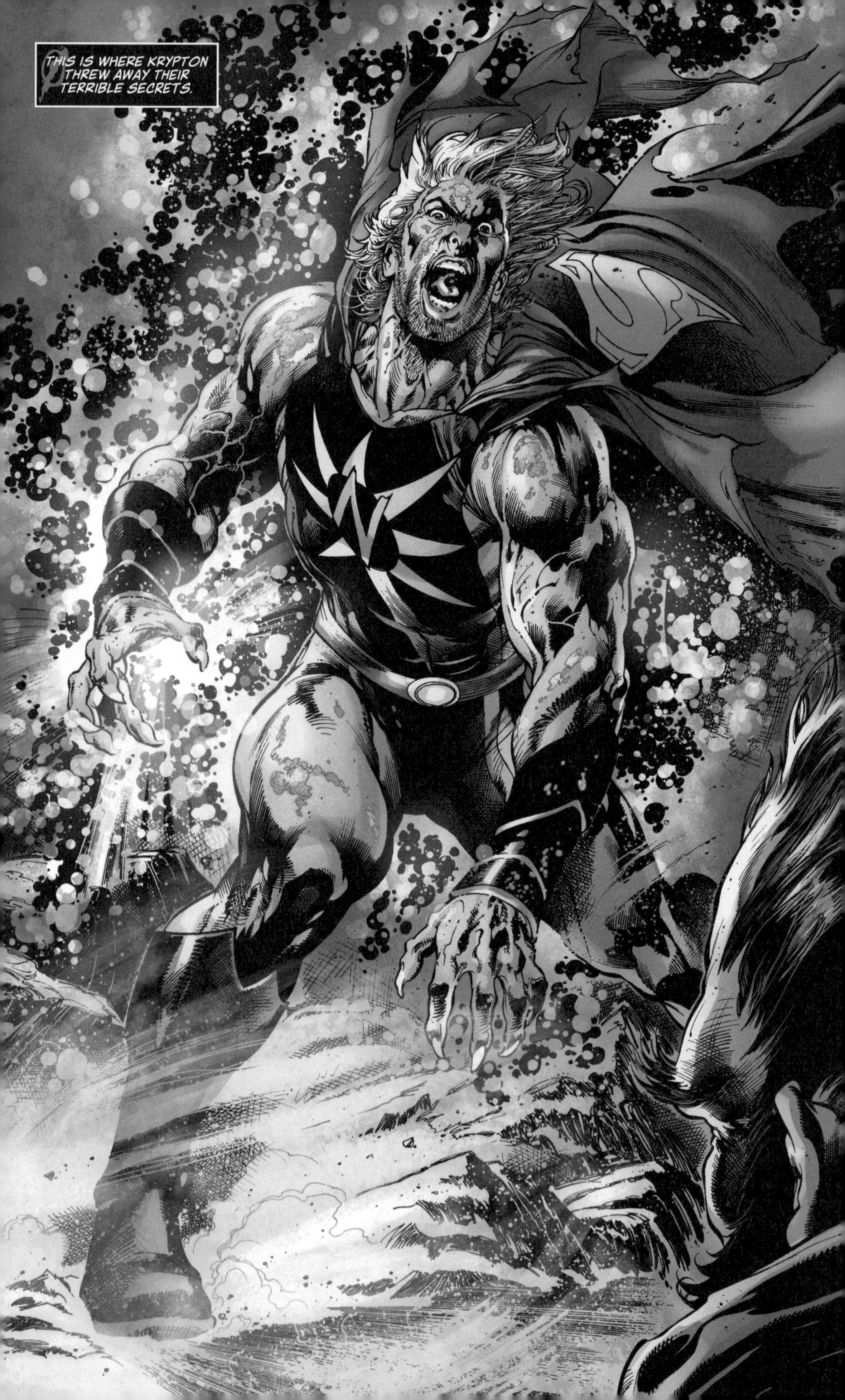
THIS IS WHERE KRYPTON THREW AWAY THEIR TERRIBLE SECRETS.

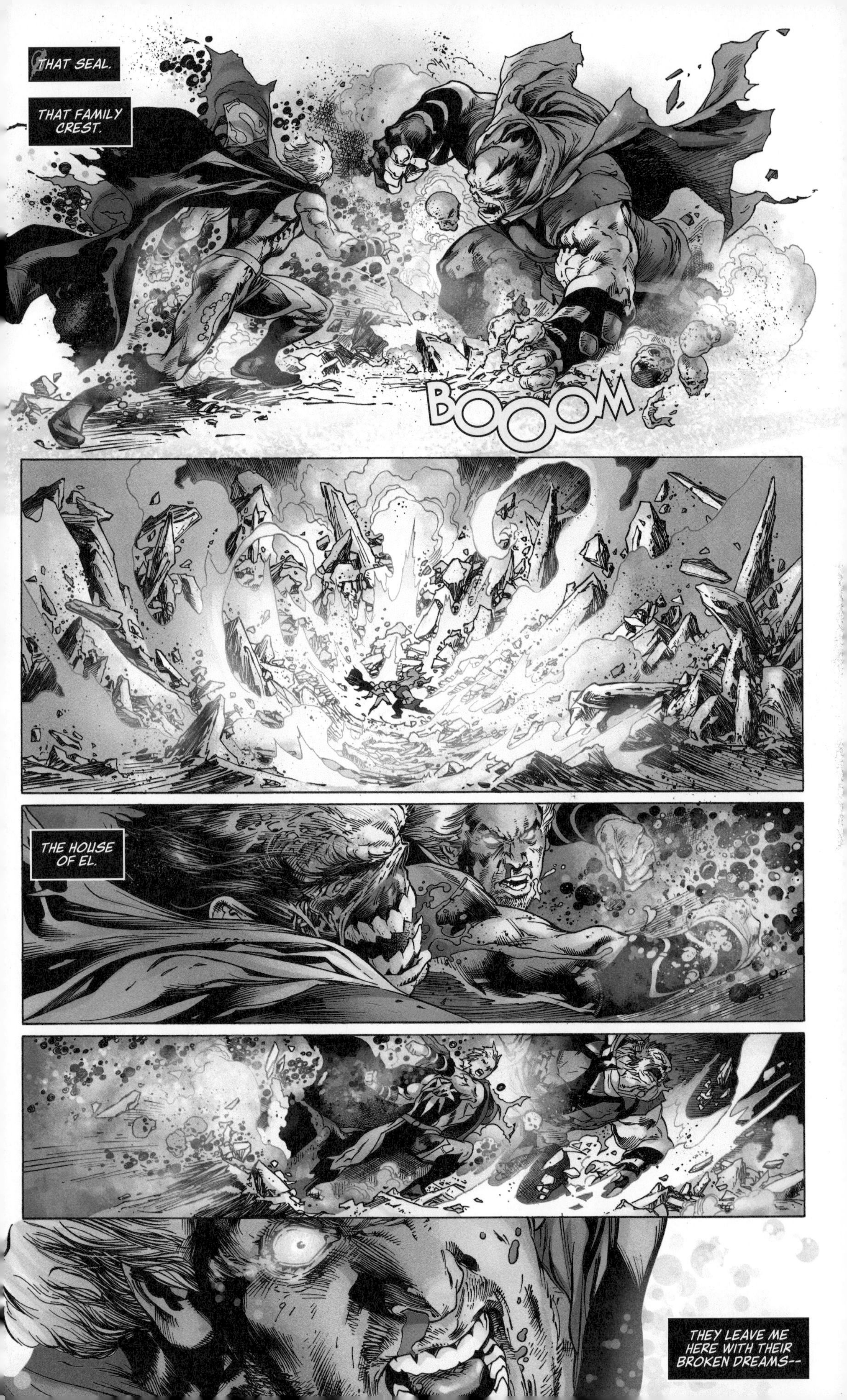
THAT SEAL.
THAT FAMILY CREST.
BOOOOM
THE HOUSE OF EL.
THEY LEAVE ME HERE WITH THEIR BROKEN DREAMS--

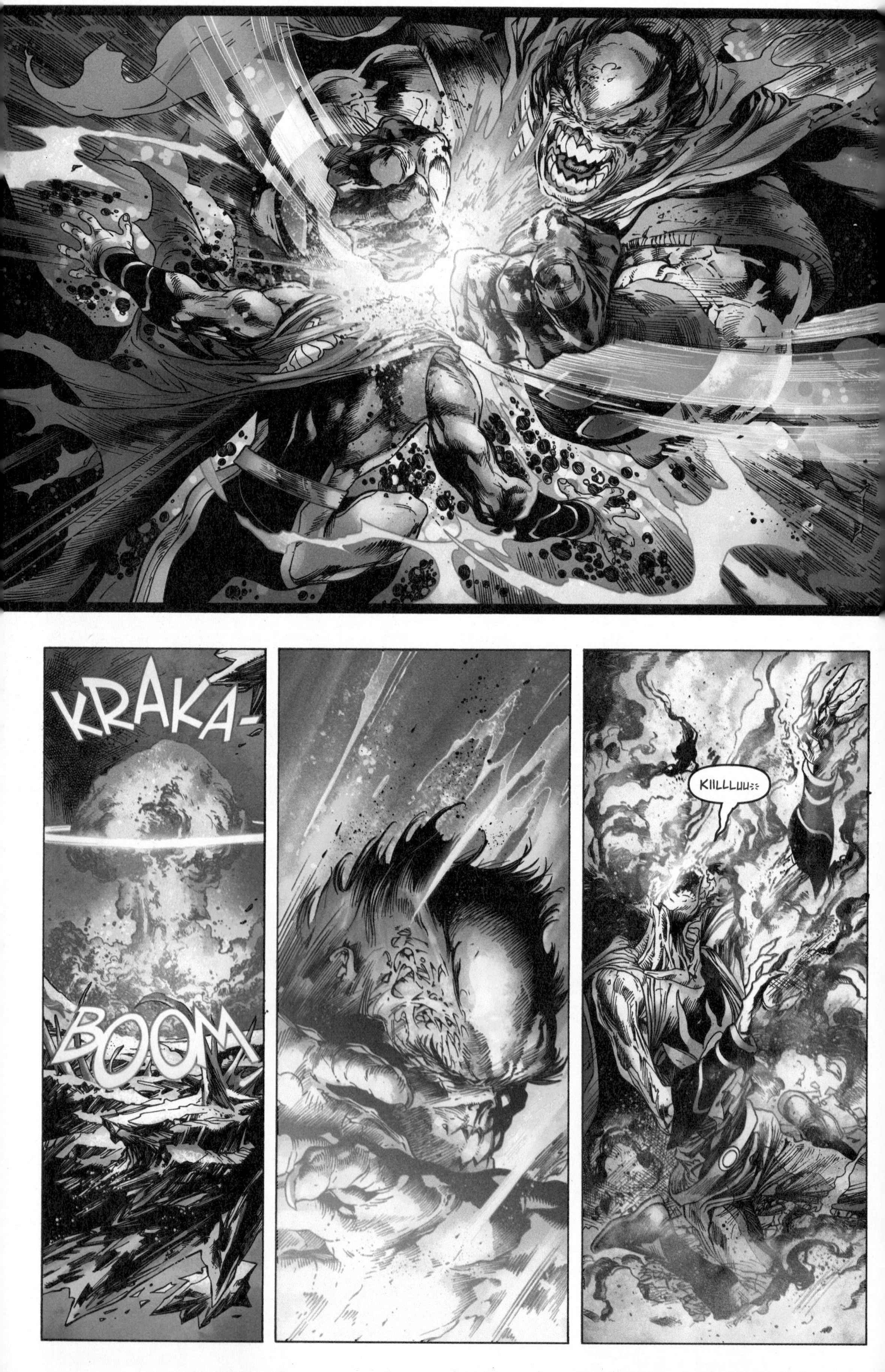
KRAKA-
BOOM
KIILLLUU

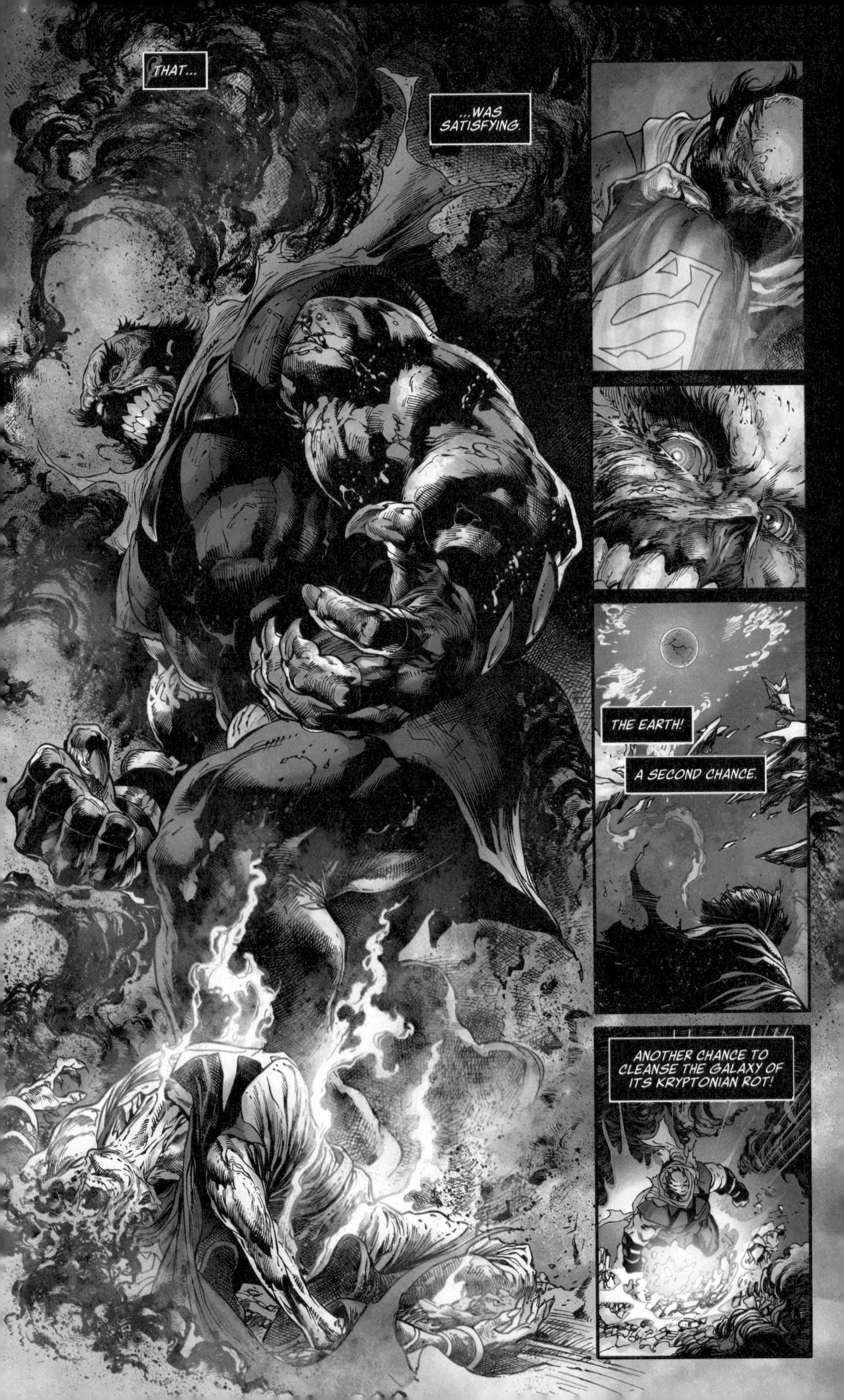
THAT...
...WAS SATISFYING.
THE EARTH!
A SECOND CHANCE.
ANOTHER CHANCE TO CLEANSE THE GALAXY OF ITS KRYPTONIAN ROT!

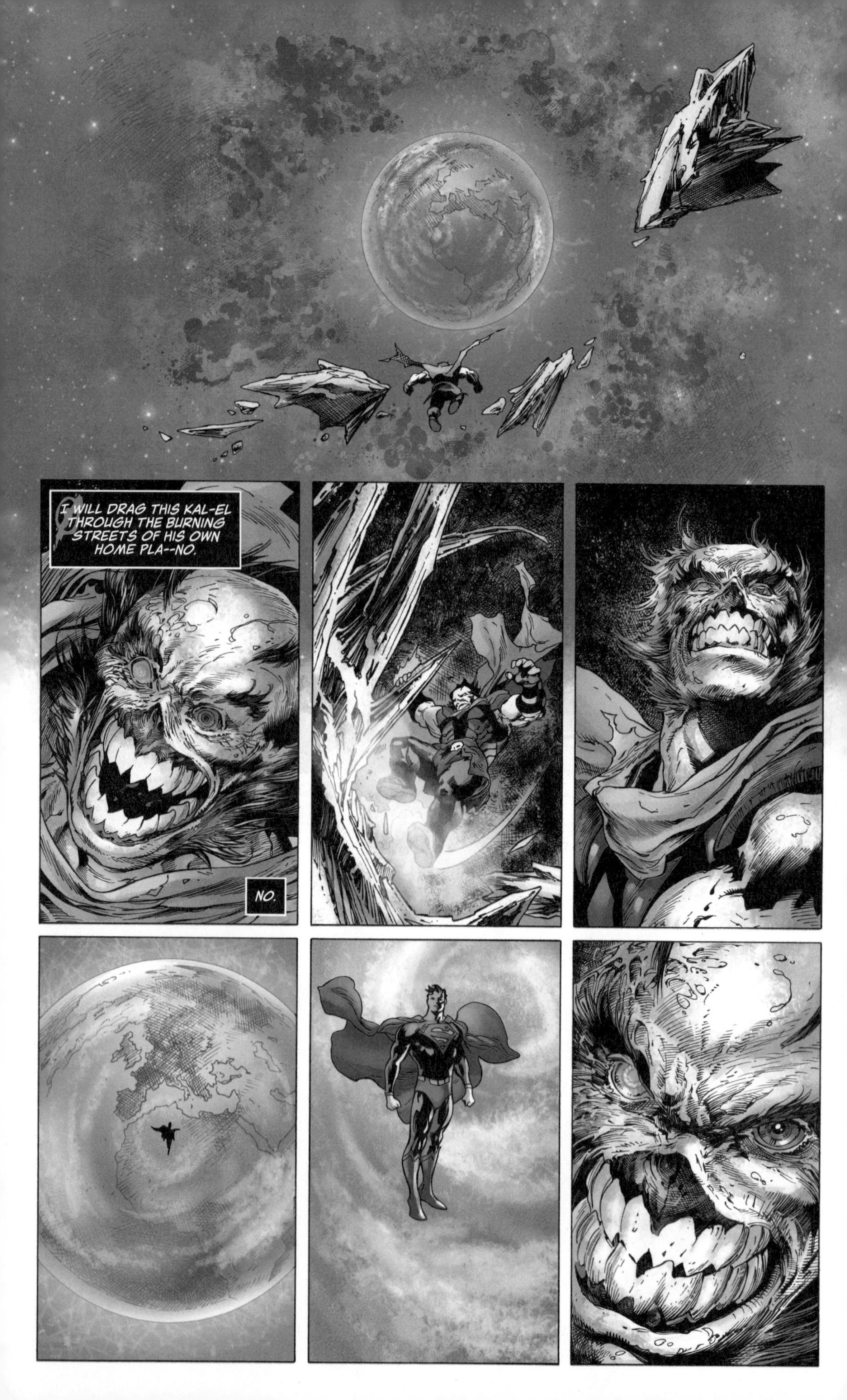
I WILL DRAG THIS KAL-EL THROUGH THE BURNING STREETS OF HIS OWN HOME PLA--NO.
NO.

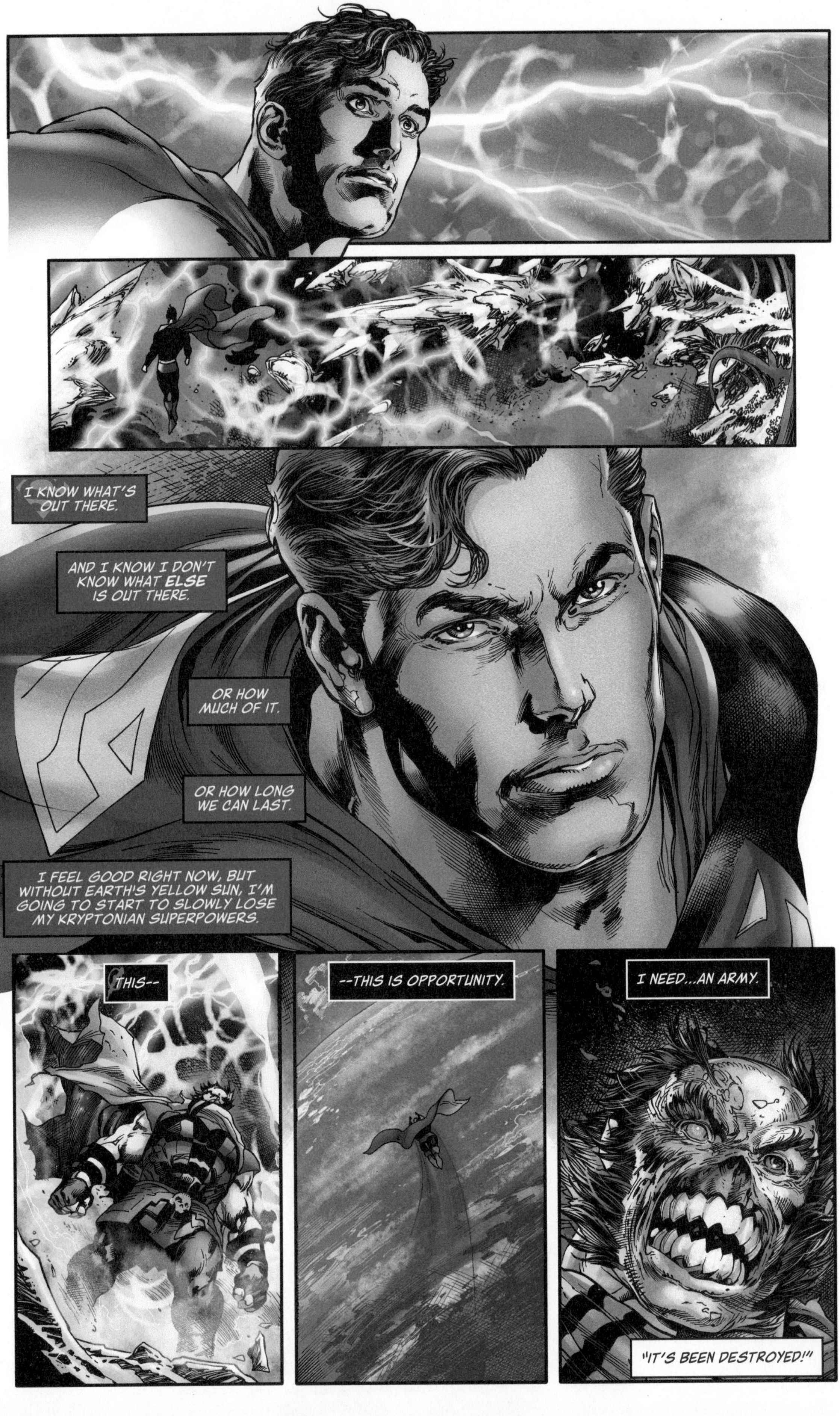
I KNOW WHAT'S OUT THERE.
AND I KNOW I DON'T KNOW WHAT ELSE IS OUT THERE.
OR HOW MUCH OF IT.
OR HOW LONG WE CAN LAST.
I FEEL GOOD RIGHT NOW, BUT WITHOUT EARTH'S YELLOW SUN, I'M GOING TO START TO SLOWLY LOSE MY KRYPTONIAN SUPERPOWERS.
THIS--
--THIS IS OPPORTUNITY.
I NEED...AN ARMY.
"IT'S BEEN DESTROYED!"

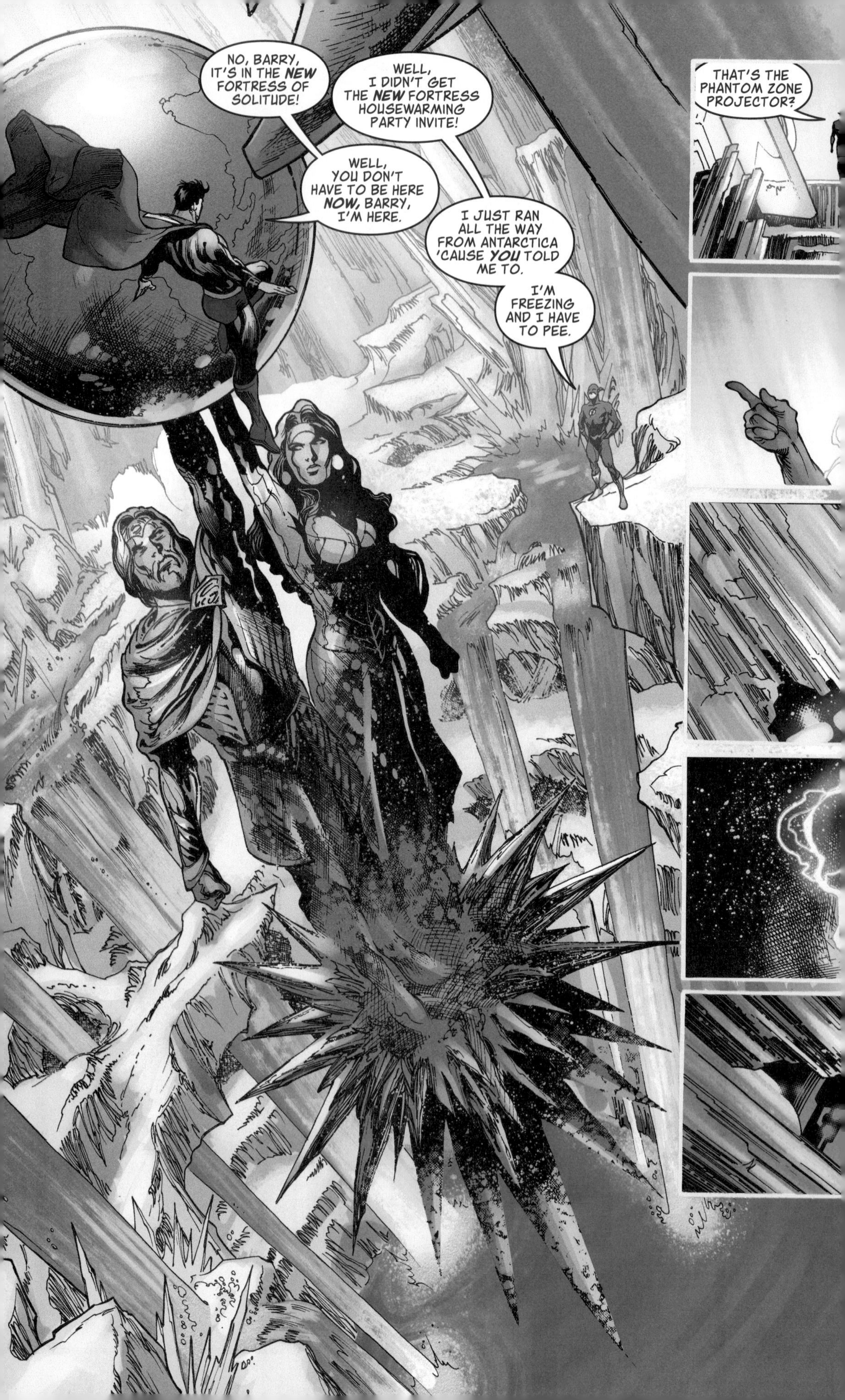
NO, BARRY, IT'S IN THE NEW FORTRESS OF SOLITUDE!
WELL, I DIDN'T GET THE NEW FORTRESS HOUSEWARMING PARTY INVITE!
WELL, YOU DON'T HAVE TO BE HERE NOW, BARRY, I'M HERE.
I JUST RAN ALL THE WAY FROM ANTARCTICA 'CAUSE YOU TOLD ME TO.
I'M FREEZING AND I HAVE TO PEE.
THAT'S THE PHANTOM ZONE PROJECTOR?

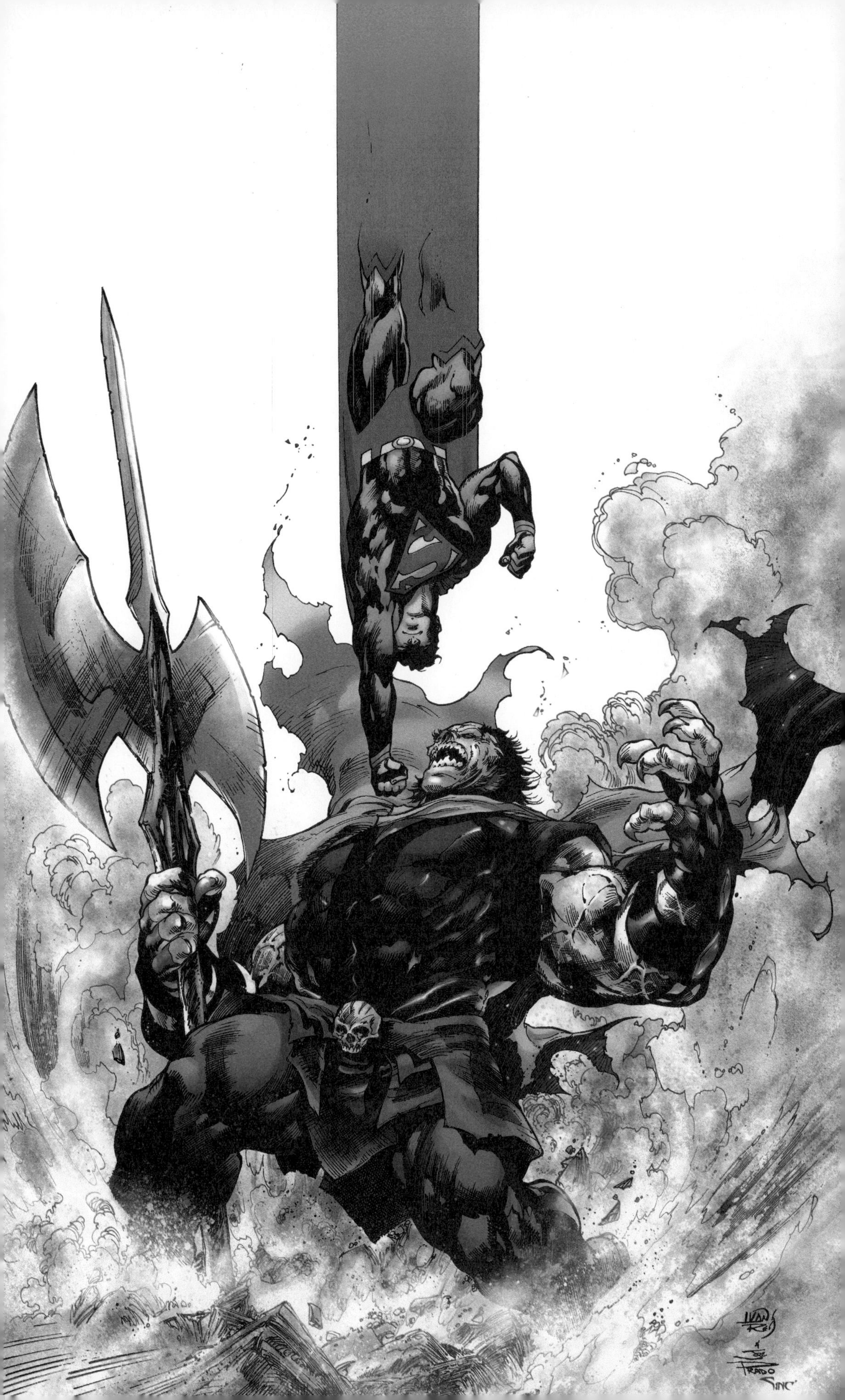

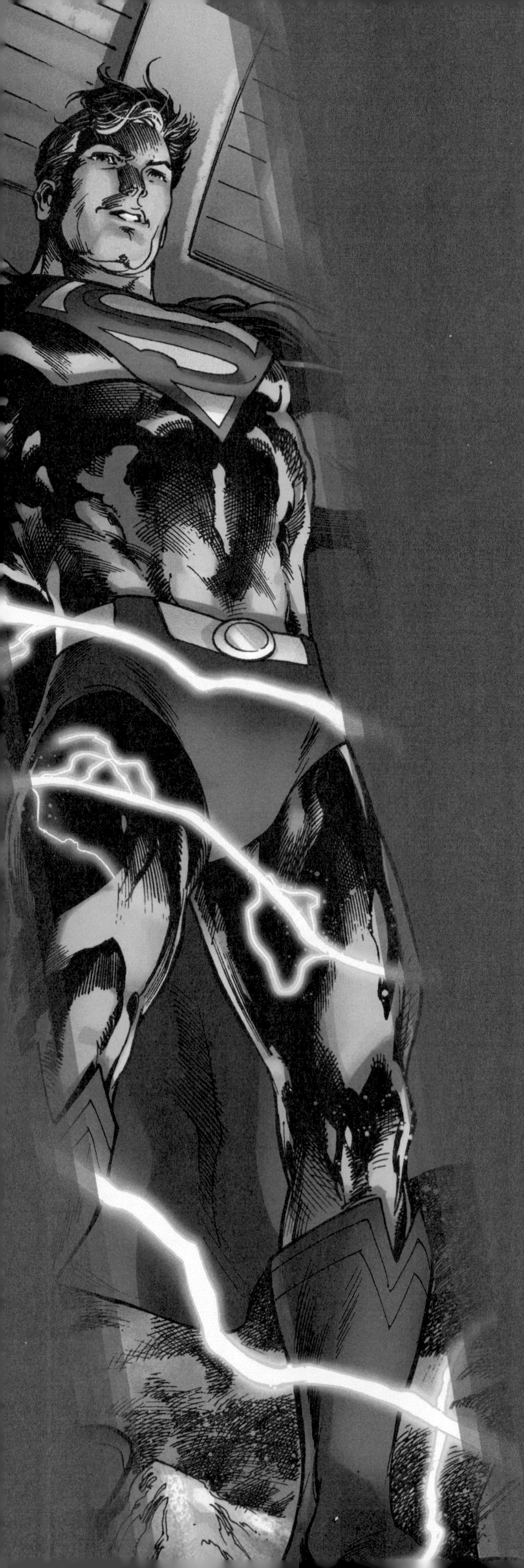

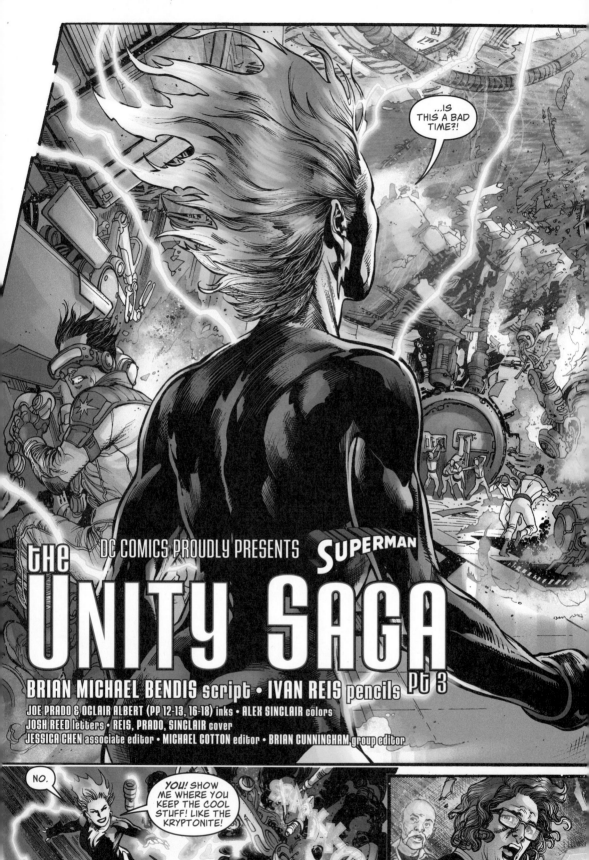

...IS THIS A BAD TIME?!

DC COMICS PROUDLY PRESENTS SUPERMAN
the UNITY SAGA pt 3

BRIAN MICHAEL BENDIS script • **IVAN REIS** pencils

JOE PRADO & OCLAIR ALBERT (PP 12-13, 16-18) inks • ALEX SINCLAIR colors
JOSH REED letters • REIS, PRADO, SINCLAIR cover
JESSICA CHEN associate editor • MICHAEL COTTON editor • BRIAN CUNNINGHAM group editor

NO.

YOU! SHOW ME WHERE YOU KEEP THE COOL STUFF! LIKE THE KRYPTONITE!

SERIOUSLY, I'M *VERY GOOD* AT MAKING THE MOST OUT OF A BAD SITUATION.

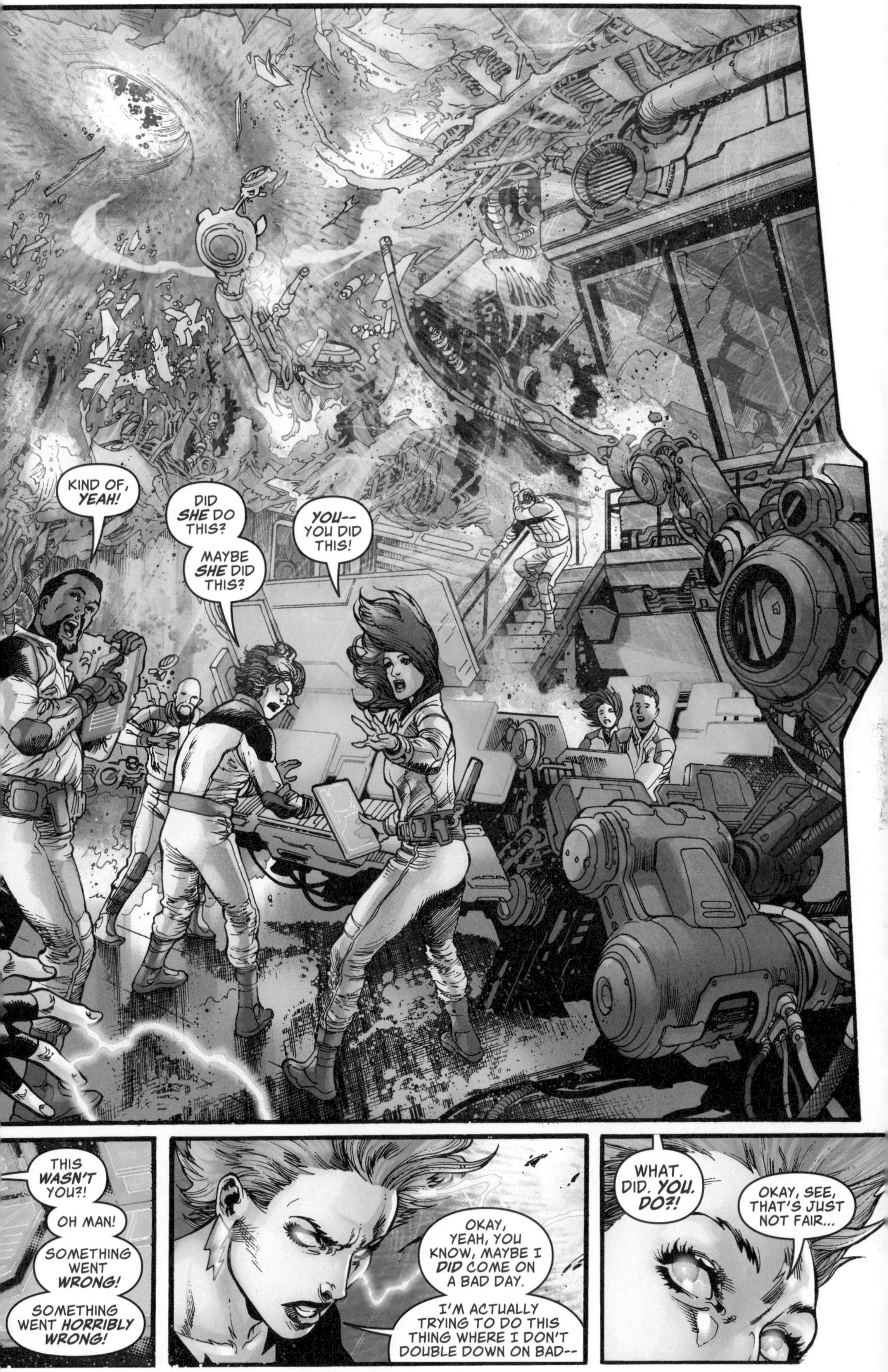
KIND OF, YEAH!
DID SHE DO THIS?
MAYBE SHE DID THIS?
YOU-- YOU DID THIS!
THIS WASN'T YOU?!
OH MAN!
SOMETHING WENT WRONG!
SOMETHING WENT HORRIBLY WRONG!
OKAY, YEAH, YOU KNOW, MAYBE I DID COME ON A BAD DAY.
I'M ACTUALLY TRYING TO DO THIS THING WHERE I DON'T DOUBLE DOWN ON BAD--
WHAT. DID. YOU. DO?!
OKAY, SEE, THAT'S JUST NOT FAIR...

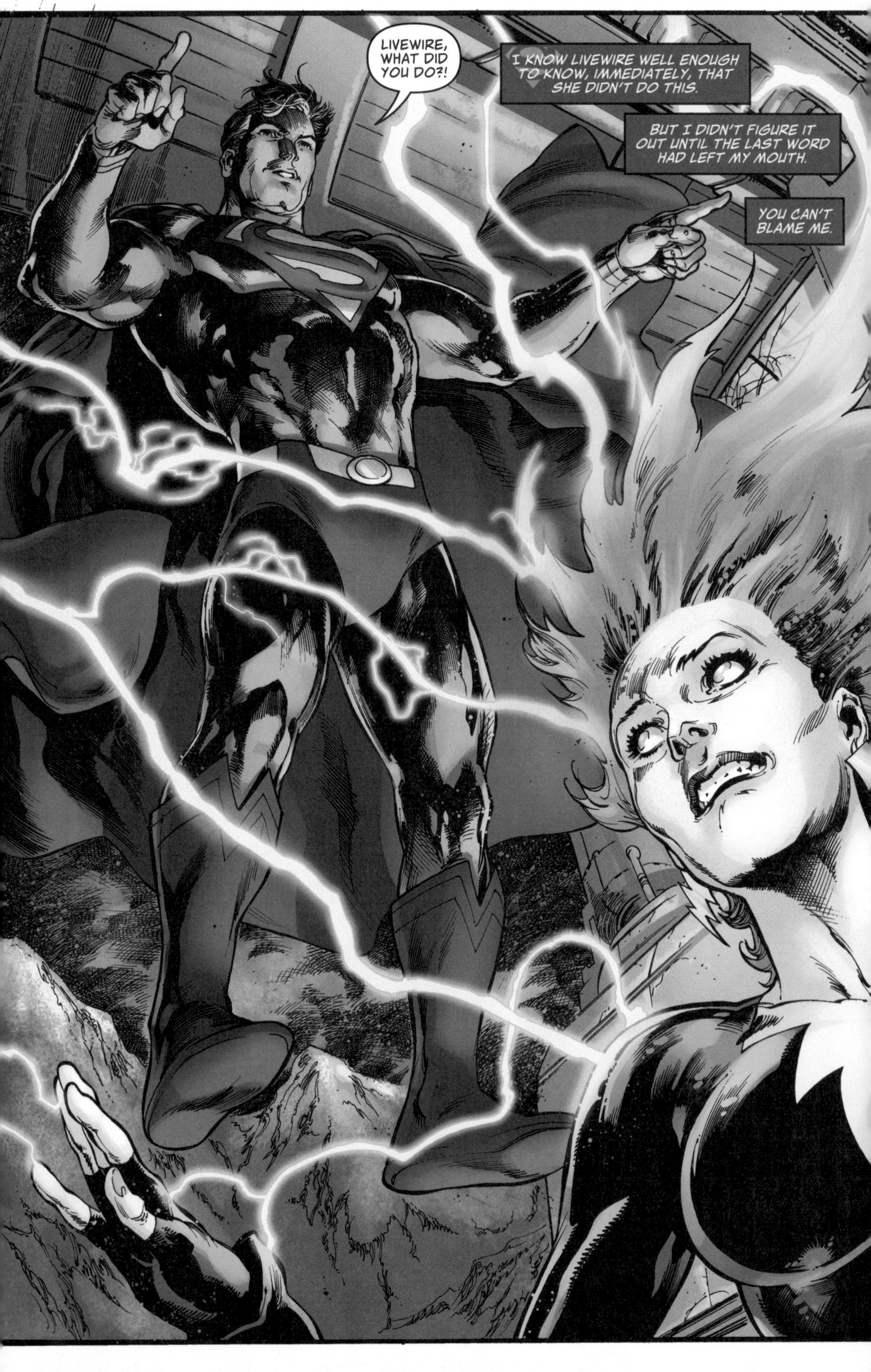
LIVEWIRE, WHAT DID YOU DO?!
I KNOW LIVEWIRE WELL ENOUGH TO KNOW, IMMEDIATELY, THAT SHE DIDN'T DO THIS.
BUT I DIDN'T FIGURE IT OUT UNTIL THE LAST WORD HAD LEFT MY MOUTH.
YOU CAN'T BLAME ME.

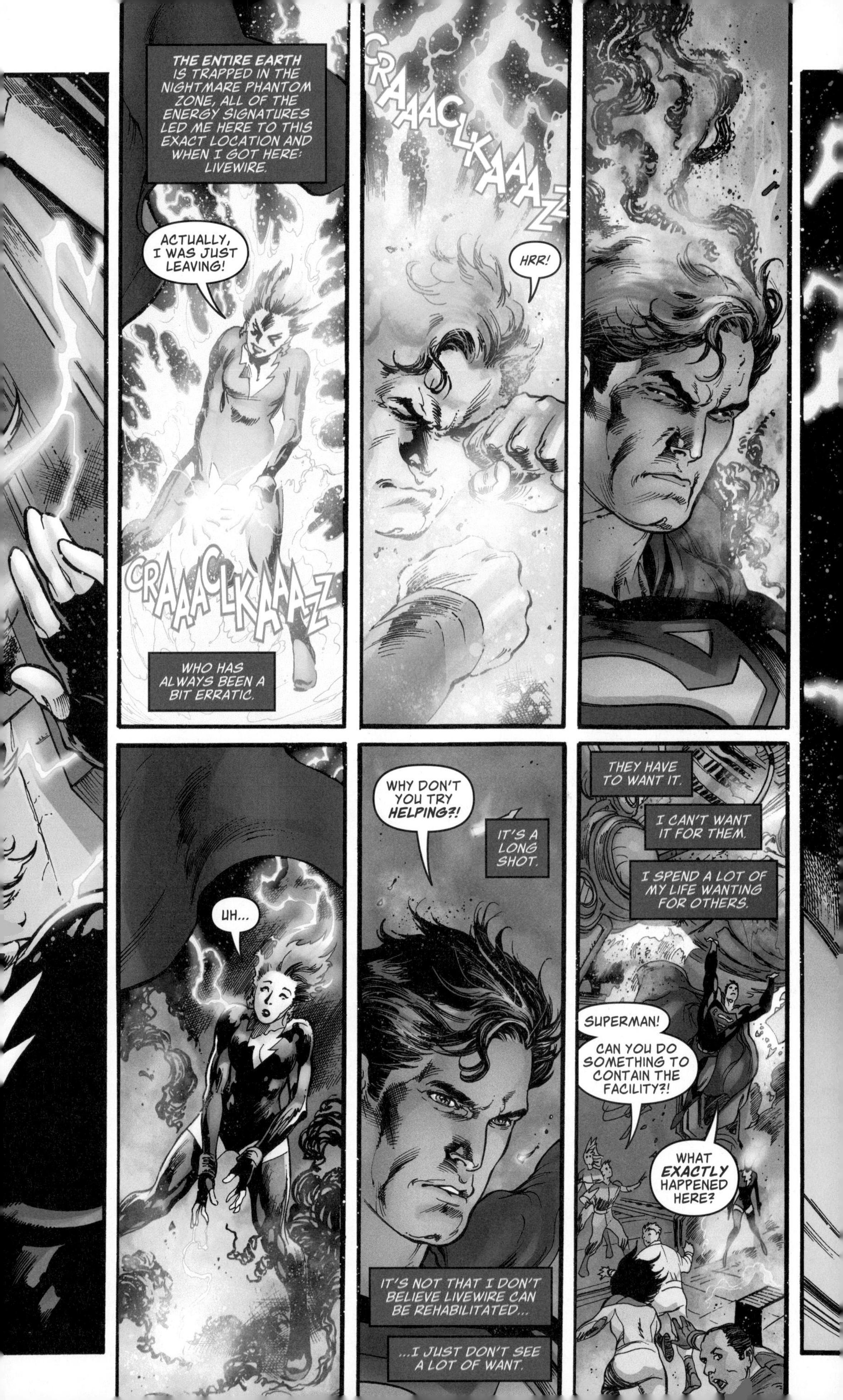
THE ENTIRE EARTH IS TRAPPED IN THE NIGHTMARE PHANTOM ZONE, ALL OF THE ENERGY SIGNATURES LED ME HERE TO THIS EXACT LOCATION AND WHEN I GOT HERE: LIVEWIRE.
ACTUALLY, I WAS JUST LEAVING!
CRAAACLKAAAZZ
WHO HAS ALWAYS BEEN A BIT ERRATIC.
CRAAACLKAAAZZ
HRR!
UH...
WHY DON'T YOU TRY HELPING?!
IT'S A LONG SHOT.
IT'S NOT THAT I DON'T BELIEVE LIVEWIRE CAN BE REHABILITATED...
...I JUST DON'T SEE A LOT OF WANT.
THEY HAVE TO WANT IT.
I CAN'T WANT IT FOR THEM.
I SPEND A LOT OF MY LIFE WANTING FOR OTHERS.
SUPERMAN!
CAN YOU DO SOMETHING TO CONTAIN THE FACILITY?!
WHAT EXACTLY HAPPENED HERE?

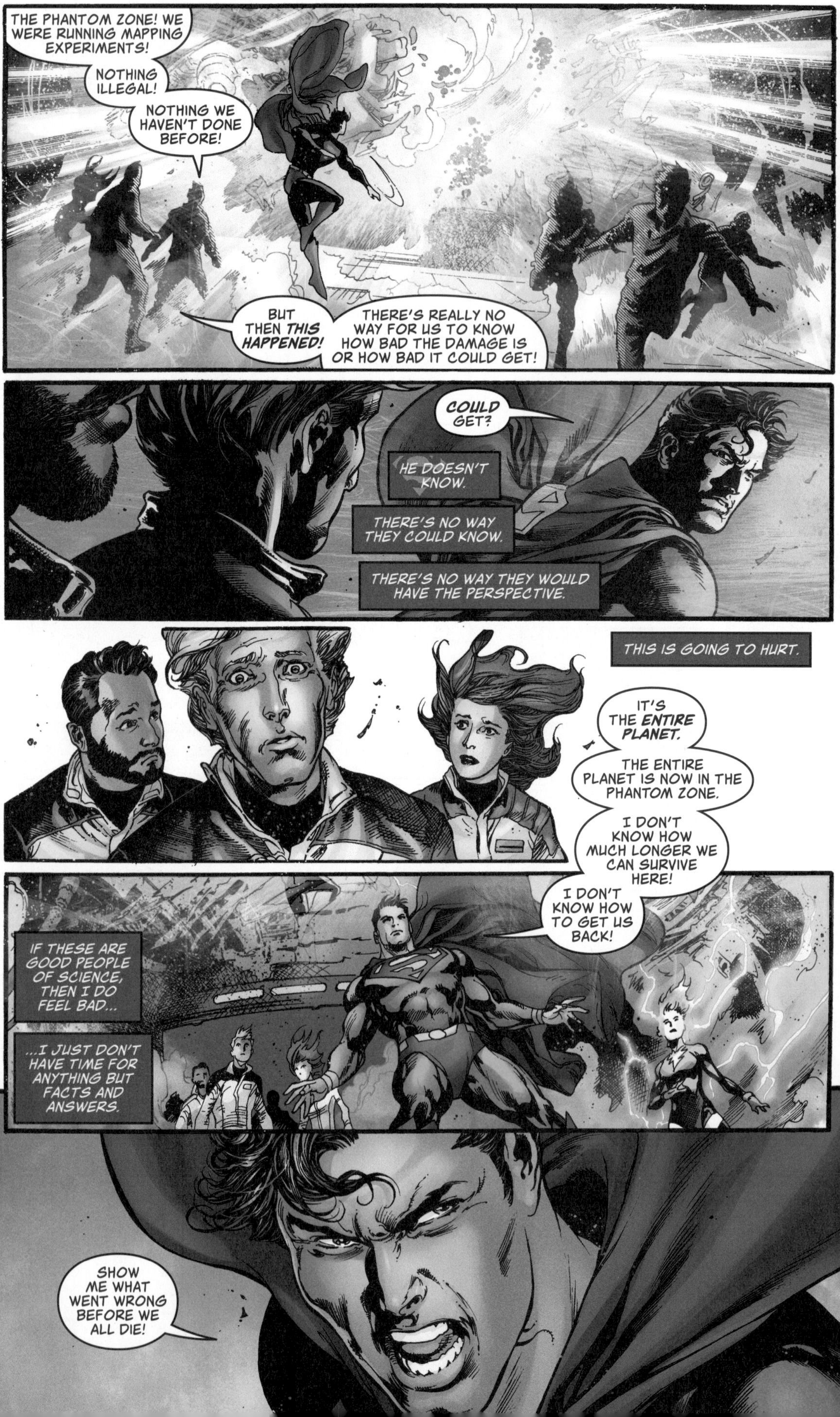
THE PHANTOM ZONE! WE WERE RUNNING MAPPING EXPERIMENTS!
NOTHING ILLEGAL!
NOTHING WE HAVEN'T DONE BEFORE!
BUT THEN **THIS HAPPENED!**
THERE'S REALLY NO WAY FOR US TO KNOW HOW BAD THE DAMAGE IS OR HOW BAD IT COULD GET!
COULD GET?
HE DOESN'T KNOW.
THERE'S NO WAY THEY COULD KNOW.
THERE'S NO WAY THEY WOULD HAVE THE PERSPECTIVE.
THIS IS GOING TO HURT.
IT'S THE **ENTIRE PLANET.**
THE ENTIRE PLANET IS NOW IN THE PHANTOM ZONE.
I DON'T KNOW HOW MUCH LONGER WE CAN SURVIVE HERE!
I DON'T KNOW HOW TO GET US BACK!
IF THESE ARE GOOD PEOPLE OF SCIENCE, THEN I DO FEEL BAD...
...I JUST DON'T HAVE TIME FOR ANYTHING BUT FACTS AND ANSWERS.
SHOW ME WHAT WENT WRONG BEFORE WE ALL DIE!

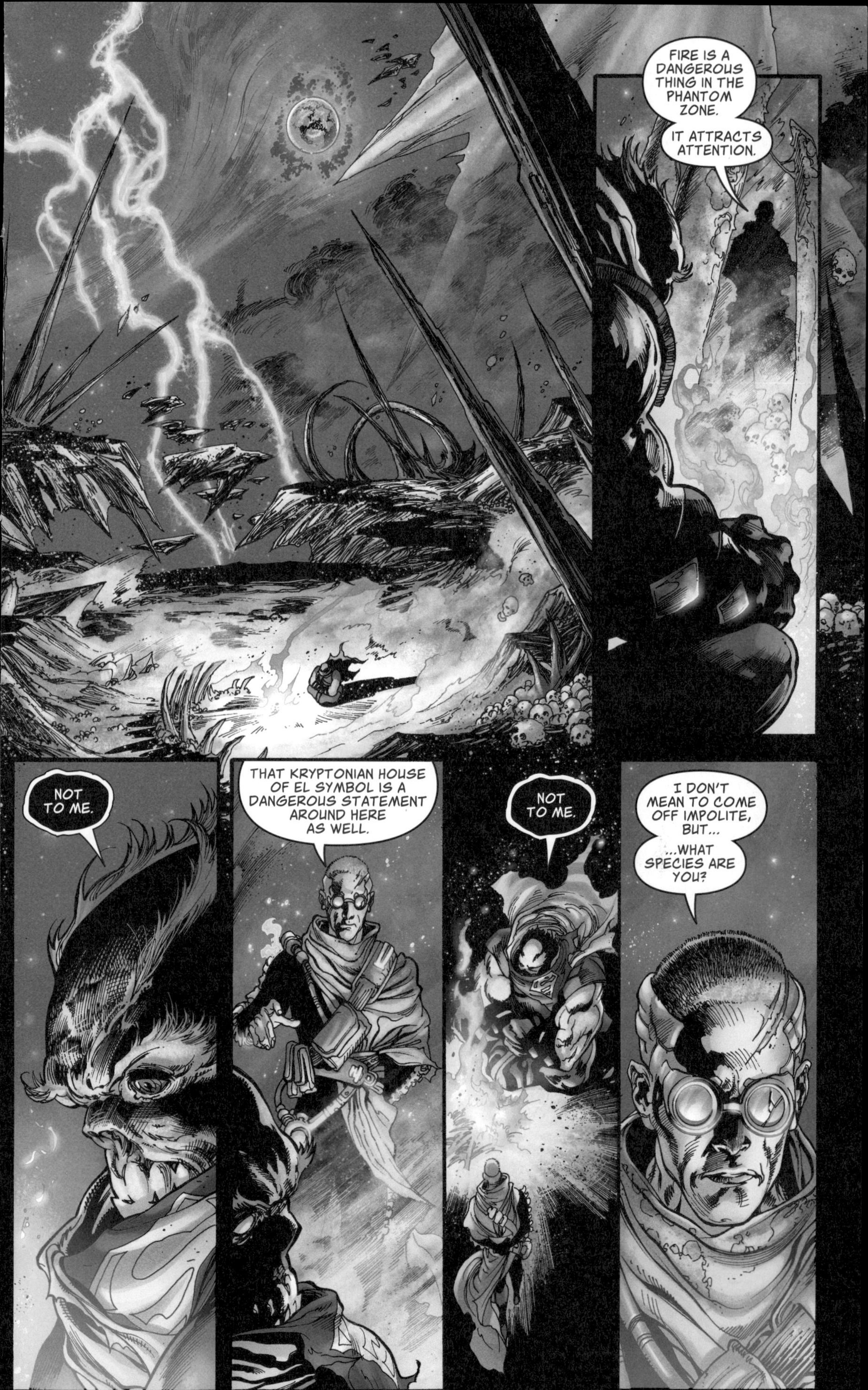
FIRE IS A DANGEROUS THING IN THE PHANTOM ZONE.
IT ATTRACTS ATTENTION.
NOT TO ME.
THAT KRYPTONIAN HOUSE OF EL SYMBOL IS A DANGEROUS STATEMENT AROUND HERE AS WELL.
NOT TO ME.
I DON'T MEAN TO COME OFF IMPOLITE, BUT...
...WHAT SPECIES ARE YOU?

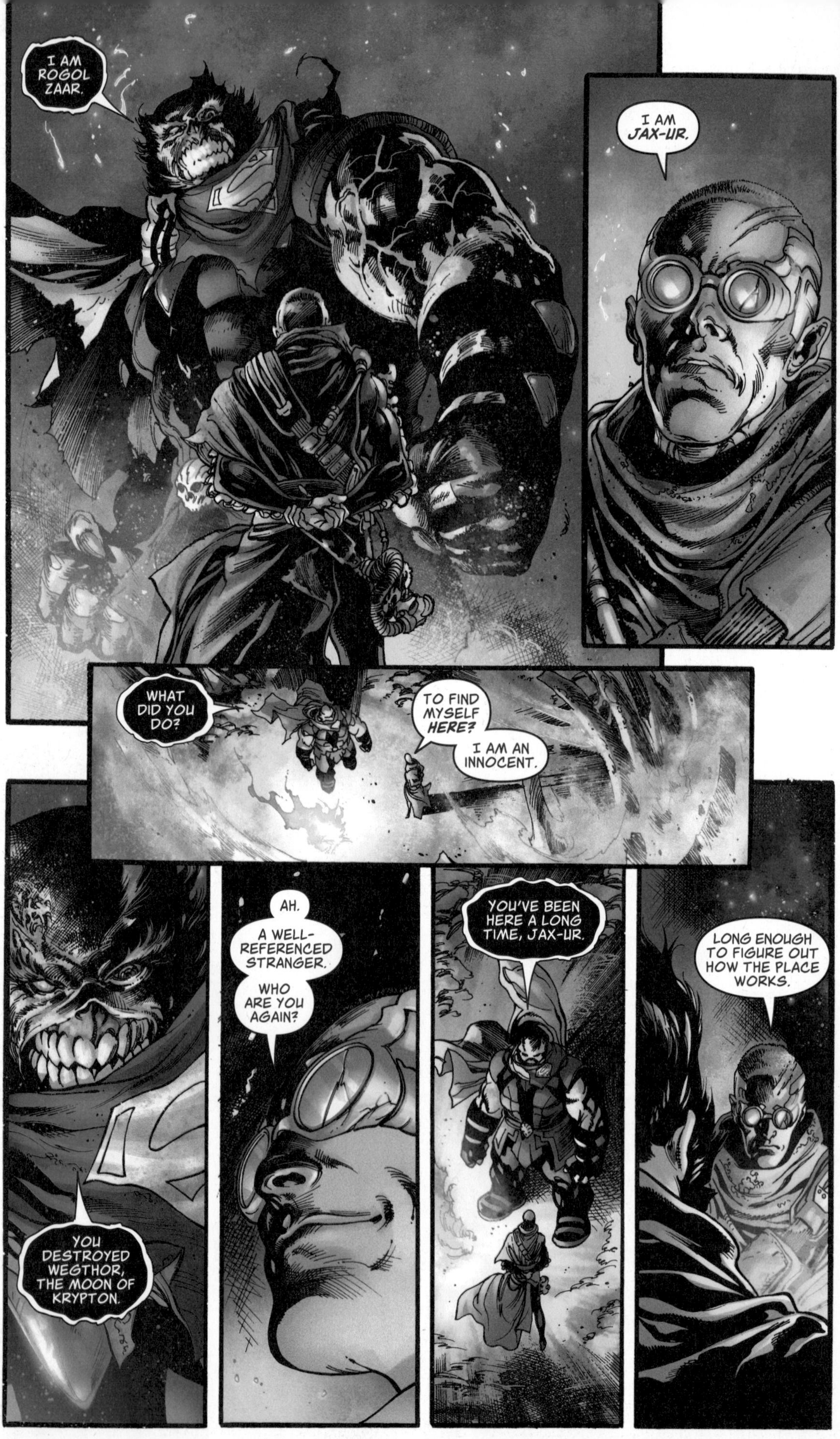
I AM ROGOL ZAAR.
I AM JAX-UR.
WHAT DID YOU DO?
TO FIND MYSELF HERE?
I AM AN INNOCENT.
YOU DESTROYED WEGTHOR, THE MOON OF KRYPTON.
AH.
A WELL-REFERENCED STRANGER.
WHO ARE YOU AGAIN?
YOU'VE BEEN HERE A LONG TIME, JAX-UR.
LONG ENOUGH TO FIGURE OUT HOW THE PLACE WORKS.

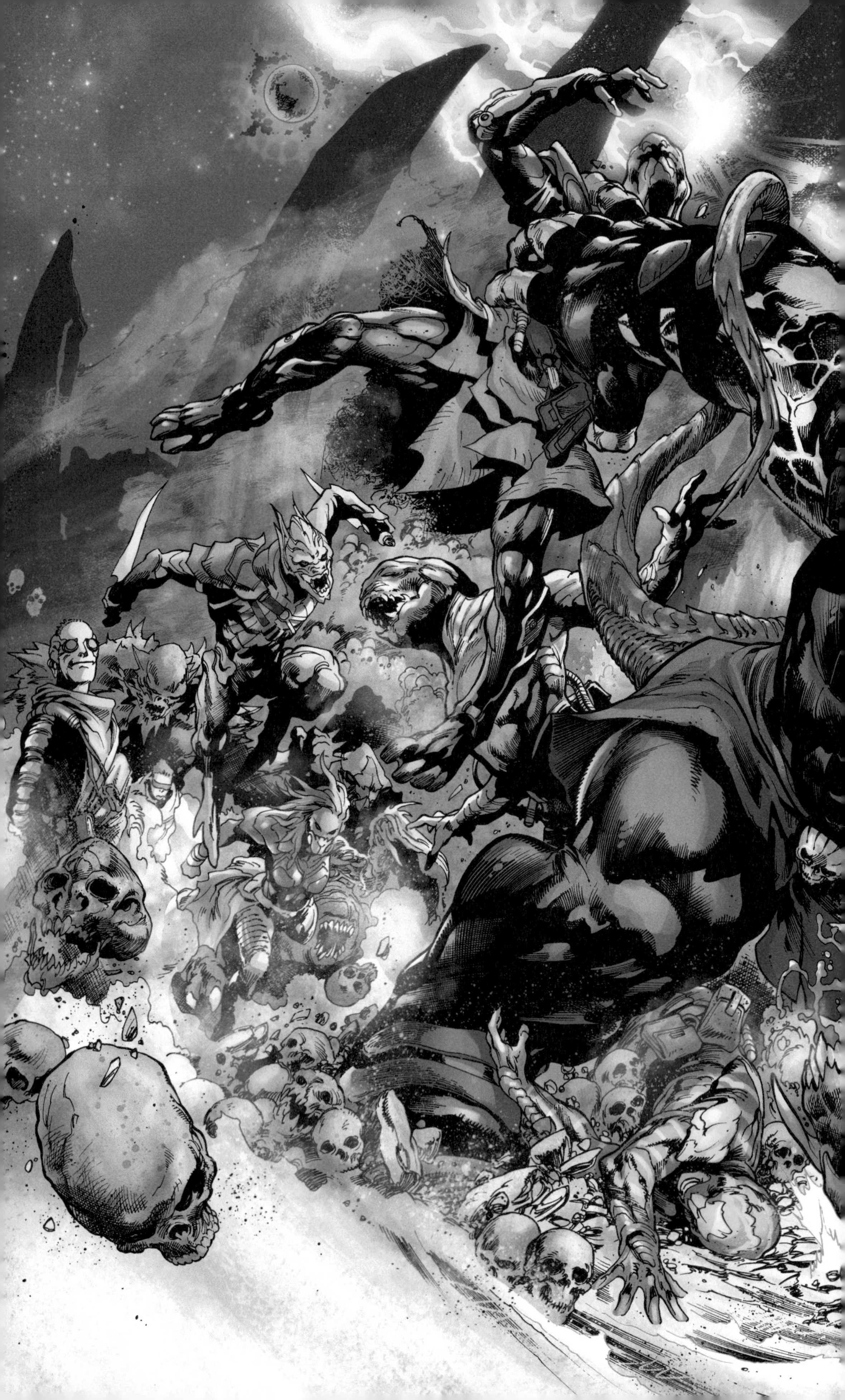

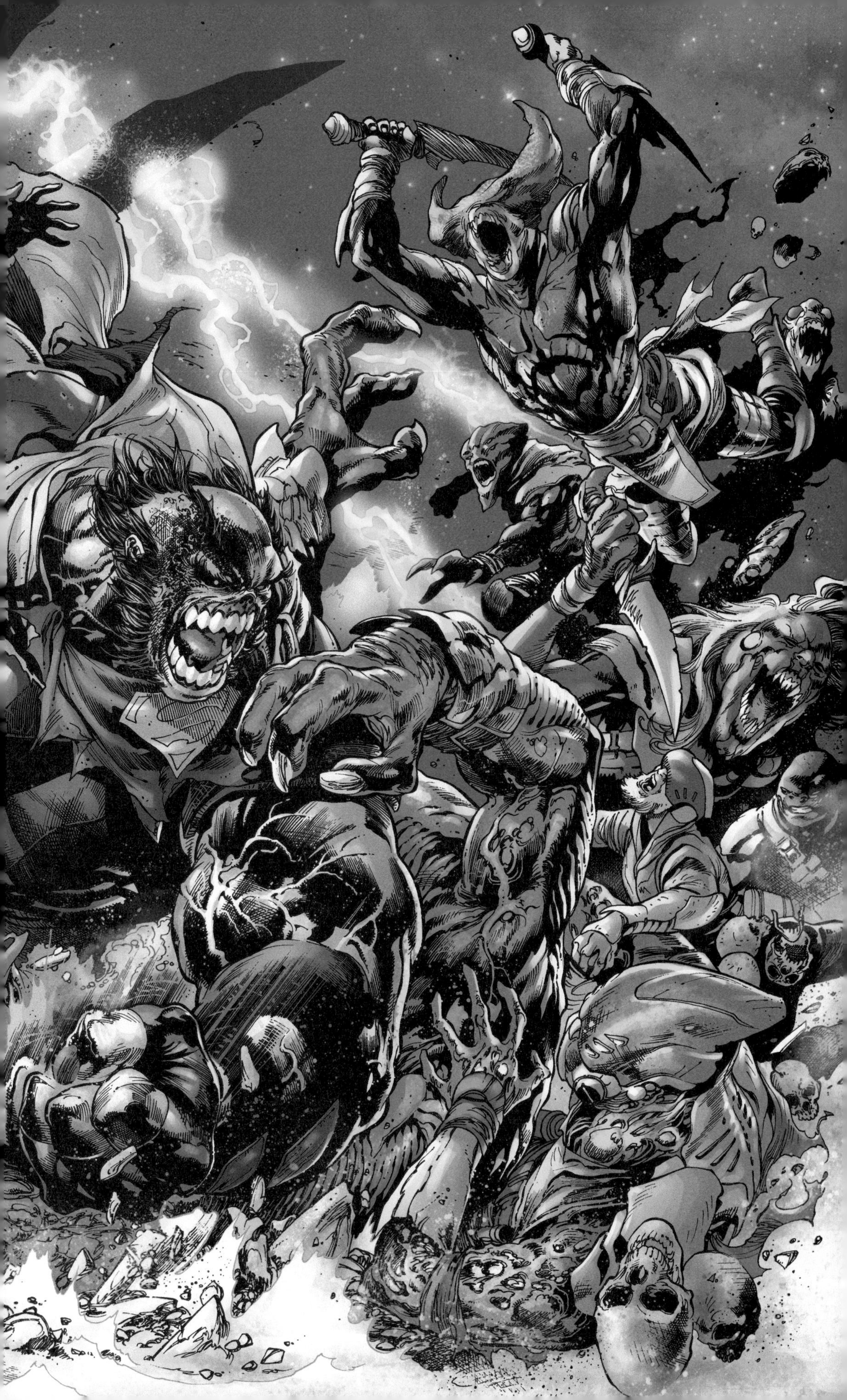

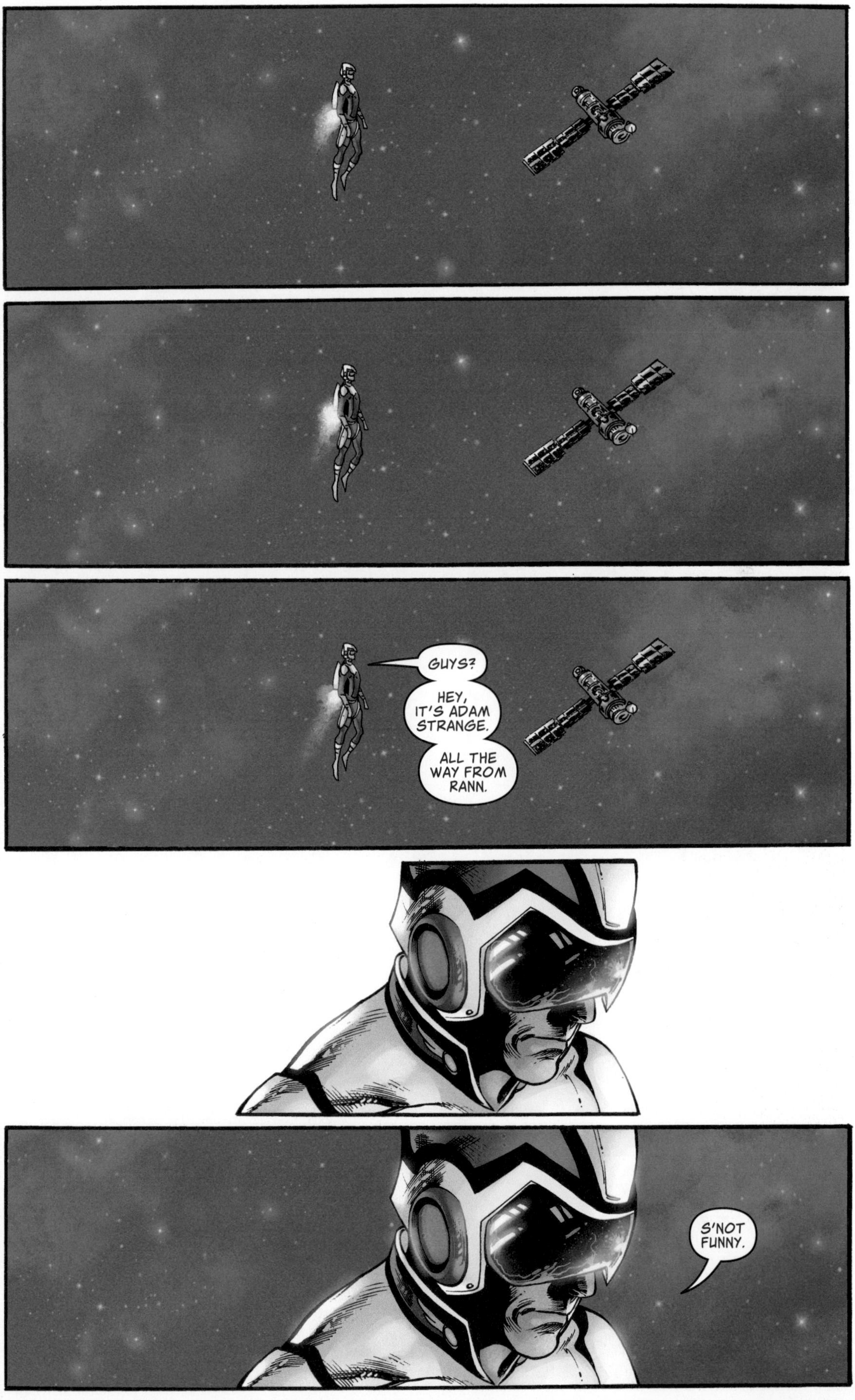
GUYS?
HEY, IT'S ADAM STRANGE.
ALL THE WAY FROM RANN.
S'NOT FUNNY.

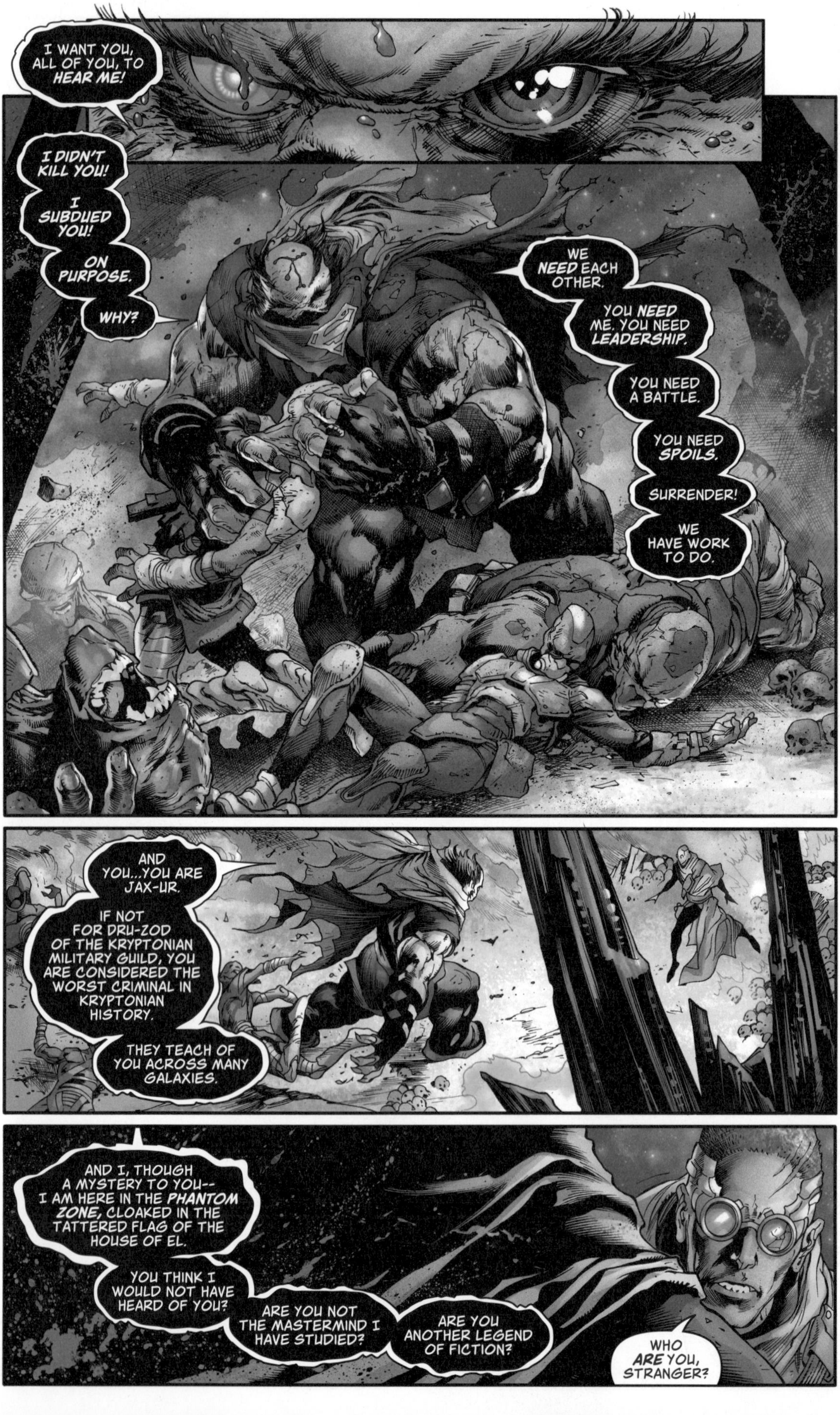

I WANT YOU, ALL OF YOU, TO HEAR ME!
I DIDN'T KILL YOU!
I SUBDUED YOU!
ON PURPOSE.
WHY?
WE NEED EACH OTHER.
YOU NEED ME. YOU NEED LEADERSHIP.
YOU NEED A BATTLE.
YOU NEED SPOILS.
SURRENDER!
WE HAVE WORK TO DO.
AND YOU...YOU ARE JAX-UR.
IF NOT FOR DRU-ZOD OF THE KRYPTONIAN MILITARY GUILD, YOU ARE CONSIDERED THE WORST CRIMINAL IN KRYPTONIAN HISTORY.
THEY TEACH OF YOU ACROSS MANY GALAXIES.
AND I, THOUGH A MYSTERY TO YOU-- I AM HERE IN THE PHANTOM ZONE, CLOAKED IN THE TATTERED FLAG OF THE HOUSE OF EL.
YOU THINK I WOULD NOT HAVE HEARD OF YOU?
ARE YOU NOT THE MASTERMIND I HAVE STUDIED?
ARE YOU ANOTHER LEGEND OF FICTION?
WHO ARE YOU, STRANGER?

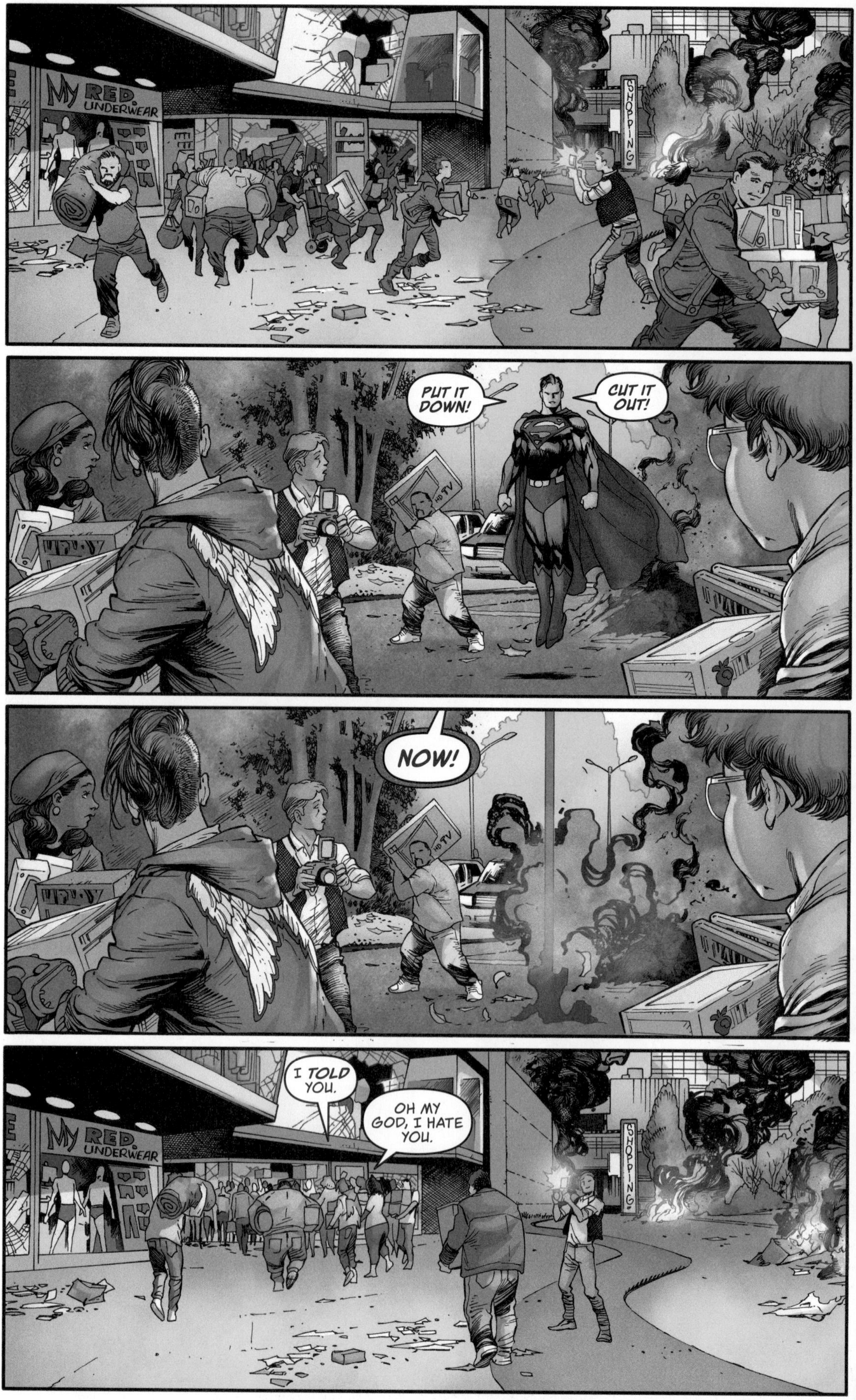
MY RED. UNDERWEAR
SHOPPING
PUT IT DOWN!
CUT IT OUT!
NOW!
I TOLD YOU.
OH MY GOD, I HATE YOU.

HALL OF JUSTICE.

"CALM *DOWN*, RAY!"

"THIS ISN'T THE TIME TO FREAK OUT!"

"*WHAT?!*"

THE EARTH CANNOT SURVIVE THIS IMMEDIATE SITUATION!

MR. TERRIFIC

WILL MAGNUS

WE ARE ABOUT TO CEASE TO EXIST UNLESS SOME-THING CHANGES IMMEDIATELY!

ACTUALLY, TECHNICALLY, NONE OF US *ACTUALLY* KNOW THAT, RAY.

WE'RE JUST GOING ON--

RAY PALMER

PUT A SOCK IN IT, TERRIFIC!

THIS IS AN *IMMEDIATE CRISIS OF INFINITE PROPORTIONS!*

LORD! EVERYONE CHILL!

TED KORD

RYAN CHOI

EVEN *IF WE* GET THE ENTIRE PLANET OUT OF HERE, WHO SAYS THE PLANETARY DAMAGE IS REVERSIBLE?

SO, YOU KNOW WHAT, TED, I *AM* GOING TO FREAK OUT!

RAY, TED, RYAN... I'VE JUST COME FROM S.T.A.R. LABS.

IT *WAS* S.T.A.R. LABS.

IT WAS *JUST* AN ACCIDENT.

I TOLD YOU!

WHAT IS *WRONG* WITH THEM?

SUPERMAN! WHAT DO WE DO?

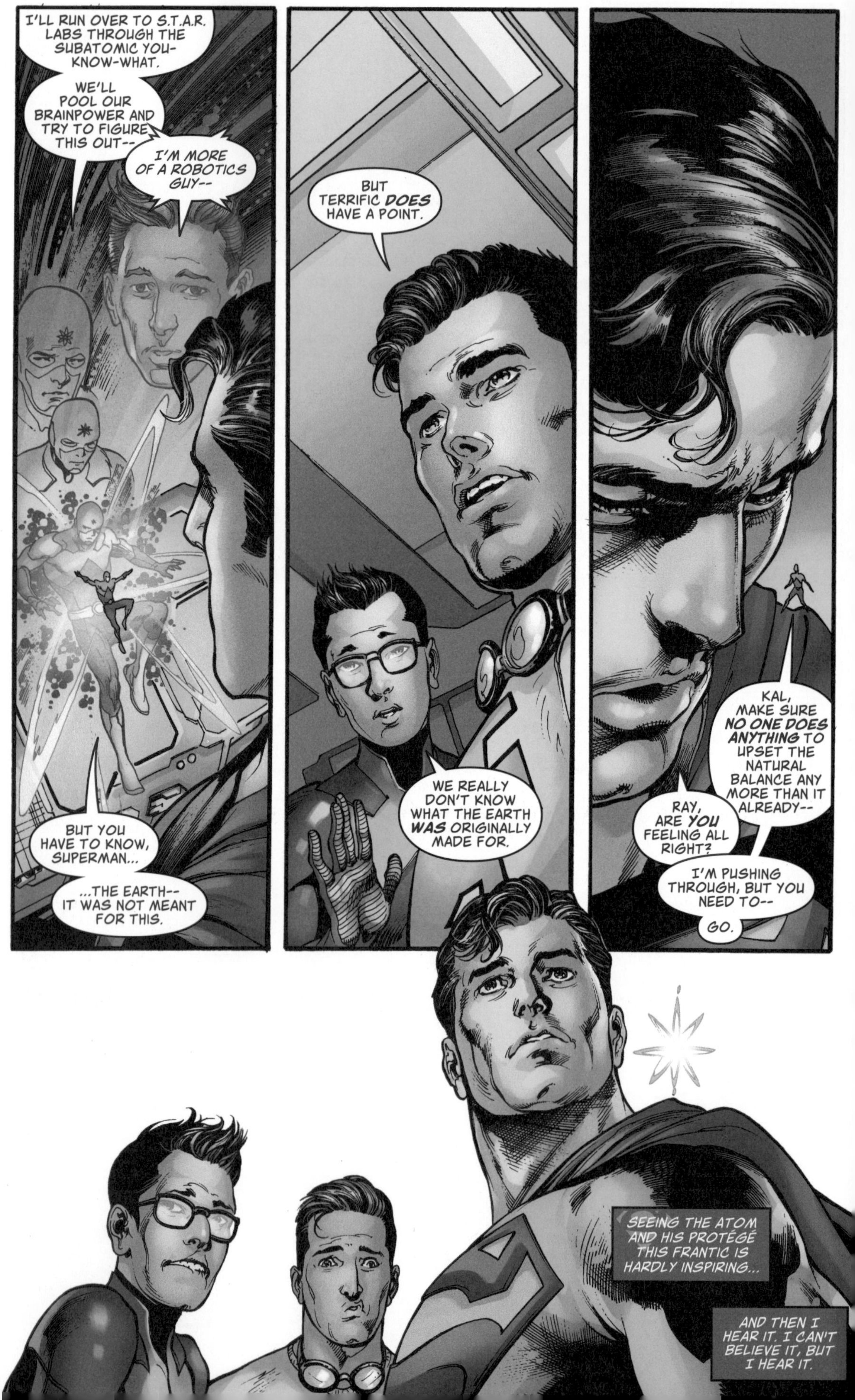

I'LL RUN OVER TO S.T.A.R. LABS THROUGH THE SUBATOMIC YOU-KNOW-WHAT.
WE'LL POOL OUR BRAINPOWER AND TRY TO FIGURE THIS OUT--
I'M MORE OF A ROBOTICS GUY--
BUT YOU HAVE TO KNOW, SUPERMAN...
...THE EARTH-- IT WAS NOT MEANT FOR THIS.
BUT TERRIFIC DOES HAVE A POINT.
WE REALLY DON'T KNOW WHAT THE EARTH WAS ORIGINALLY MADE FOR.
KAL, MAKE SURE NO ONE DOES ANYTHING TO UPSET THE NATURAL BALANCE ANY MORE THAN IT ALREADY--
RAY, ARE YOU FEELING ALL RIGHT?
I'M PUSHING THROUGH, BUT YOU NEED TO--
GO.
SEEING THE ATOM AND HIS PROTÉGÉ THIS FRANTIC IS HARDLY INSPIRING...
AND THEN I HEAR IT. I CAN'T BELIEVE IT, BUT I HEAR IT.

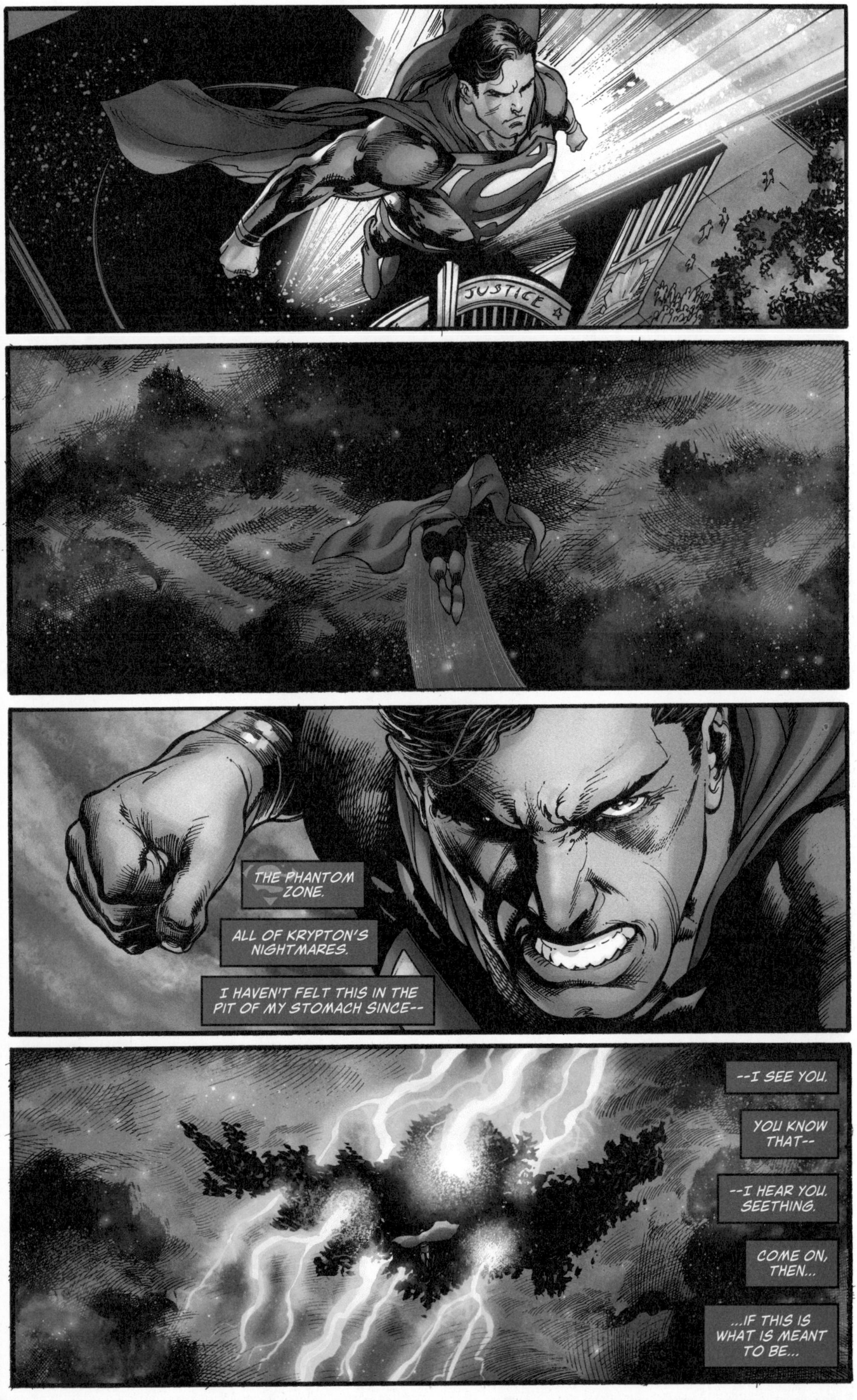
JUSTICE
THE PHANTOM ZONE.
ALL OF KRYPTON'S NIGHTMARES.
I HAVEN'T FELT THIS IN THE PIT OF MY STOMACH SINCE--
--I SEE YOU.
YOU KNOW THAT--
--I HEAR YOU. SEETHING.
COME ON, THEN...
...IF THIS IS WHAT IS MEANT TO BE...

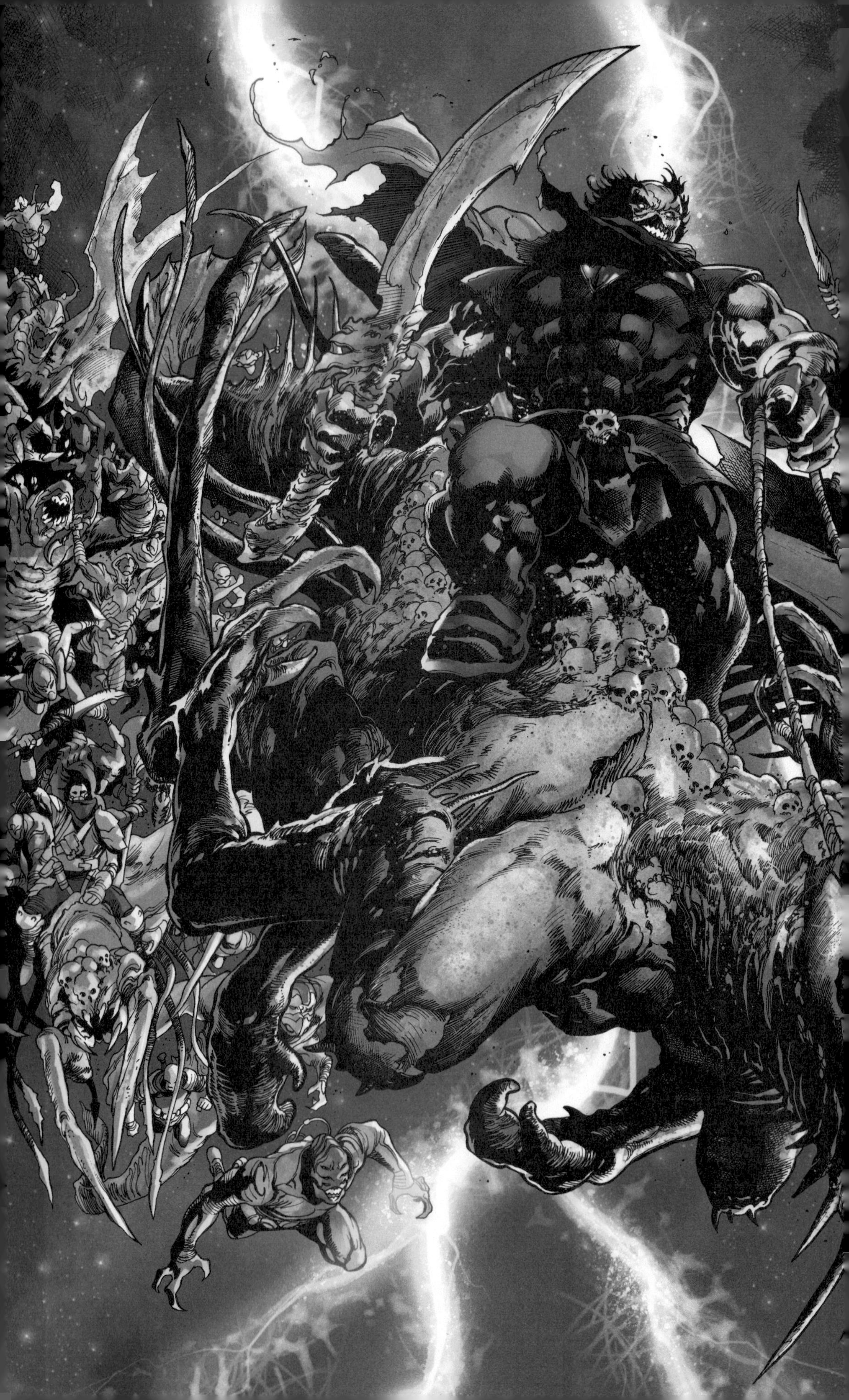

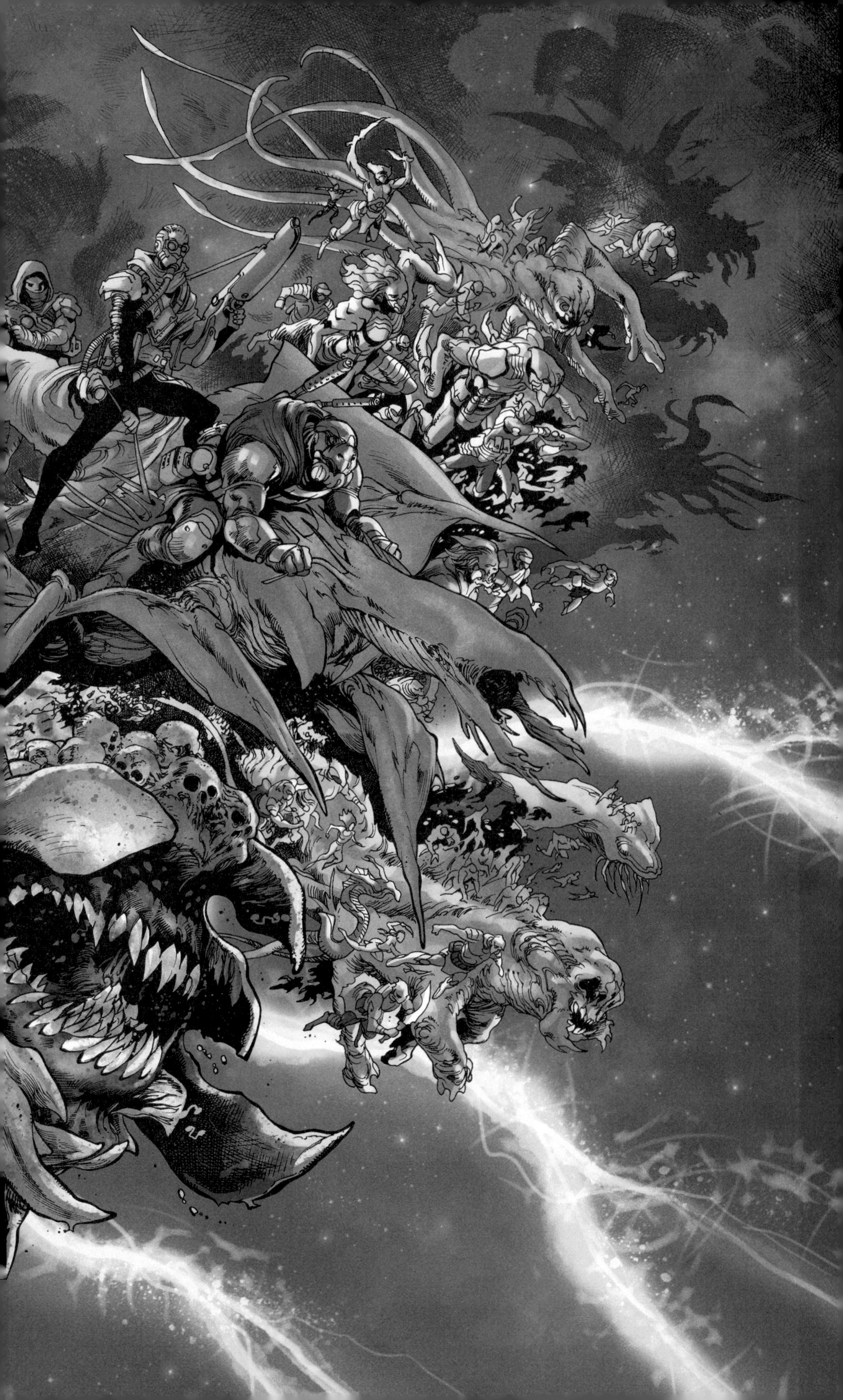

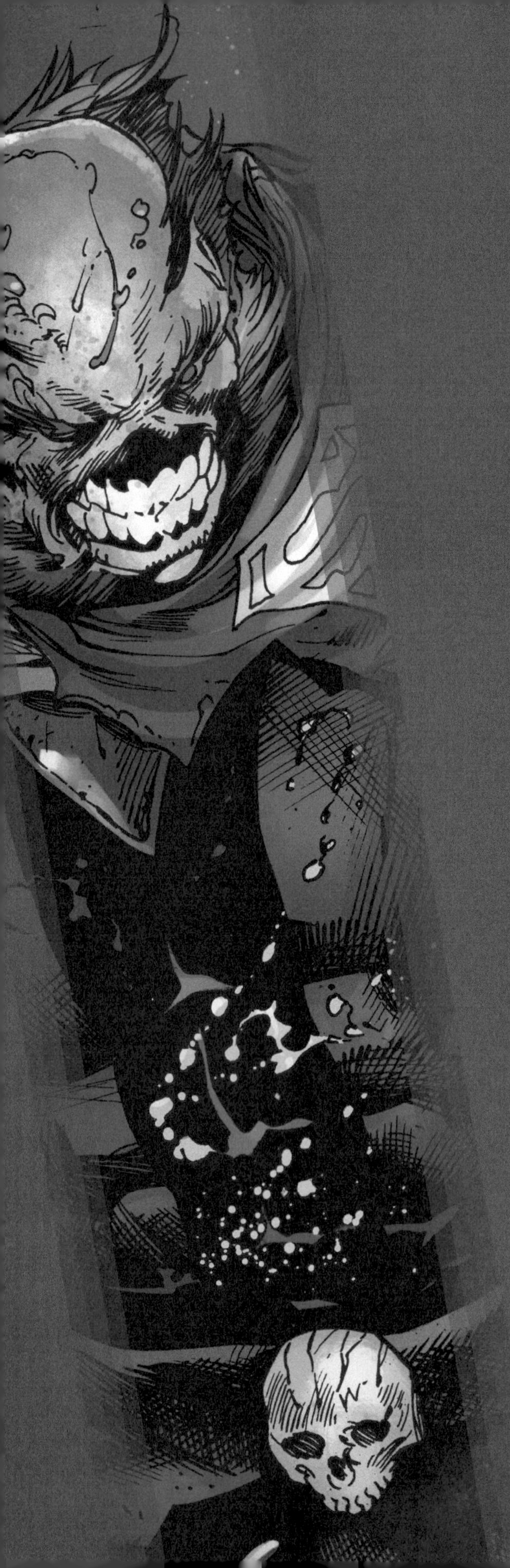

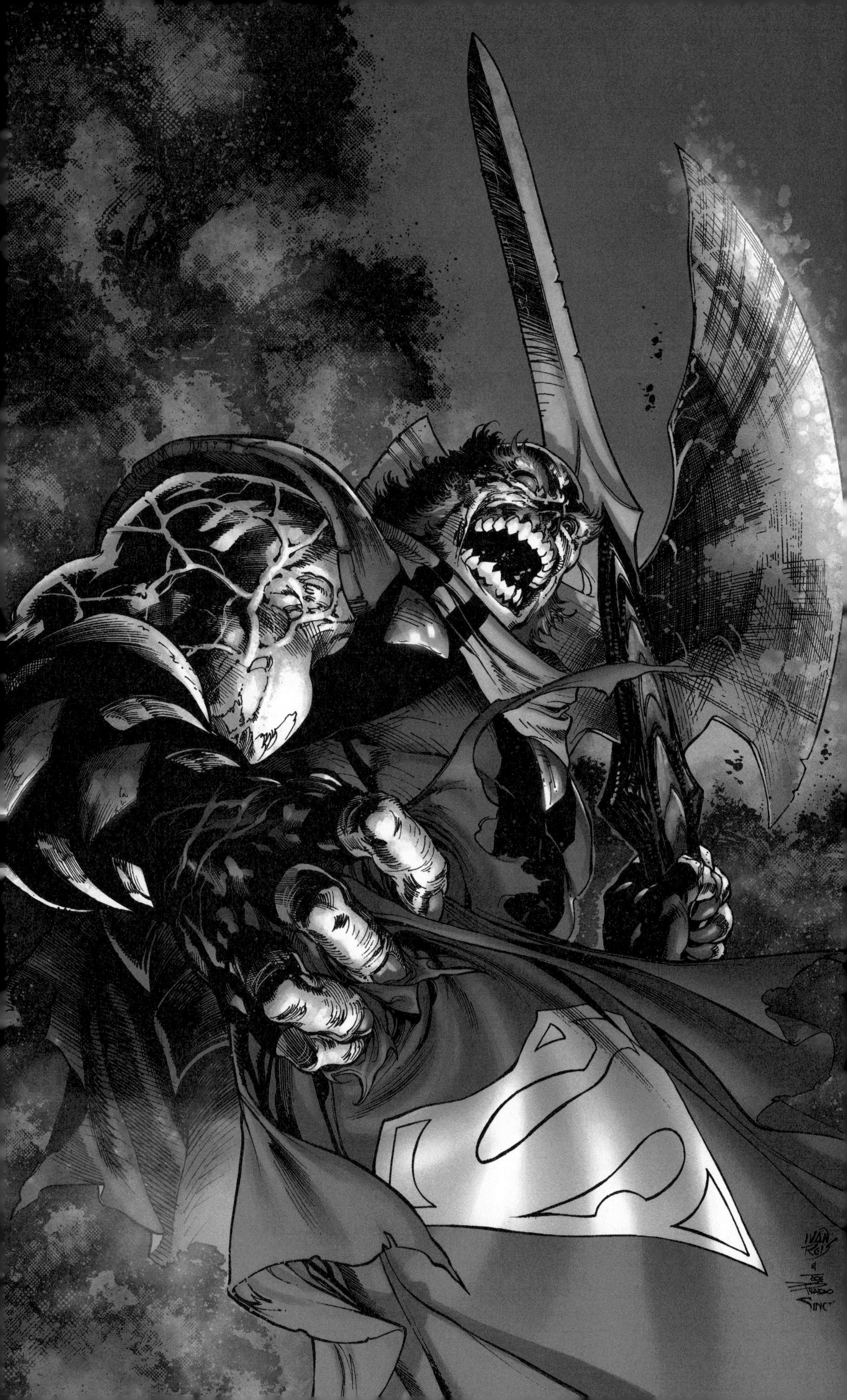

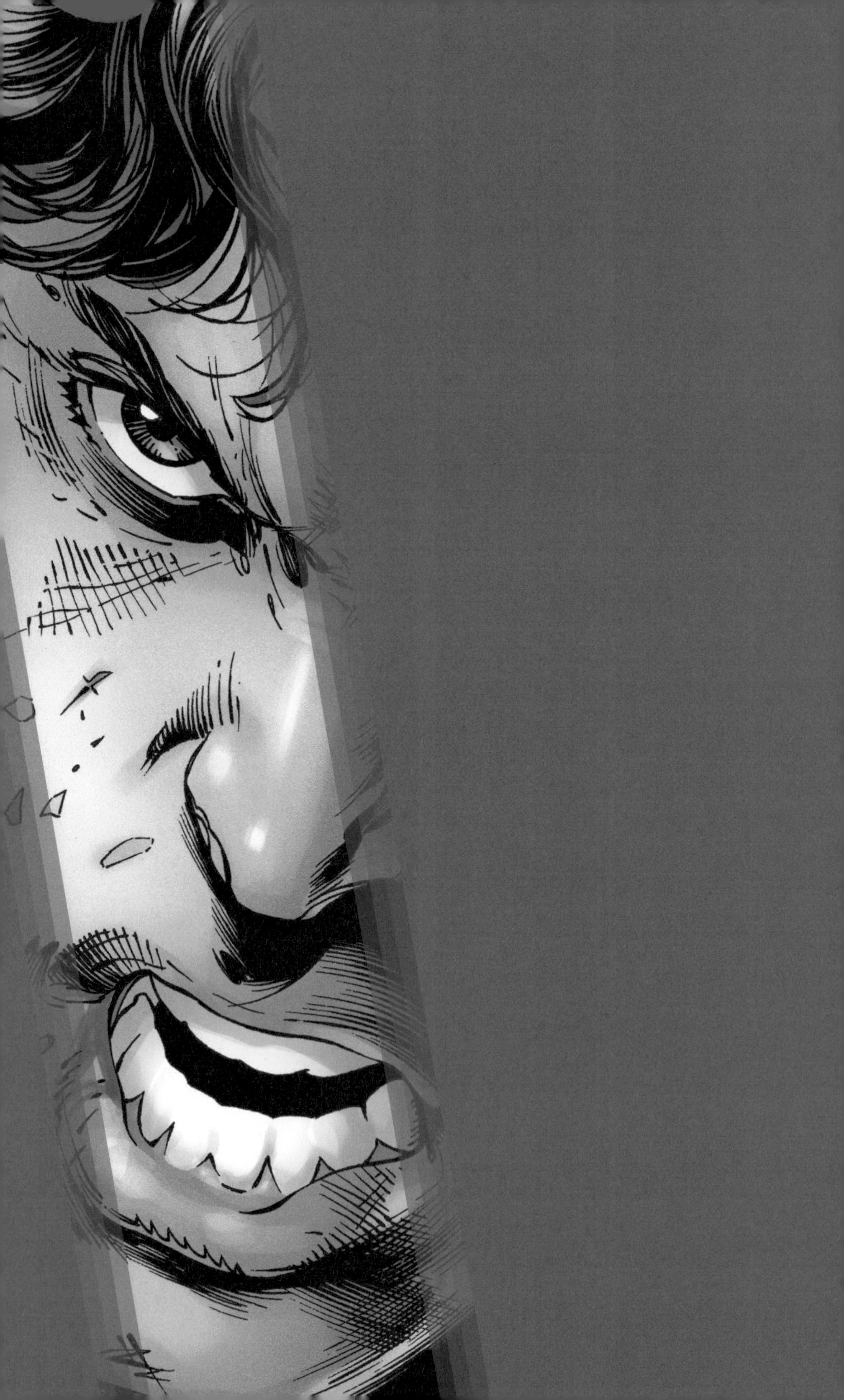

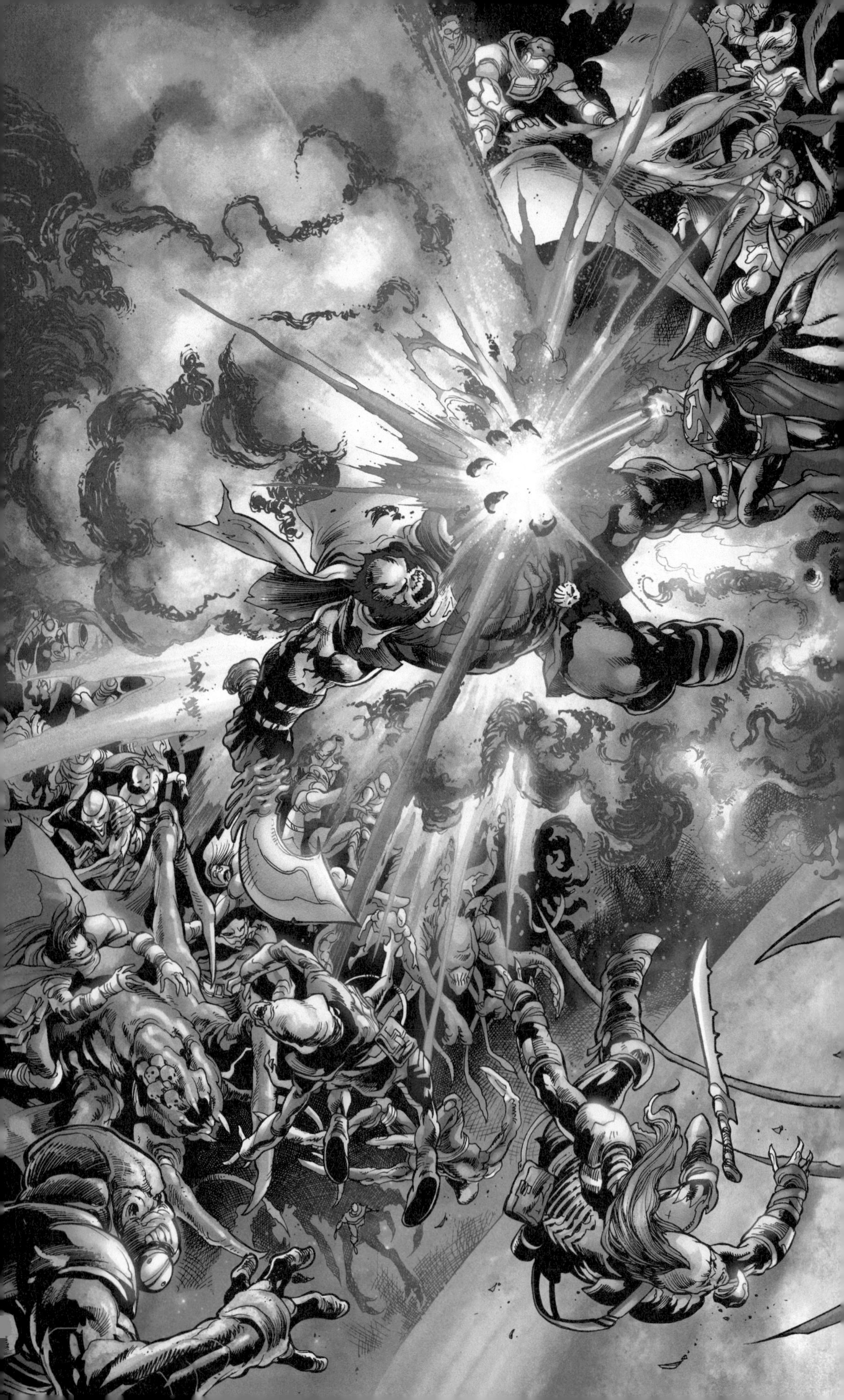

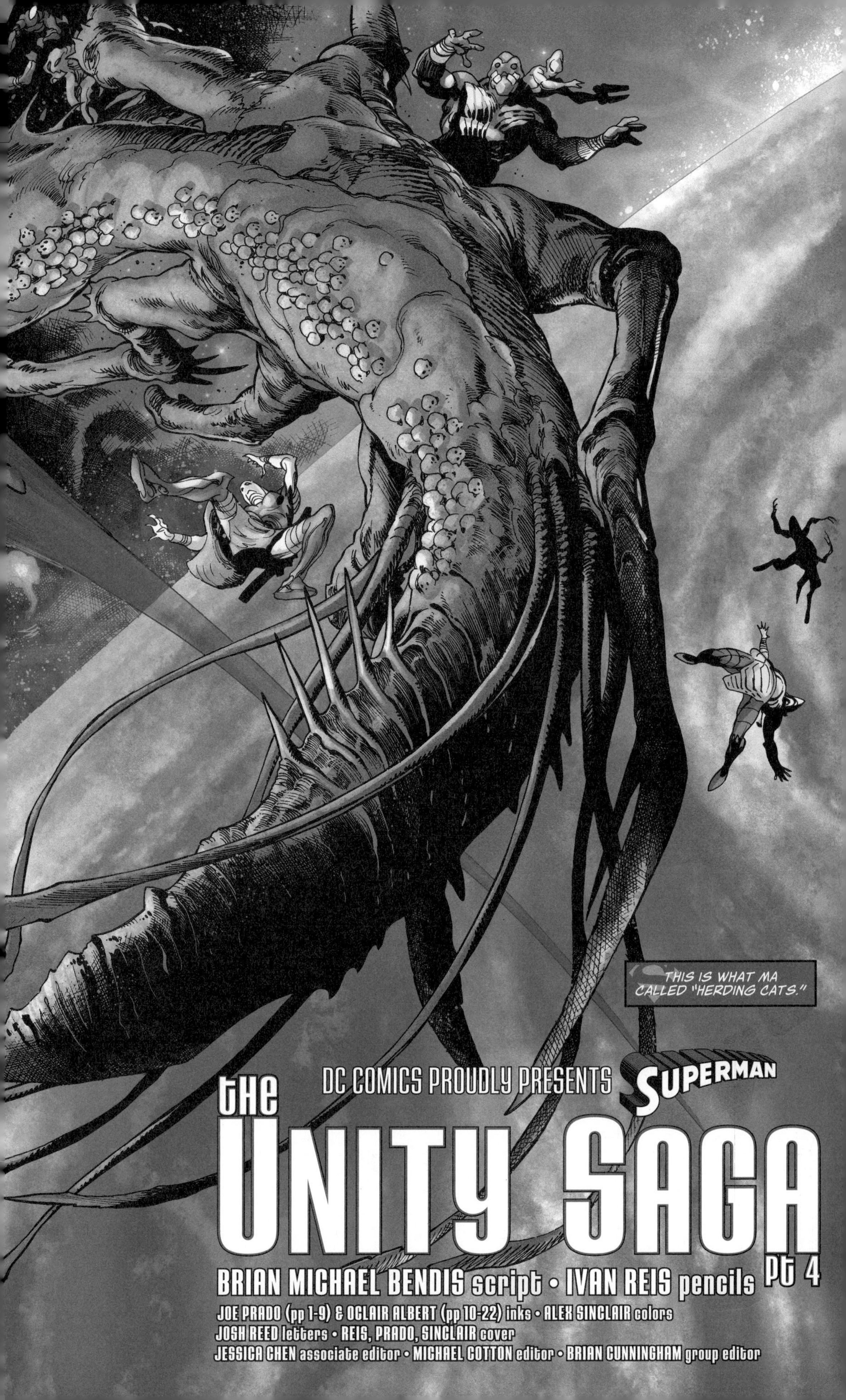
THIS IS WHAT MA CALLED "HERDING CATS."
DC COMICS PROUDLY PRESENTS SUPERMAN
THE UNITY SAGA PT 4
BRIAN MICHAEL BENDIS script • IVAN REIS pencils
JOE PRADO (pp 1-9) & OCLAIR ALBERT (pp 10-22) inks • ALEX SINCLAIR colors
JOSH REED letters • REIS, PRADO, SINCLAIR cover
JESSICA CHEN associate editor • MICHAEL COTTON editor • BRIAN CUNNINGHAM group editor

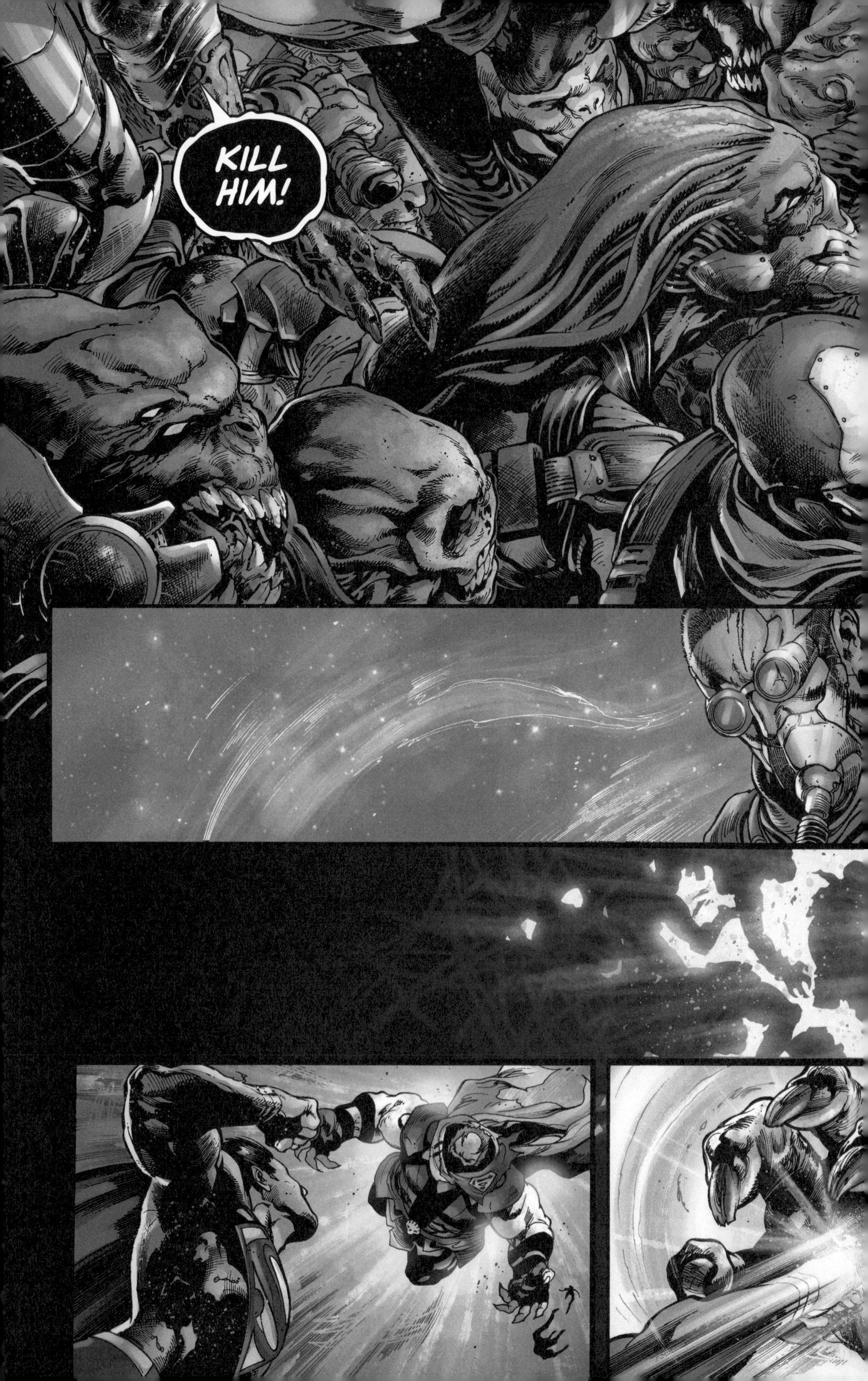
KILL HIM!

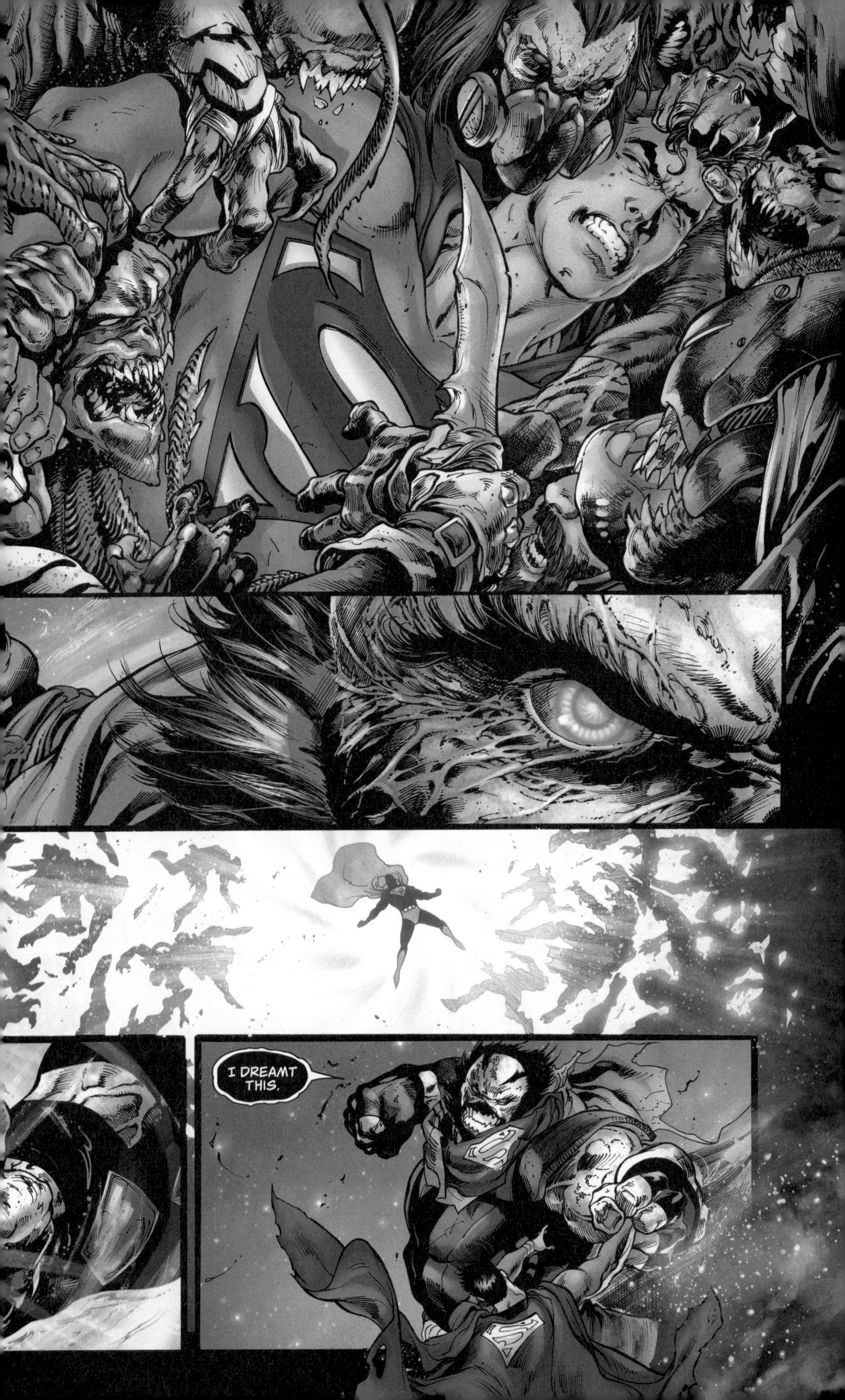
I DREAMT THIS.

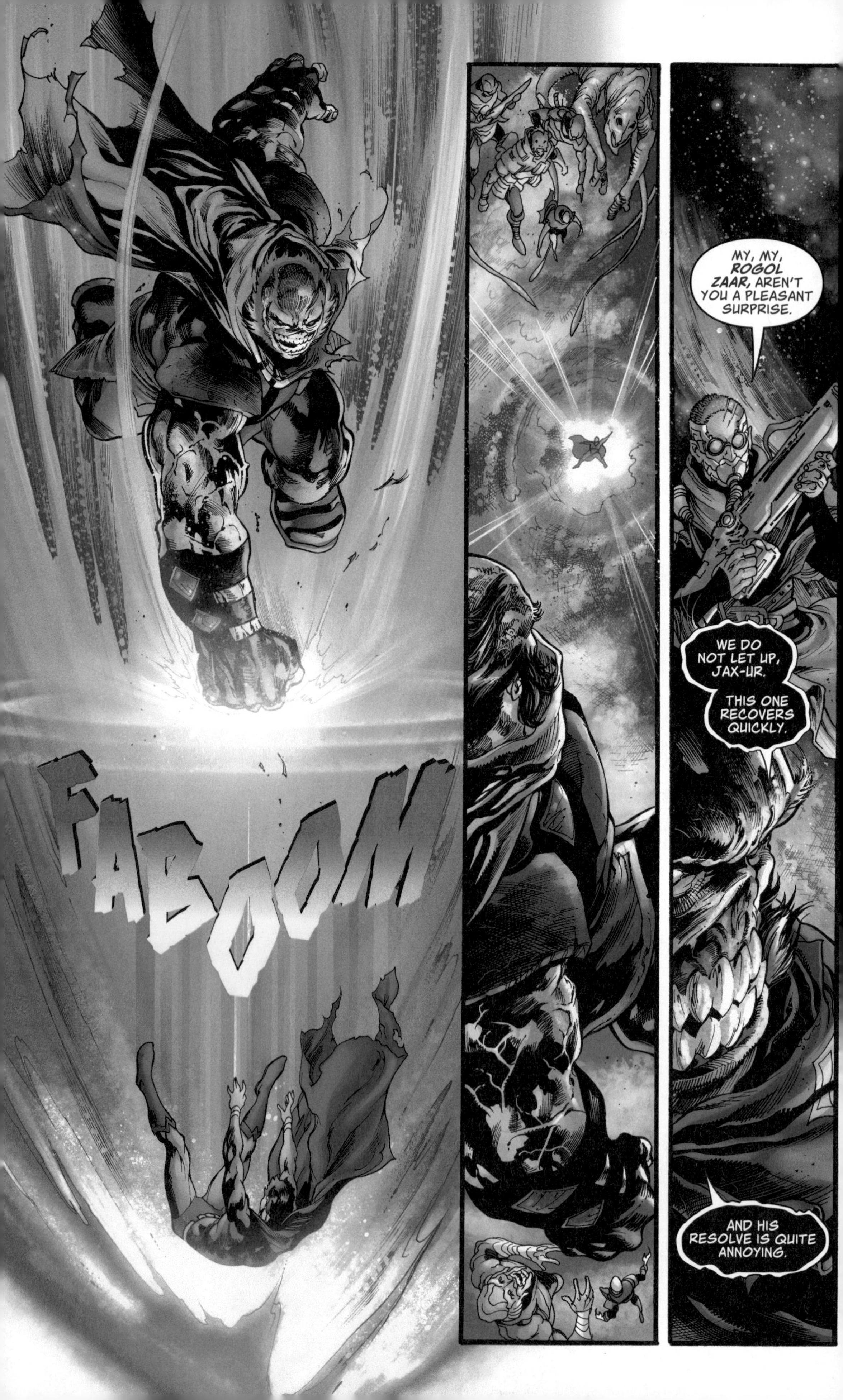
FABOOM
MY, MY, ROGOL ZAAR, AREN'T YOU A PLEASANT SURPRISE.
WE DO NOT LET UP, JAX-UR.
THIS ONE RECOVERS QUICKLY.
AND HIS RESOLVE IS QUITE ANNOYING.

DO NOT GIVE AN *EL* A MOMENT TO BREATHE, LET ALONE...

"NOT FAAAAIIIRRR!

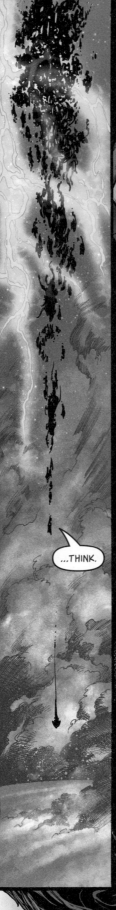

...THINK.

"NOT FAAAAIIIRRR!

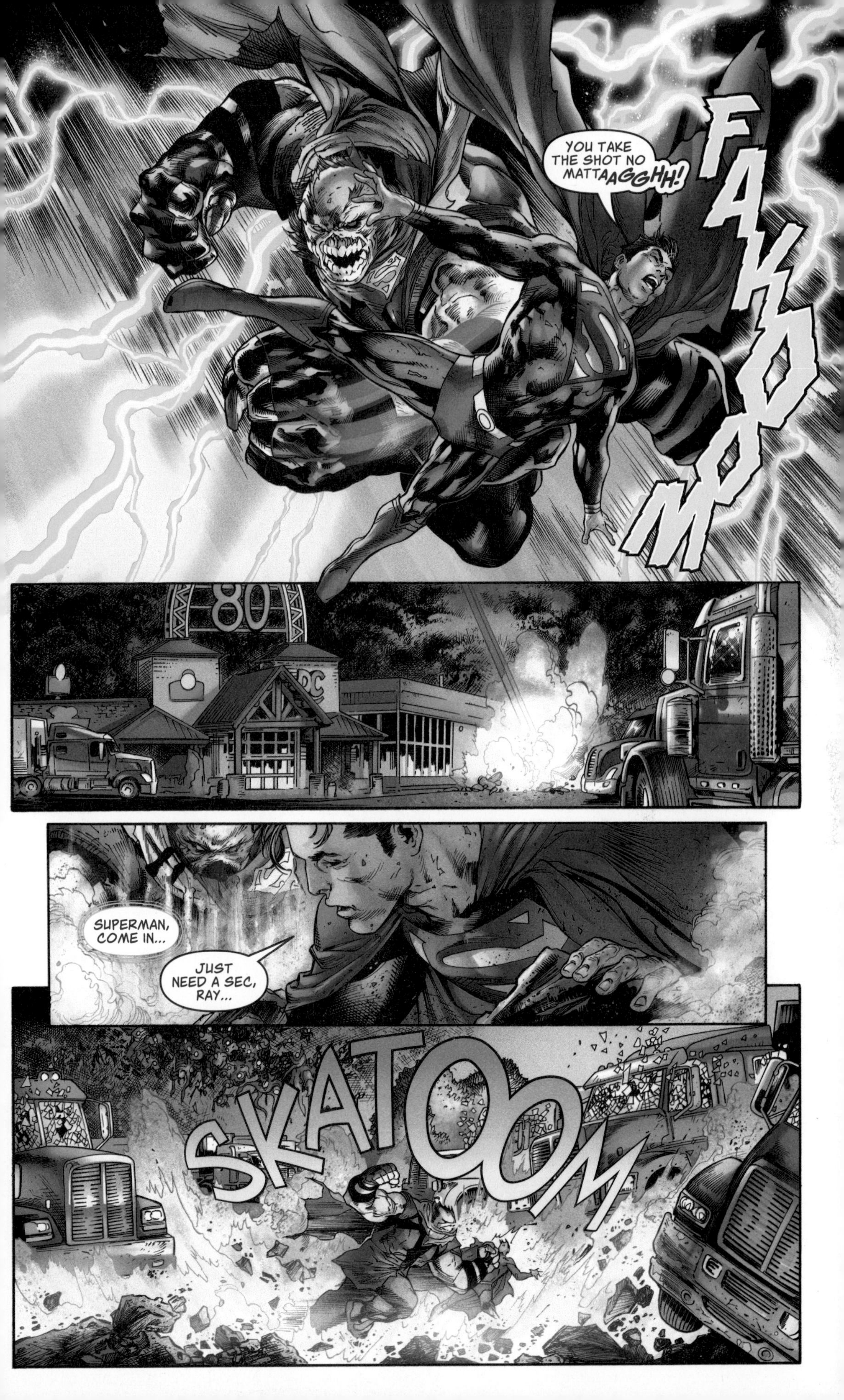
YOU TAKE THE SHOT NO MATTAAGGHH!
FAKOOM
SUPERMAN, COME IN...
JUST NEED A SEC, RAY...
SKATOOM

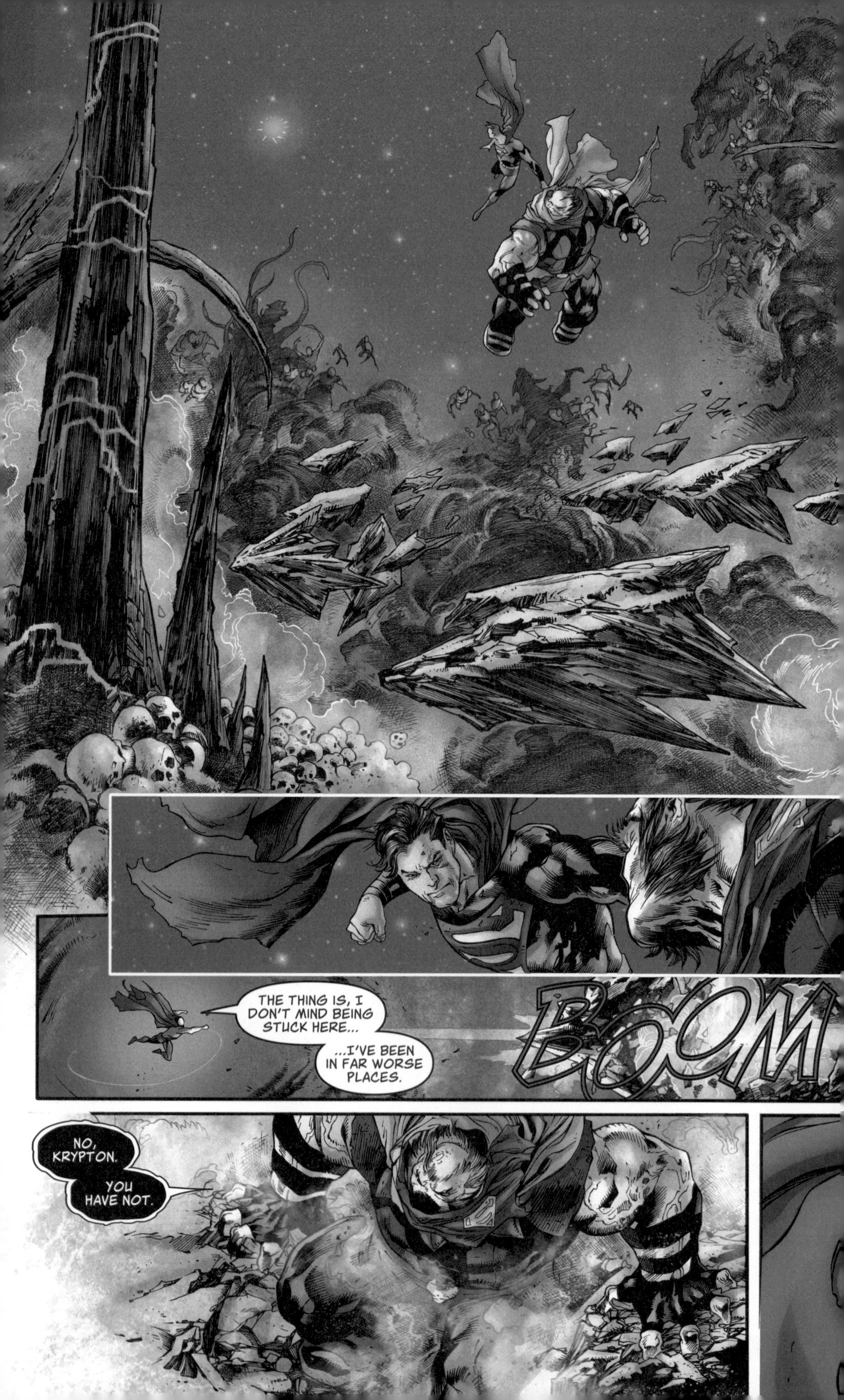
THE THING IS, I DON'T MIND BEING STUCK HERE...
...I'VE BEEN IN FAR WORSE PLACES.
BOOM
NO, KRYPTON.
YOU HAVE NOT.

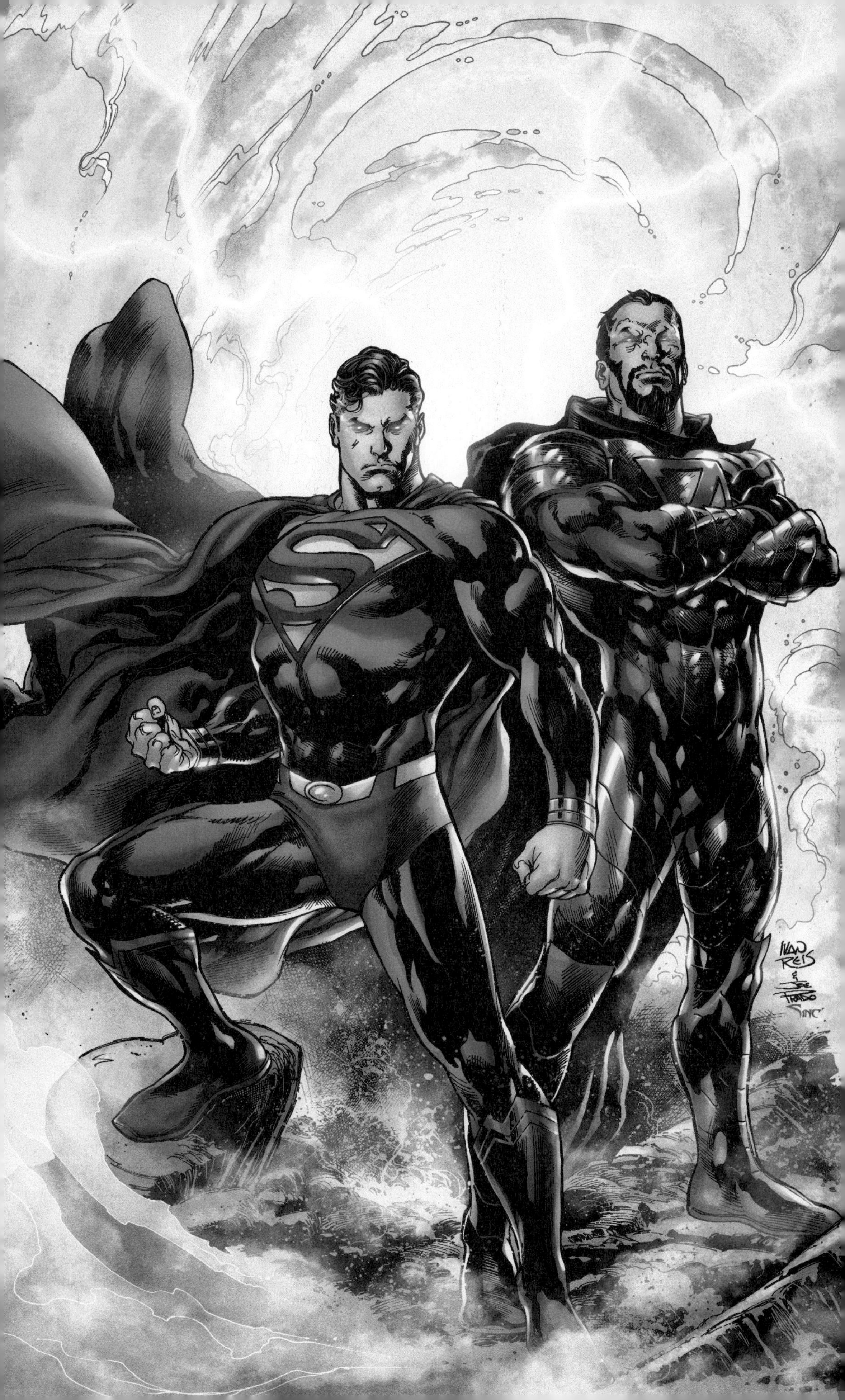

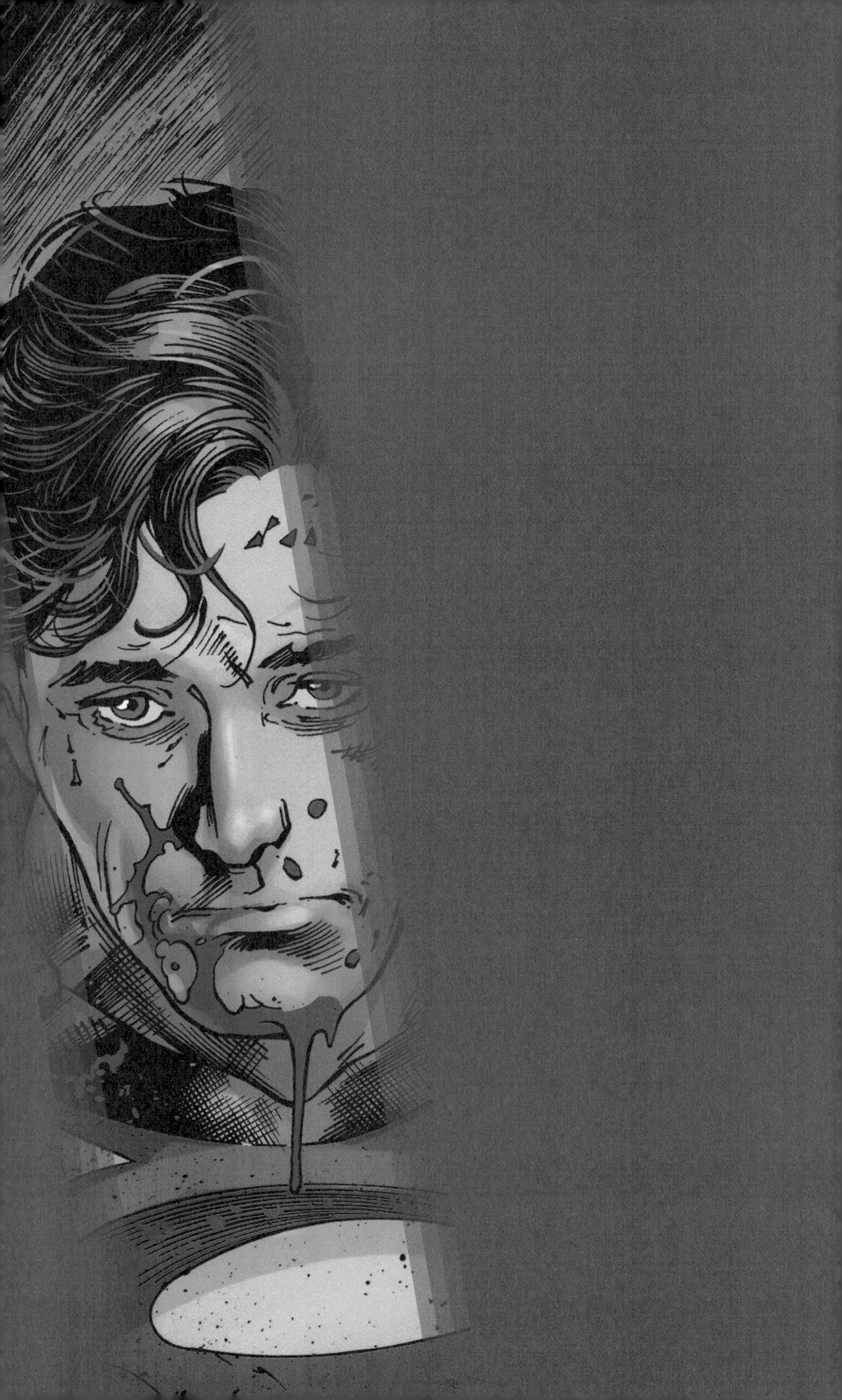

DC COMICS PROUDLY PRESENTS

SUPERMAN

the UNITY SAGA pt

BRIAN MICHAEL BENDIS script • IVAN REIS pencils

JOE PRADO (pp 1-6, 23-24) & OCLAIR ALBERT (pp 7-22) inks

ALEX SINCLAIR colors • JOSH REED letters

REIS, PRADO, SINCLAIR cover

JESSICA CHEN associate editor • MIKE COTTON editor

BRIAN CUNNINGHAM group editor

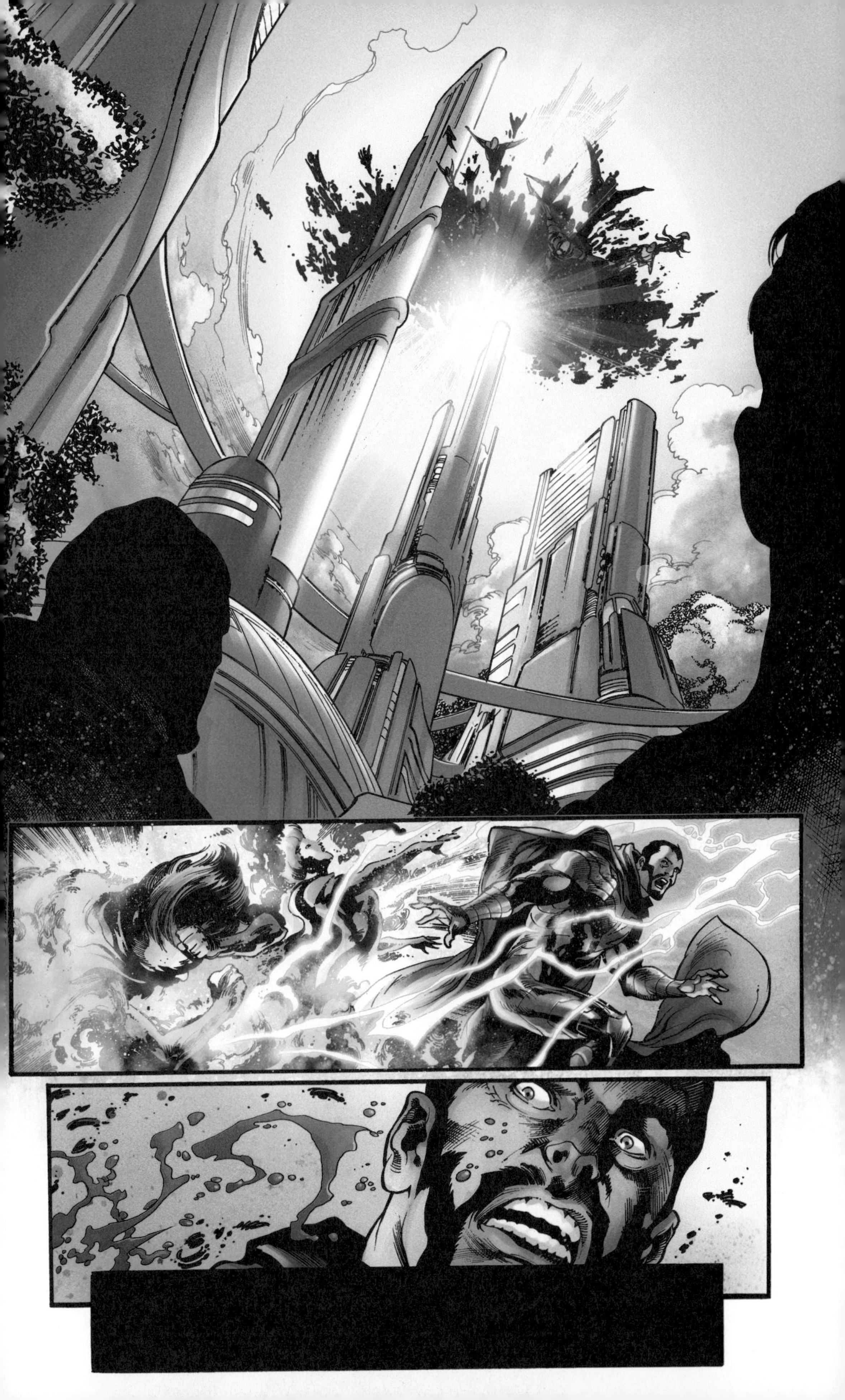

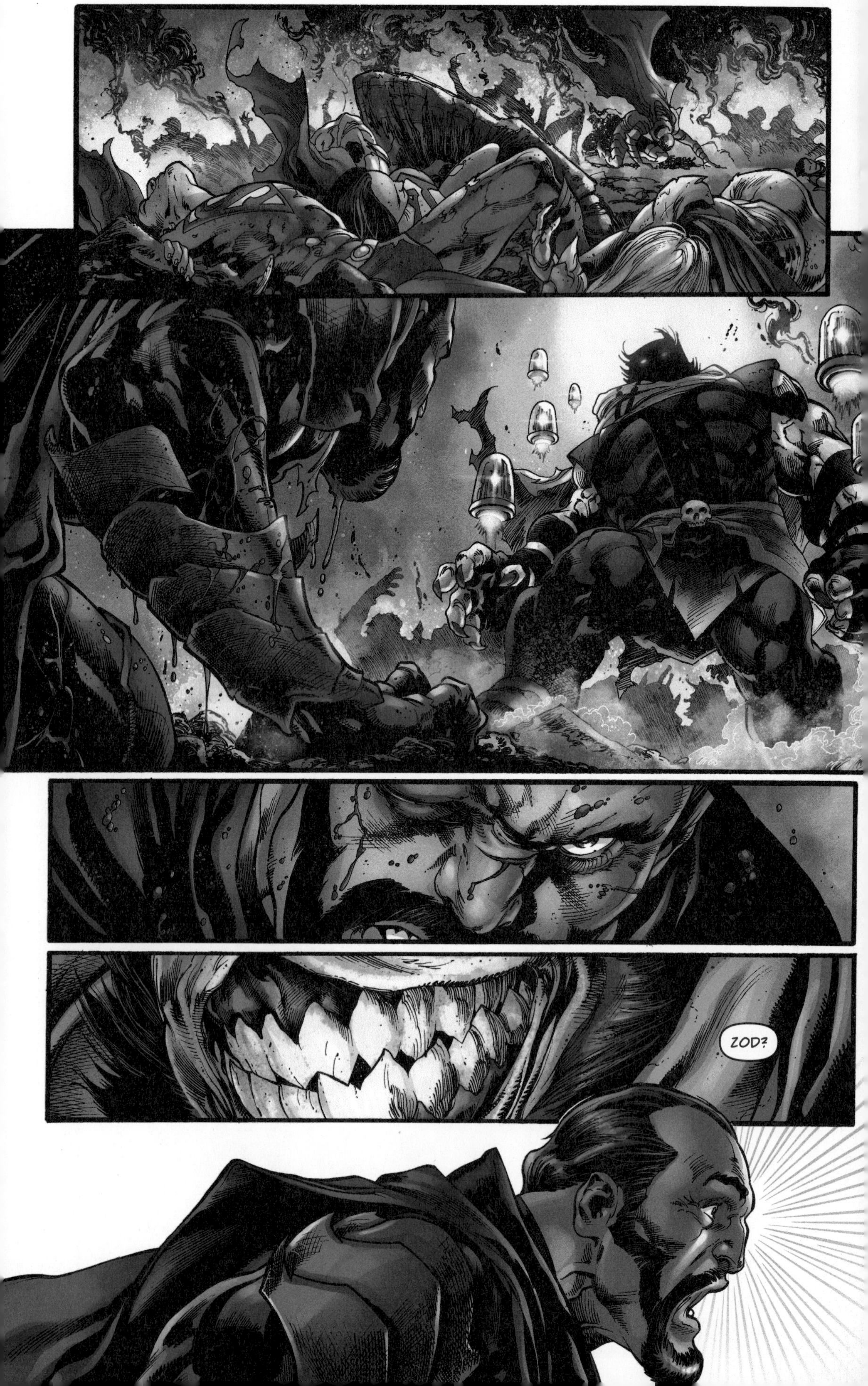
ZOD?

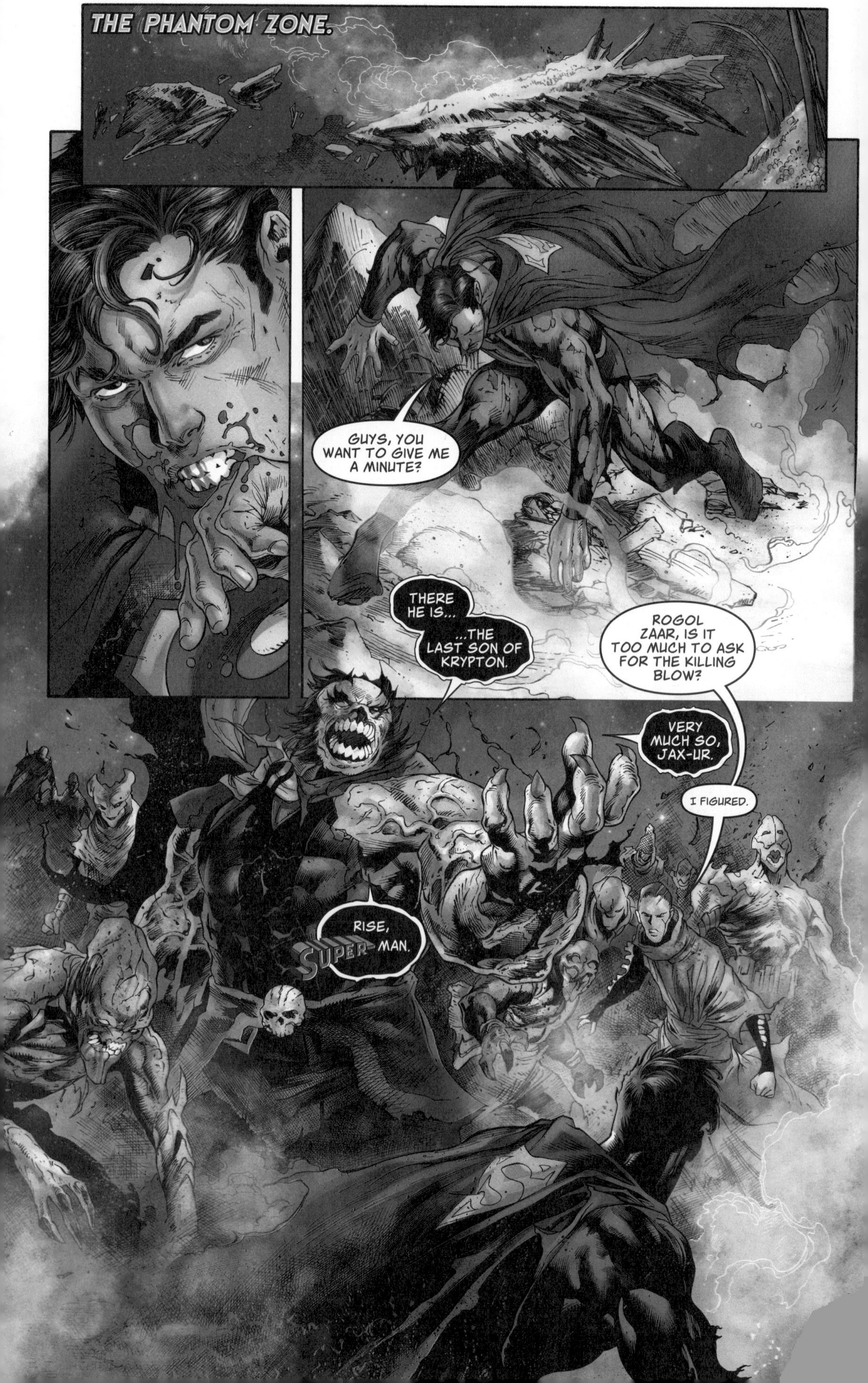
THE PHANTOM ZONE.
GUYS, YOU WANT TO GIVE ME A MINUTE?
THERE HE IS...
...THE LAST SON OF KRYPTON.
ROGOL ZAAR, IS IT TOO MUCH TO ASK FOR THE KILLING BLOW?
VERY MUCH SO, JAX-UR.
I FIGURED.
RISE, SUPER-MAN.

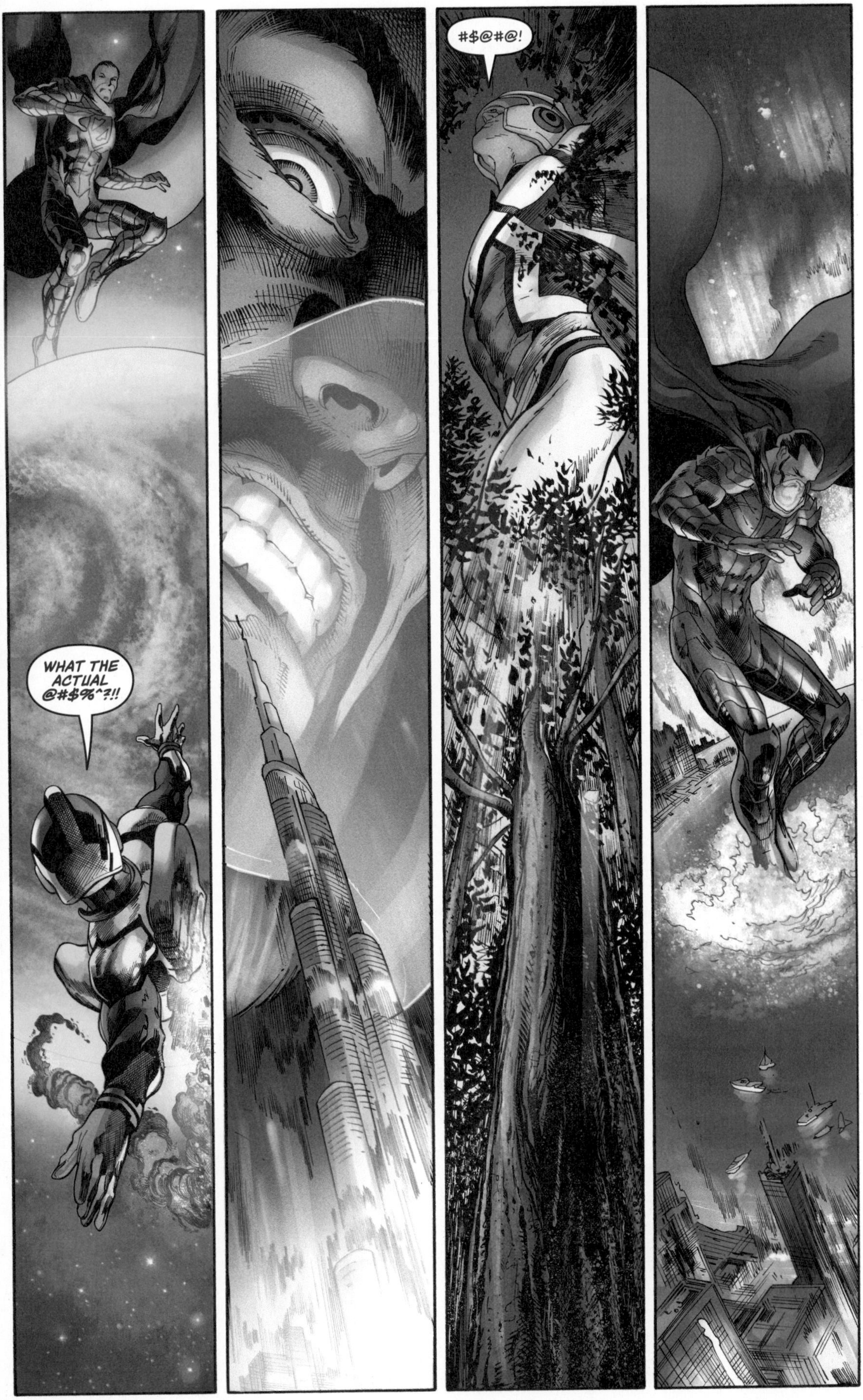
WHAT THE ACTUAL @#$%^?!!
#$@#@!

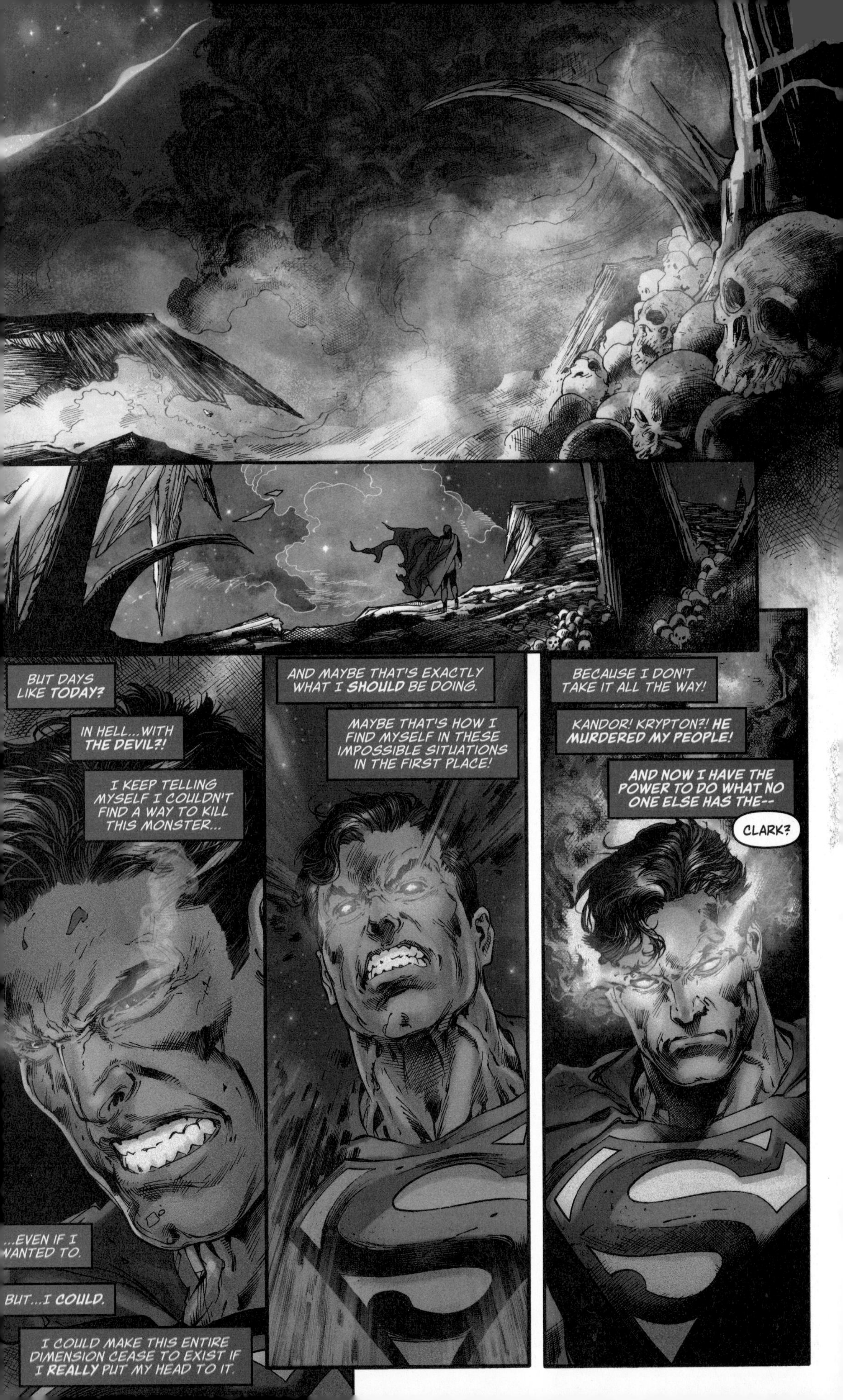
BUT DAYS LIKE TODAY?
IN HELL...WITH THE DEVIL?!
I KEEP TELLING MYSELF I COULDN'T FIND A WAY TO KILL THIS MONSTER...
...EVEN IF I WANTED TO.
BUT...I COULD.
I COULD MAKE THIS ENTIRE DIMENSION CEASE TO EXIST IF I REALLY PUT MY HEAD TO IT.
AND MAYBE THAT'S EXACTLY WHAT I SHOULD BE DOING.
MAYBE THAT'S HOW I FIND MYSELF IN THESE IMPOSSIBLE SITUATIONS IN THE FIRST PLACE!
BECAUSE I DON'T TAKE IT ALL THE WAY!
KANDOR! KRYPTON?! HE MURDERED MY PEOPLE!
AND NOW I HAVE THE POWER TO DO WHAT NO ONE ELSE HAS THE--
CLARK?

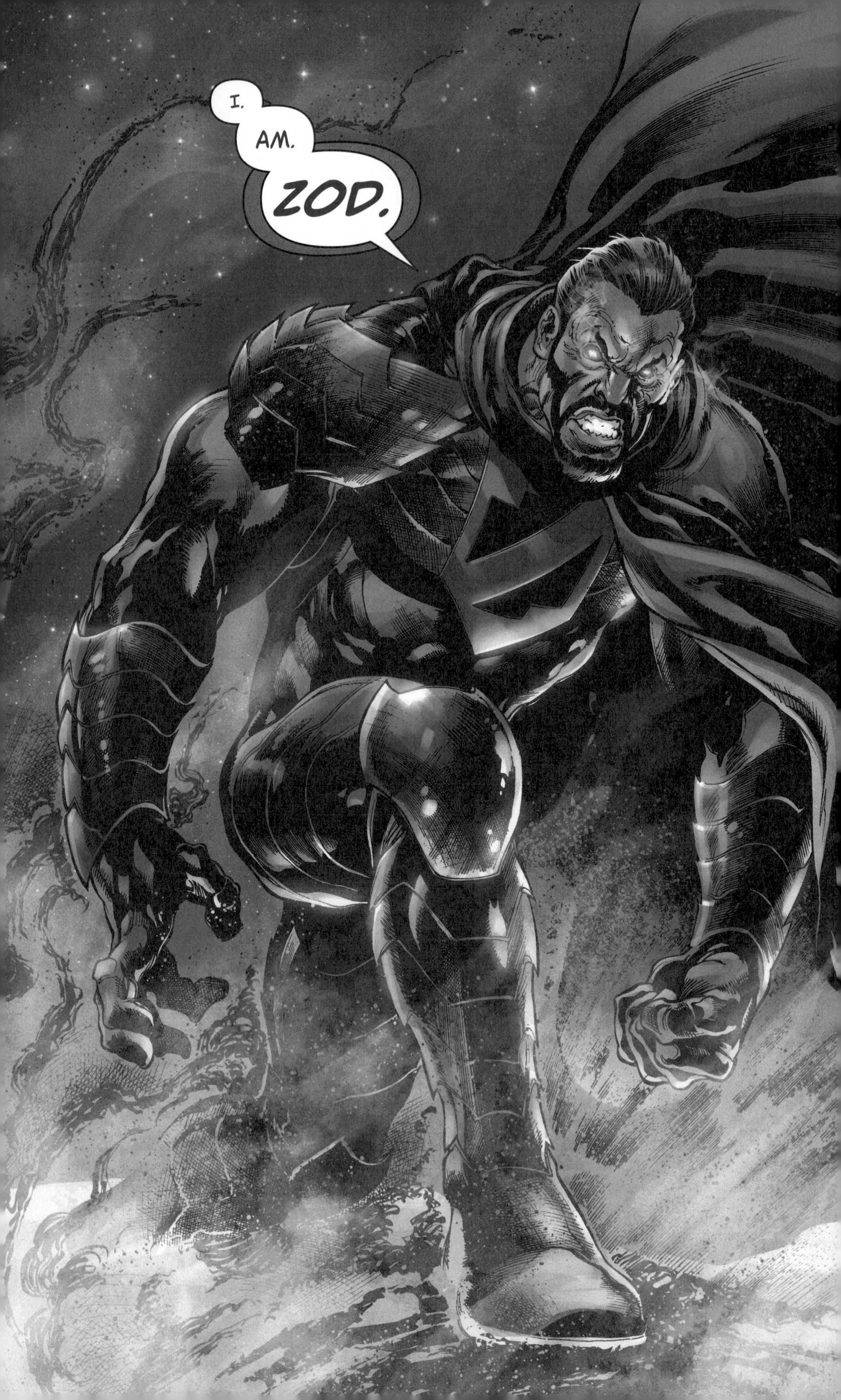
I.
AM.
ZOD.

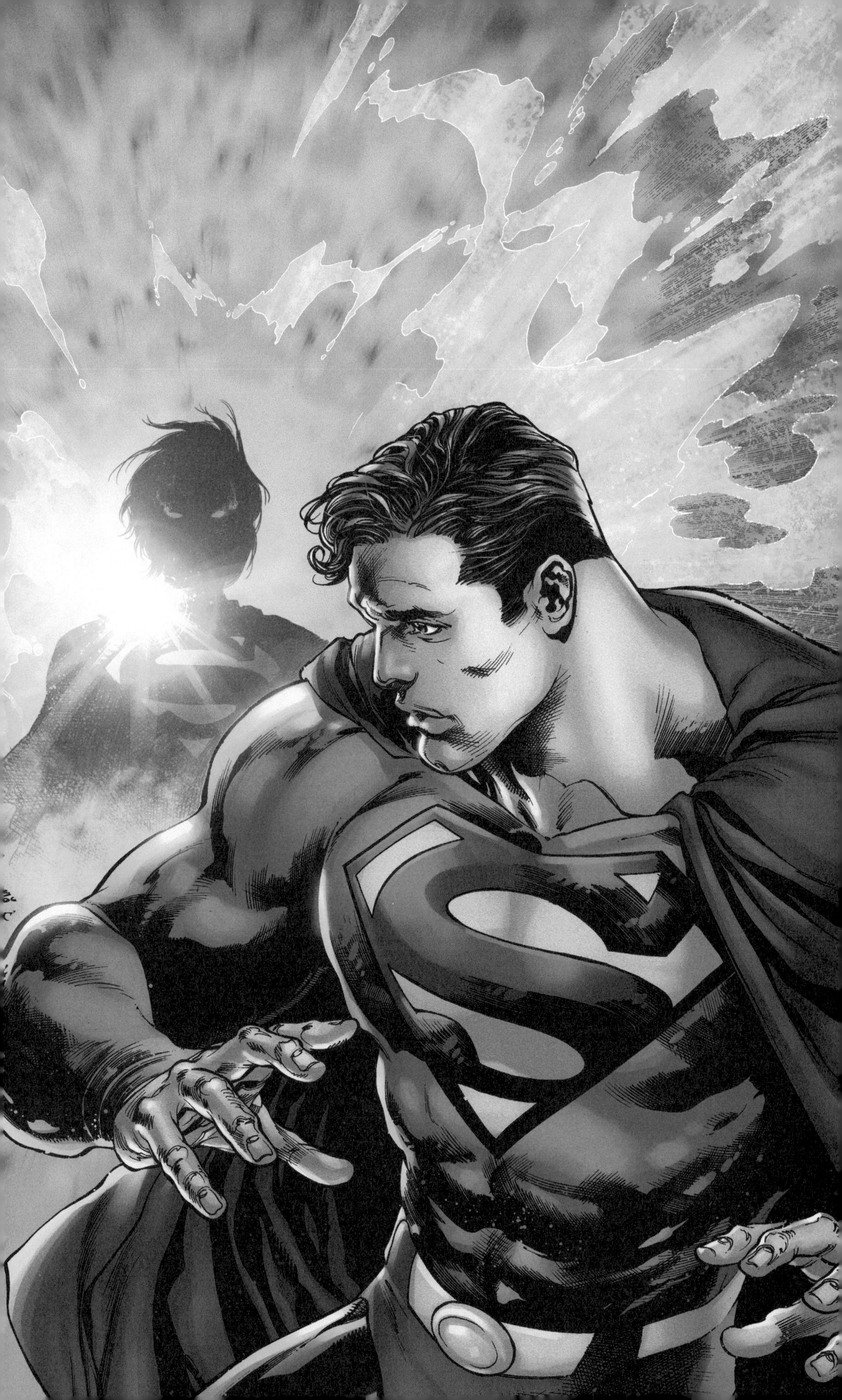

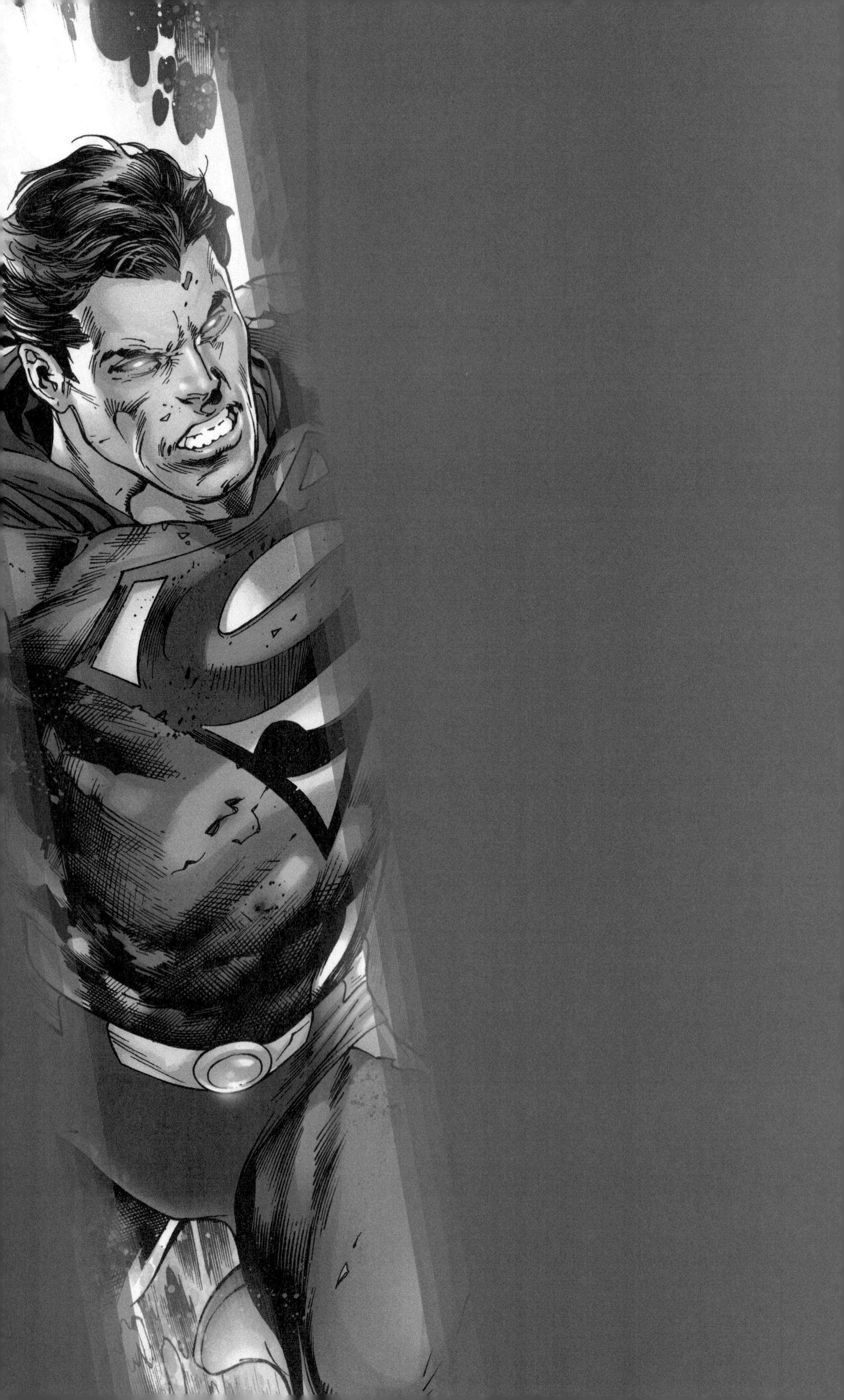

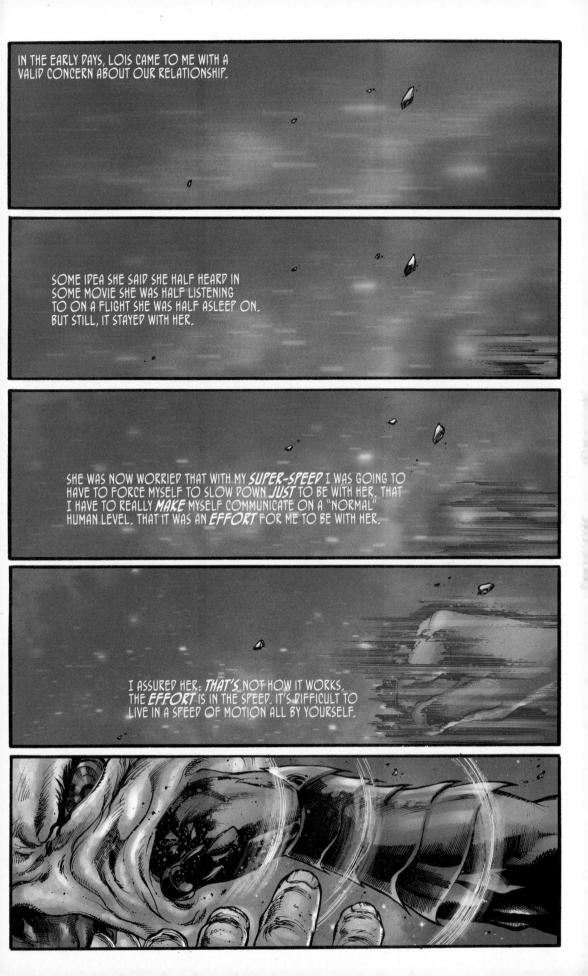

IN THE EARLY DAYS, LOIS CAME TO ME WITH A VALID CONCERN ABOUT OUR RELATIONSHIP.

SOME IDEA SHE SAID SHE HALF HEARD IN SOME MOVIE SHE WAS HALF LISTENING TO ON A FLIGHT SHE WAS HALF ASLEEP ON. BUT STILL, IT STAYED WITH HER.

SHE WAS NOW WORRIED THAT WITH MY *SUPER-SPEED* I WAS GOING TO HAVE TO FORCE MYSELF TO SLOW DOWN *JUST* TO BE WITH HER. THAT I HAVE TO REALLY *MAKE* MYSELF COMMUNICATE ON A "NORMAL" HUMAN LEVEL. THAT IT WAS AN *EFFORT* FOR ME TO BE WITH HER.

I ASSURED HER: *THAT'S* NOT HOW IT WORKS. THE *EFFORT* IS IN THE SPEED. IT'S DIFFICULT TO LIVE IN A SPEED OF MOTION ALL BY YOURSELF.

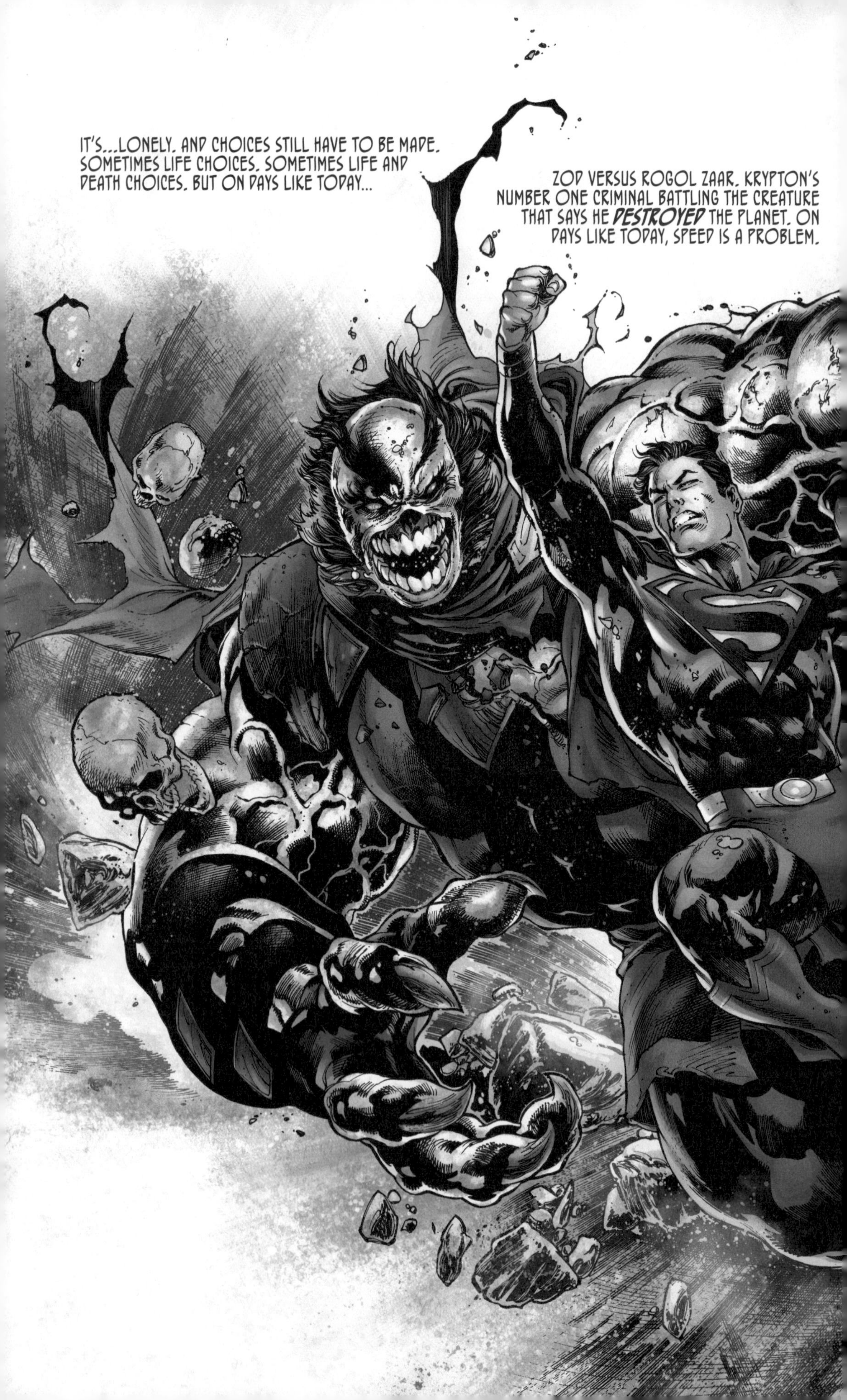
IT'S...LONELY. AND CHOICES STILL HAVE TO BE MADE. SOMETIMES LIFE CHOICES. SOMETIMES LIFE AND DEATH CHOICES. BUT ON DAYS LIKE TODAY...
ZOD VERSUS ROGOL ZAAR. KRYPTON'S NUMBER ONE CRIMINAL BATTLING THE CREATURE THAT SAYS HE DESTROYED THE PLANET. ON DAYS LIKE TODAY, SPEED IS A PROBLEM.

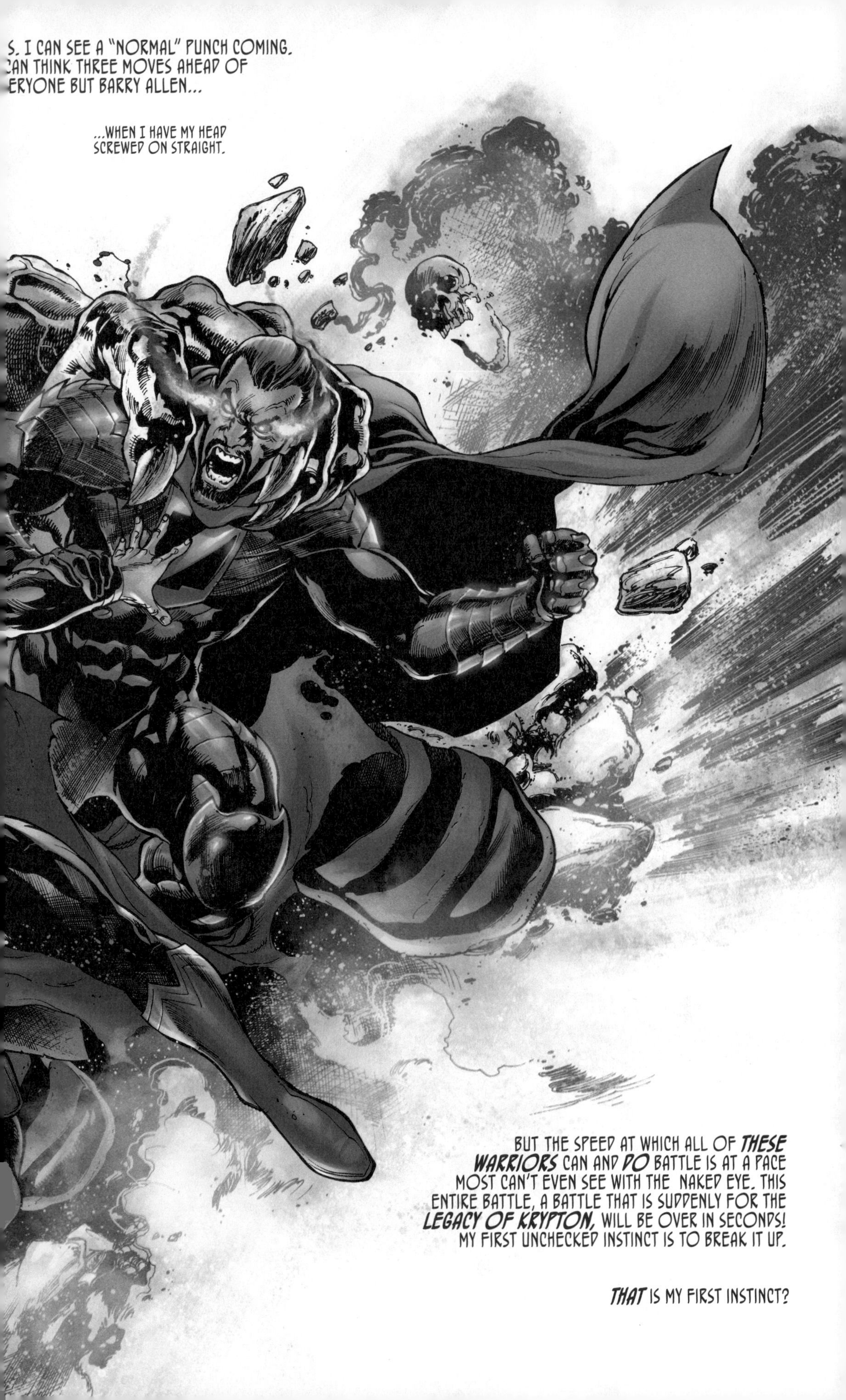
S. I CAN SEE A "NORMAL" PUNCH COMING. :AN THINK THREE MOVES AHEAD OF ERYONE BUT BARRY ALLEN...
...WHEN I HAVE MY HEAD SCREWED ON STRAIGHT.
BUT THE SPEED AT WHICH ALL OF *THESE WARRIORS* CAN AND *DO* BATTLE IS AT A PACE MOST CAN'T EVEN SEE WITH THE NAKED EYE. THIS ENTIRE BATTLE, A BATTLE THAT IS SUDDENLY FOR THE *LEGACY OF KRYPTON,* WILL BE OVER IN SECONDS! MY FIRST UNCHECKED INSTINCT IS TO BREAK IT UP.
THAT IS MY FIRST INSTINCT?

DC COMICS PROUDLY PRESENTS

SUPERMAN

the UNITY SAGA pt 6

BRIAN MICHAEL BENDIS script
IVAN REIS pencils

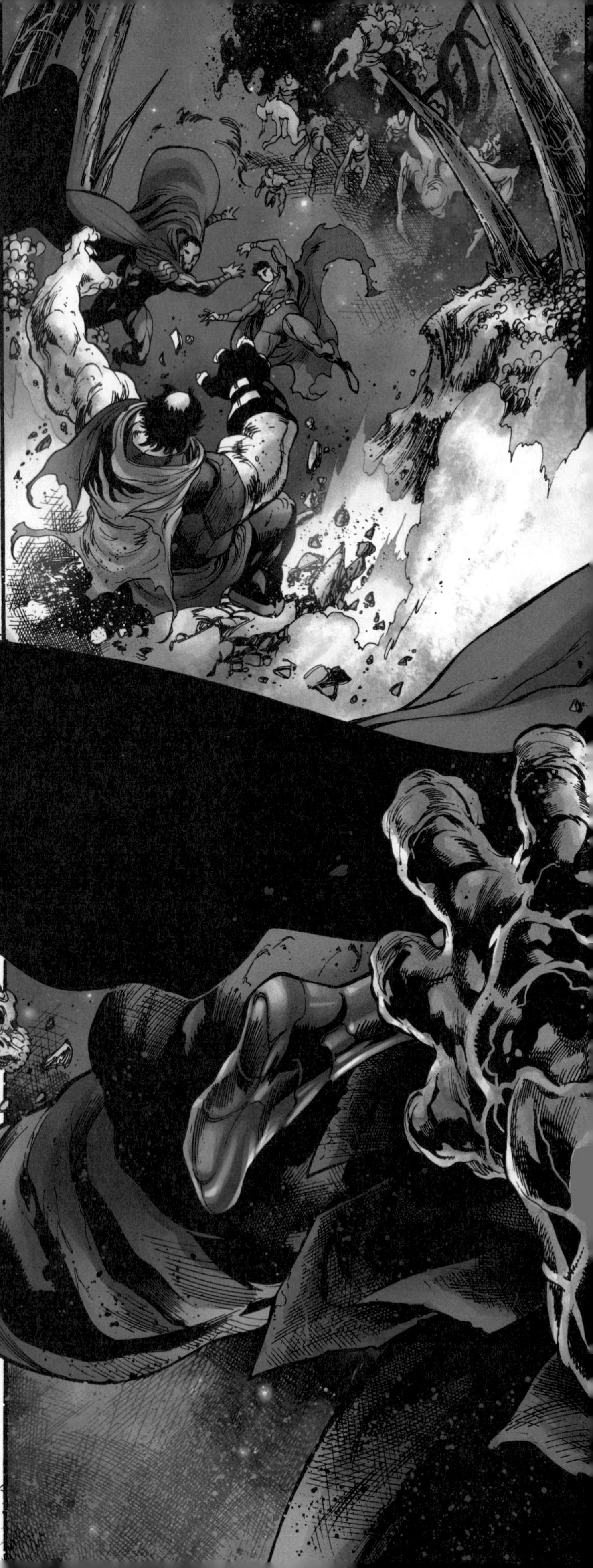

JOE PRADO & OCLAIR ALBERT inks
ALEX SINCLAIR colors
JOSH REED letters
REIS, PRADO, SINCLAIR cover
JESSICA CHEN associate editor
MIKE COTTON editor
BRIAN CUNNINGHAM group editor

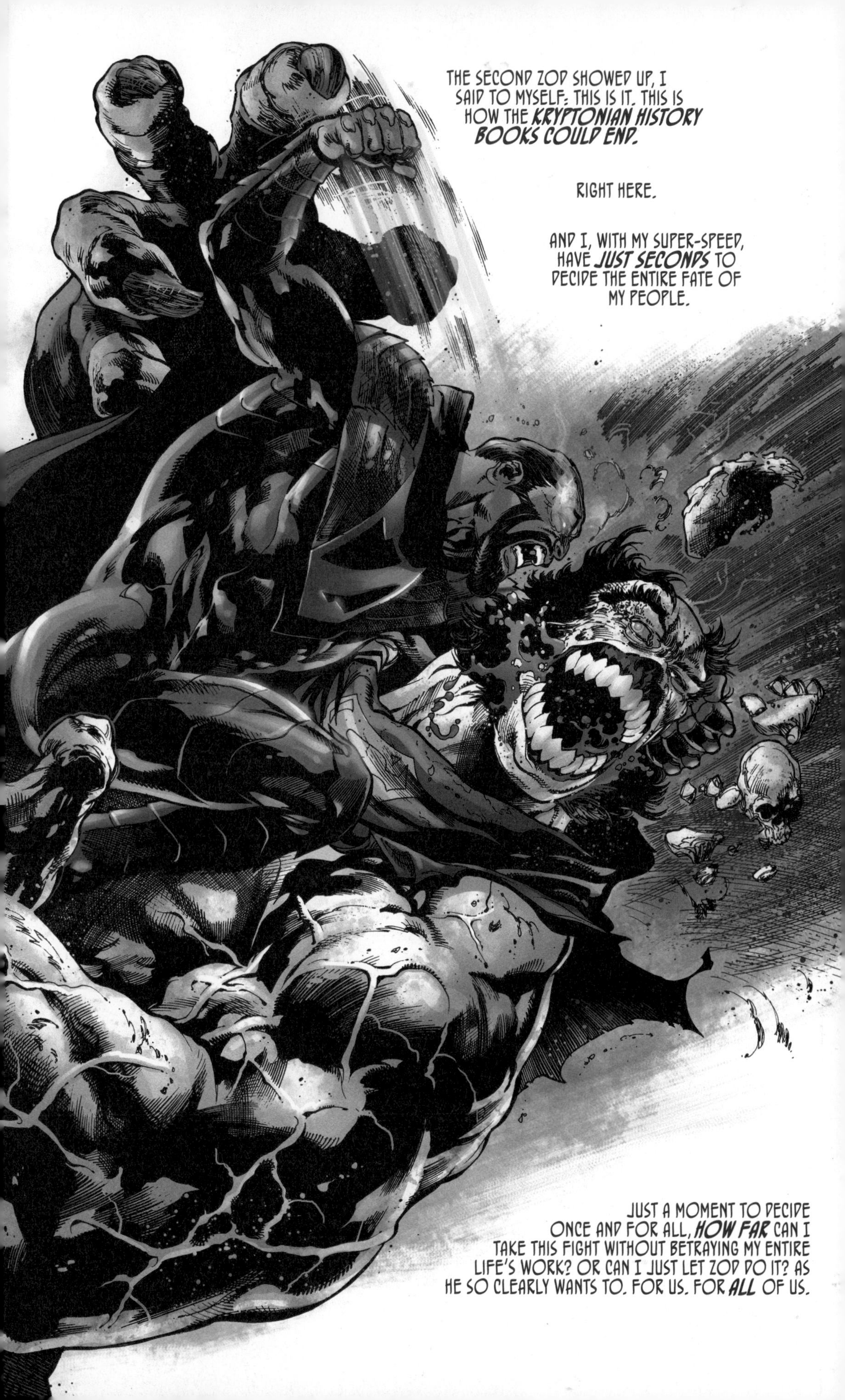
THE SECOND ZOD SHOWED UP, I SAID TO MYSELF: THIS IS IT. THIS IS HOW THE KRYPTONIAN HISTORY BOOKS COULD END.
RIGHT HERE.
AND I, WITH MY SUPER-SPEED, HAVE JUST SECONDS TO DECIDE THE ENTIRE FATE OF MY PEOPLE.
JUST A MOMENT TO DECIDE ONCE AND FOR ALL, HOW FAR CAN I TAKE THIS FIGHT WITHOUT BETRAYING MY ENTIRE LIFE'S WORK? OR CAN I JUST LET ZOD DO IT? AS HE SO CLEARLY WANTS TO. FOR US. FOR ALL OF US.

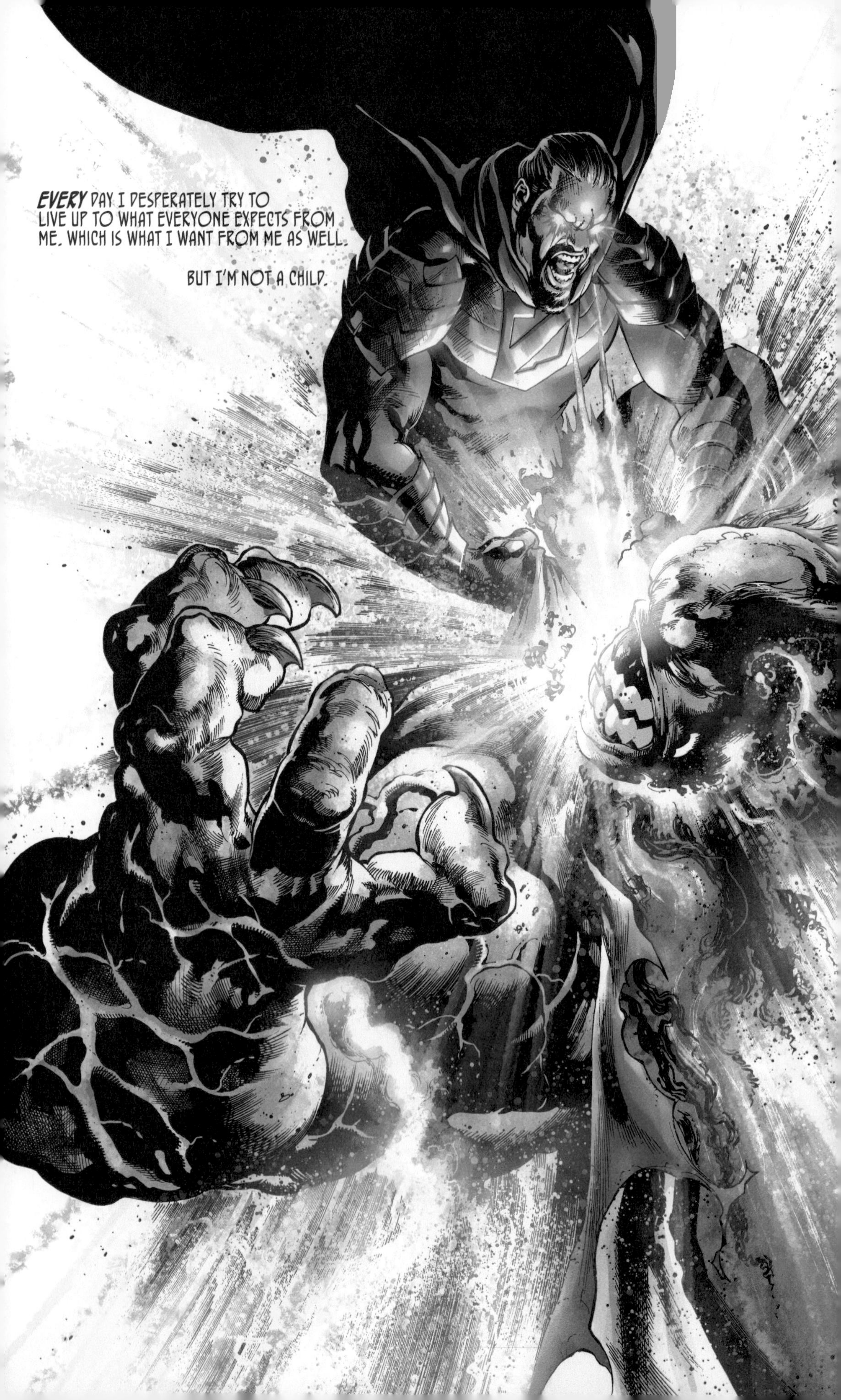
EVERY DAY I DESPERATELY TRY TO LIVE UP TO WHAT EVERYONE EXPECTS FROM ME. WHICH IS WHAT I WANT FROM ME AS WELL.
BUT I'M NOT A CHILD.

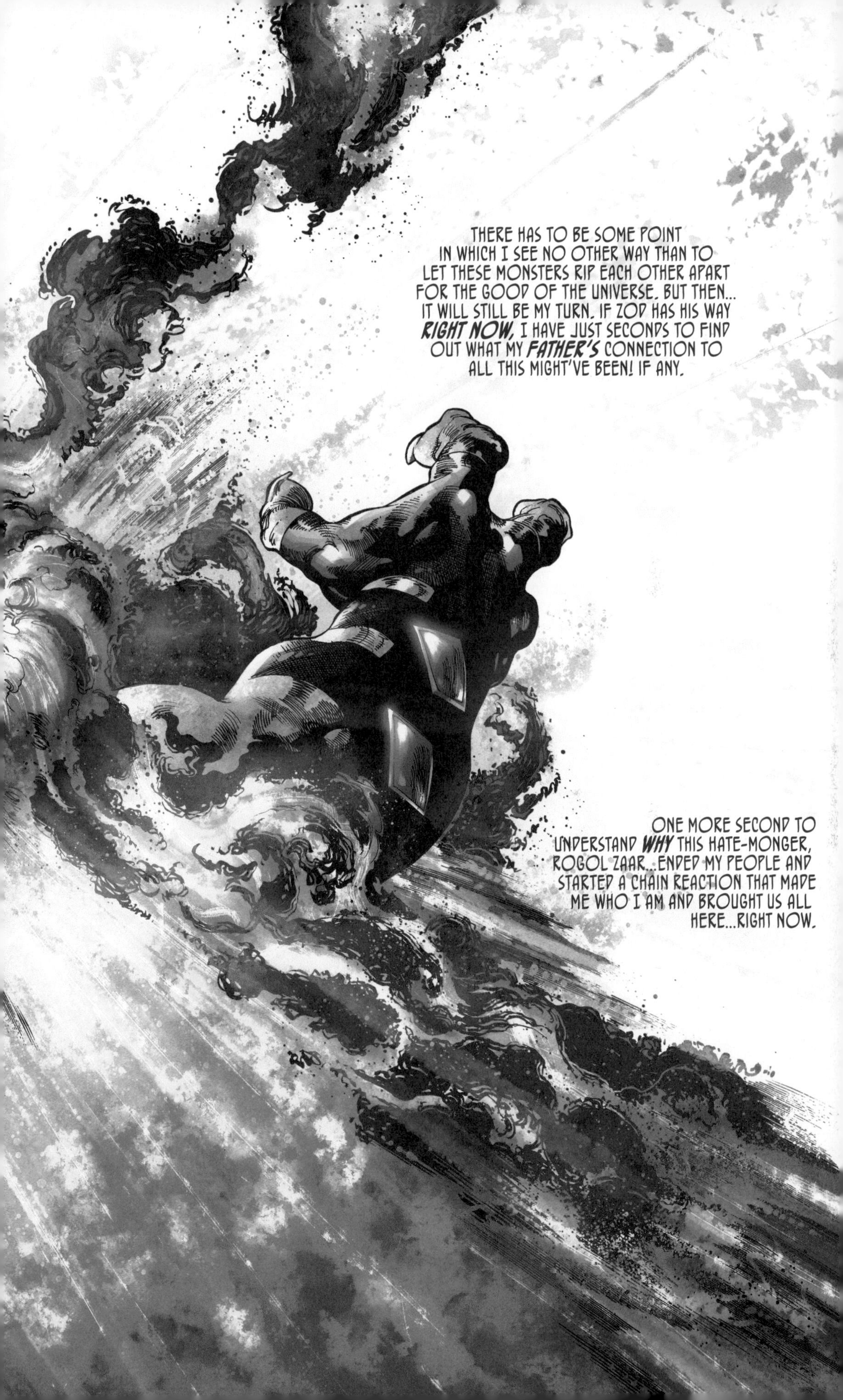
THERE HAS TO BE SOME POINT IN WHICH I SEE NO OTHER WAY THAN TO LET THESE MONSTERS RIP EACH OTHER APART FOR THE GOOD OF THE UNIVERSE. BUT THEN... IT WILL STILL BE MY TURN. IF ZOD HAS HIS WAY RIGHT NOW, I HAVE JUST SECONDS TO FIND OUT WHAT MY FATHER'S CONNECTION TO ALL THIS MIGHT'VE BEEN! IF ANY.
ONE MORE SECOND TO UNDERSTAND WHY THIS HATE-MONGER, ROGOL ZAAR...ENDED MY PEOPLE AND STARTED A CHAIN REACTION THAT MADE ME WHO I AM AND BROUGHT US ALL HERE...RIGHT NOW.

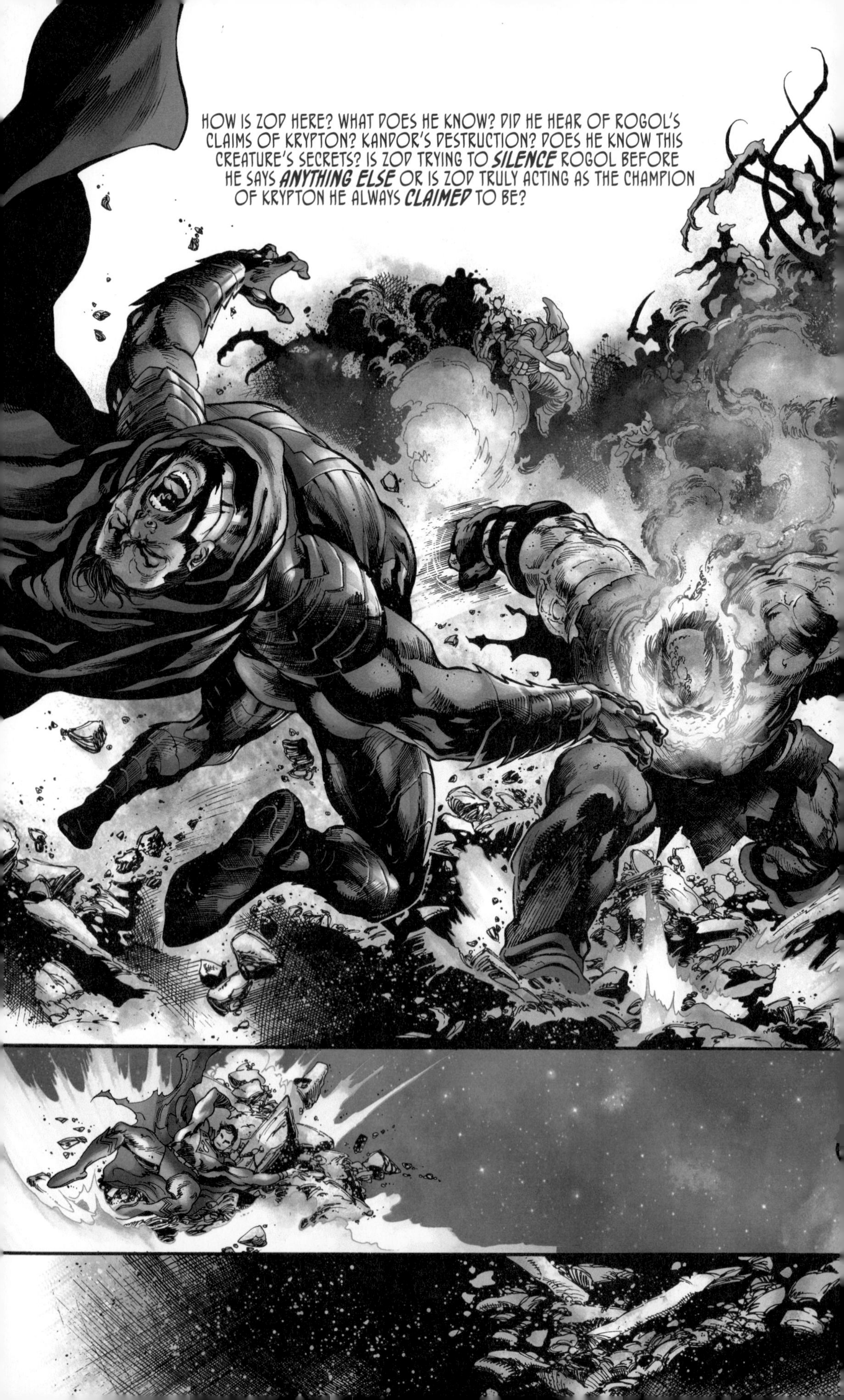
HOW IS ZOD HERE? WHAT DOES HE KNOW? DID HE HEAR OF ROGOL'S CLAIMS OF KRYPTON? KANDOR'S DESTRUCTION? DOES HE KNOW THIS CREATURE'S SECRETS? IS ZOD TRYING TO *SILENCE* ROGOL BEFORE HE SAYS *ANYTHING ELSE* OR IS ZOD TRULY ACTING AS THE CHAMPION OF KRYPTON HE ALWAYS *CLAIMED* TO BE?

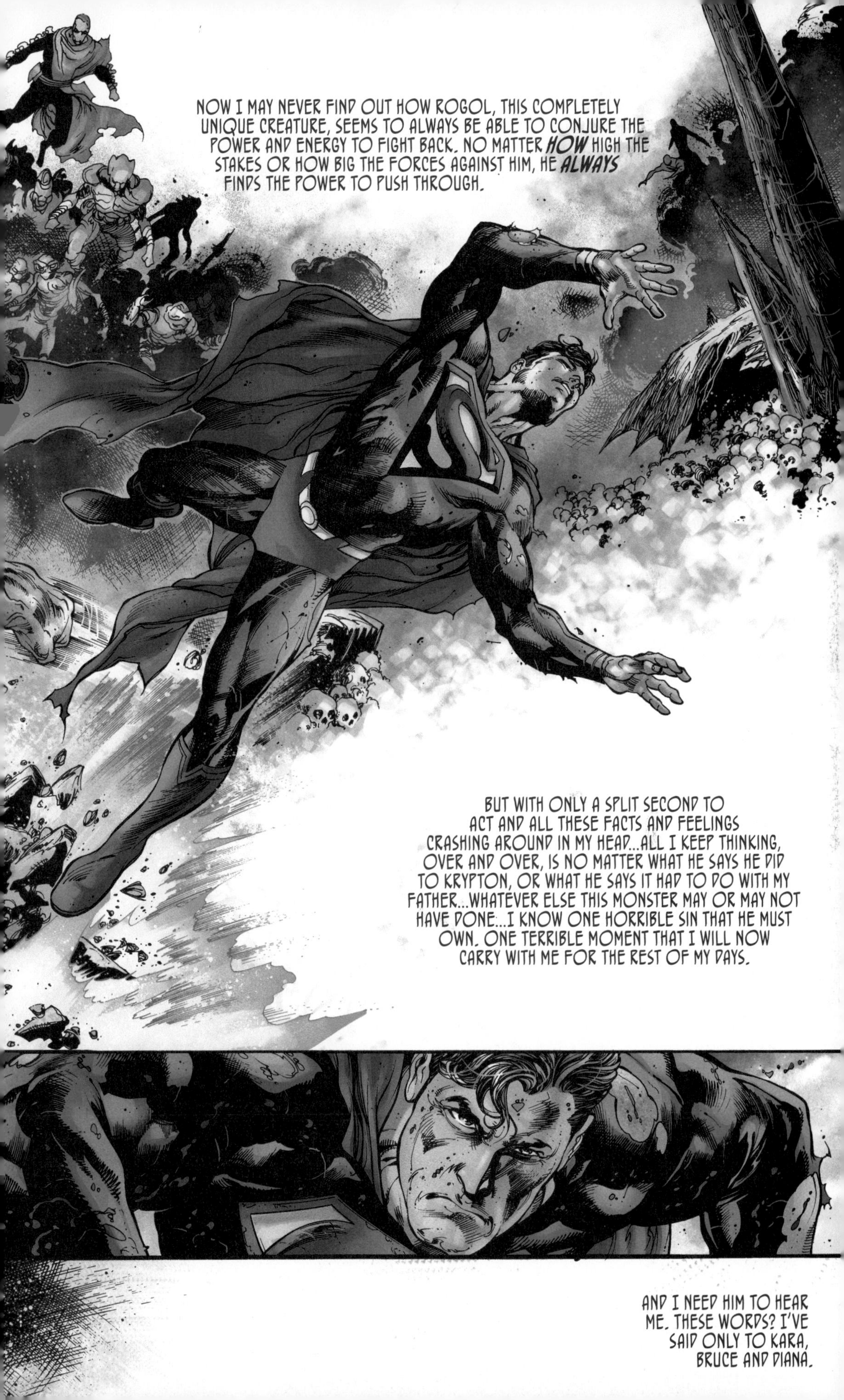
NOW I MAY NEVER FIND OUT HOW ROGOL, THIS COMPLETELY UNIQUE CREATURE, SEEMS TO ALWAYS BE ABLE TO CONJURE THE POWER AND ENERGY TO FIGHT BACK. NO MATTER HOW HIGH THE STAKES OR HOW BIG THE FORCES AGAINST HIM, HE ALWAYS FINDS THE POWER TO PUSH THROUGH.
BUT WITH ONLY A SPLIT SECOND TO ACT AND ALL THESE FACTS AND FEELINGS CRASHING AROUND IN MY HEAD...ALL I KEEP THINKING, OVER AND OVER, IS NO MATTER WHAT HE SAYS HE DID TO KRYPTON, OR WHAT HE SAYS IT HAD TO DO WITH MY FATHER...WHATEVER ELSE THIS MONSTER MAY OR MAY NOT HAVE DONE...I KNOW ONE HORRIBLE SIN THAT HE MUST OWN. ONE TERRIBLE MOMENT THAT I WILL NOW CARRY WITH ME FOR THE REST OF MY DAYS.
AND I NEED HIM TO HEAR ME. THESE WORDS? I'VE SAID ONLY TO KARA, BRUCE AND DIANA.

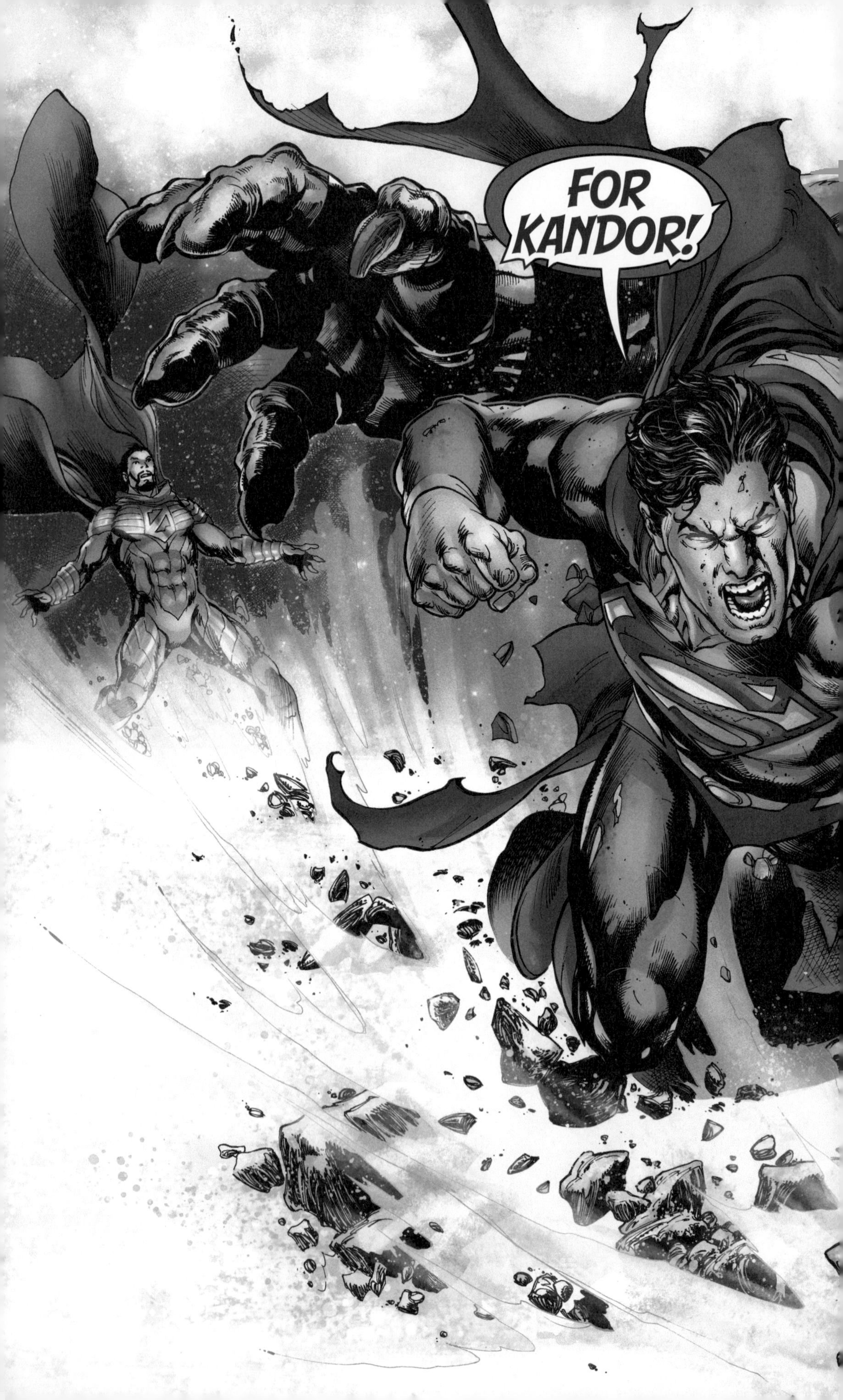
FOR KANDOR!

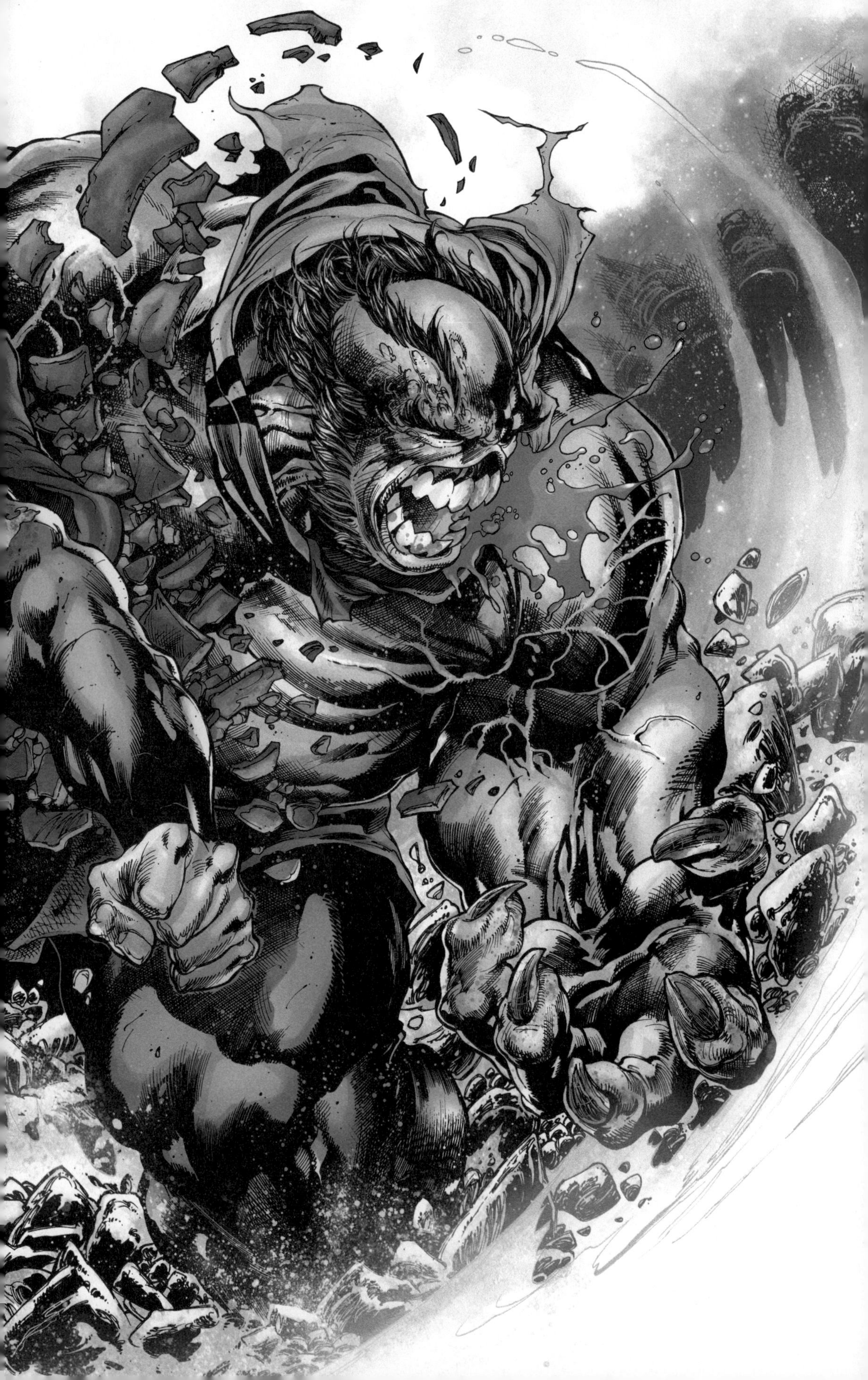

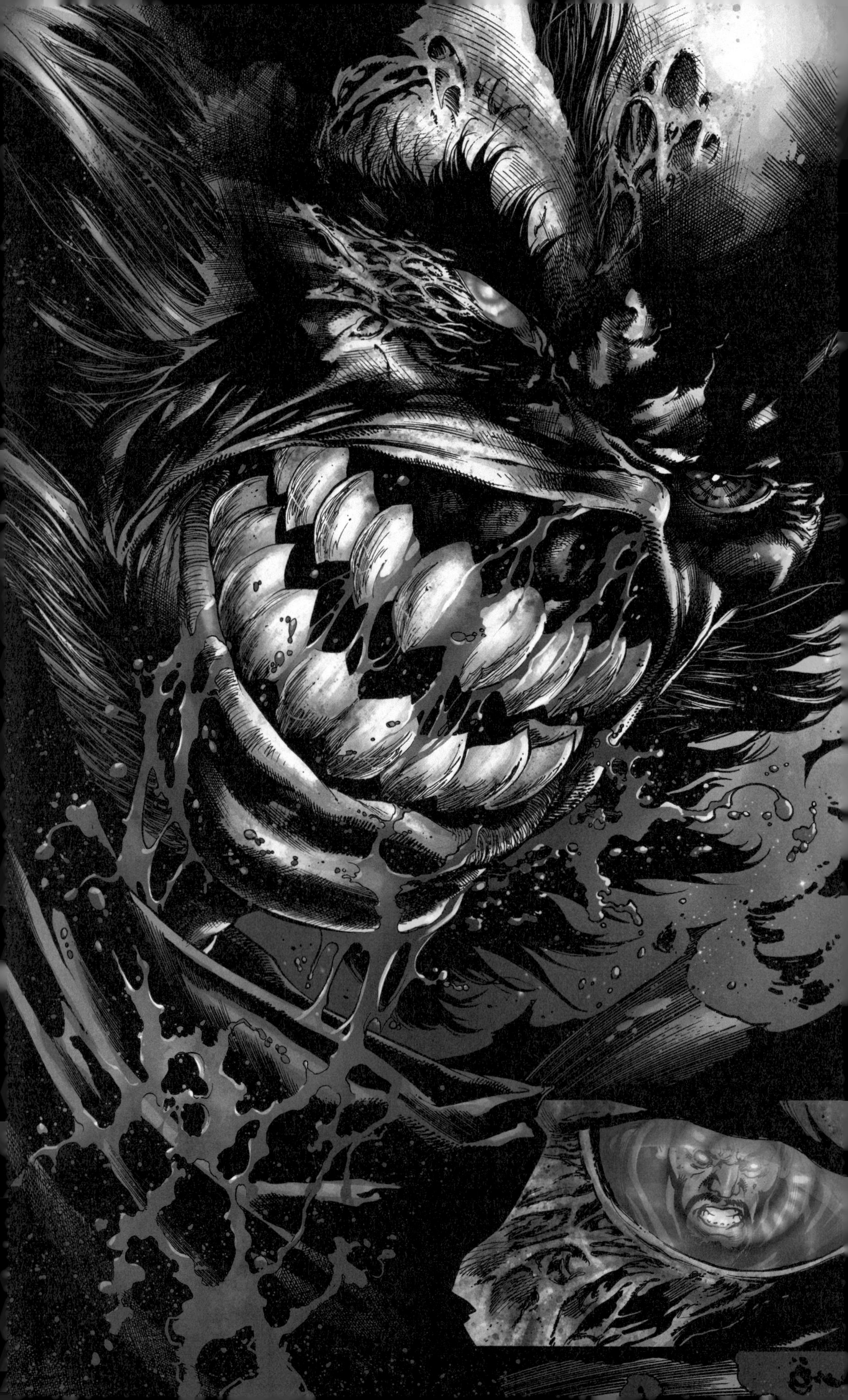

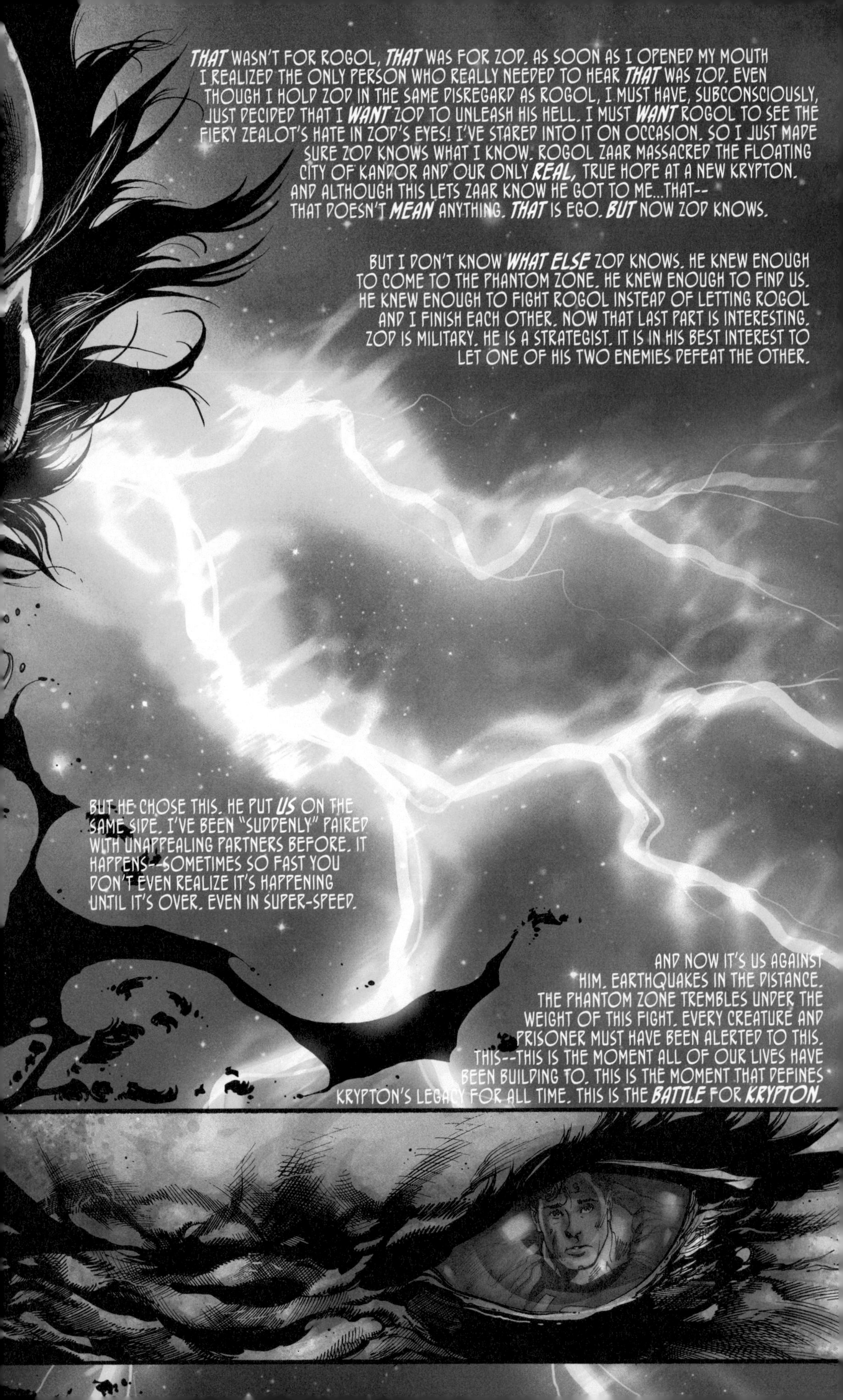
THAT WASN'T FOR ROGOL, THAT WAS FOR ZOD. AS SOON AS I OPENED MY MOUTH I REALIZED THE ONLY PERSON WHO REALLY NEEDED TO HEAR THAT WAS ZOD. EVEN THOUGH I HOLD ZOD IN THE SAME DISREGARD AS ROGOL, I MUST HAVE, SUBCONSCIOUSLY, JUST DECIDED THAT I WANT ZOD TO UNLEASH HIS HELL. I MUST WANT ROGOL TO SEE THE FIERY ZEALOT'S HATE IN ZOD'S EYES! I'VE STARED INTO IT ON OCCASION. SO I JUST MADE SURE ZOD KNOWS WHAT I KNOW. ROGOL ZAAR MASSACRED THE FLOATING CITY OF KANDOR AND OUR ONLY REAL, TRUE HOPE AT A NEW KRYPTON. AND ALTHOUGH THIS LETS ZAAR KNOW HE GOT TO ME...THAT-- THAT DOESN'T MEAN ANYTHING. THAT IS EGO. BUT NOW ZOD KNOWS.
BUT I DON'T KNOW WHAT ELSE ZOD KNOWS. HE KNEW ENOUGH TO COME TO THE PHANTOM ZONE. HE KNEW ENOUGH TO FIND US. HE KNEW ENOUGH TO FIGHT ROGOL INSTEAD OF LETTING ROGOL AND I FINISH EACH OTHER. NOW THAT LAST PART IS INTERESTING. ZOD IS MILITARY. HE IS A STRATEGIST. IT IS IN HIS BEST INTEREST TO LET ONE OF HIS TWO ENEMIES DEFEAT THE OTHER.
BUT HE CHOSE THIS. HE PUT US ON THE SAME SIDE. I'VE BEEN "SUDDENLY" PAIRED WITH UNAPPEALING PARTNERS BEFORE. IT HAPPENS--SOMETIMES SO FAST YOU DON'T EVEN REALIZE IT'S HAPPENING UNTIL IT'S OVER. EVEN IN SUPER-SPEED.
AND NOW IT'S US AGAINST HIM. EARTHQUAKES IN THE DISTANCE. THE PHANTOM ZONE TREMBLES UNDER THE WEIGHT OF THIS FIGHT. EVERY CREATURE AND PRISONER MUST HAVE BEEN ALERTED TO THIS. THIS--THIS IS THE MOMENT ALL OF OUR LIVES HAVE BEEN BUILDING TO. THIS IS THE MOMENT THAT DEFINES KRYPTON'S LEGACY FOR ALL TIME. THIS IS THE BATTLE FOR KRYPTON.

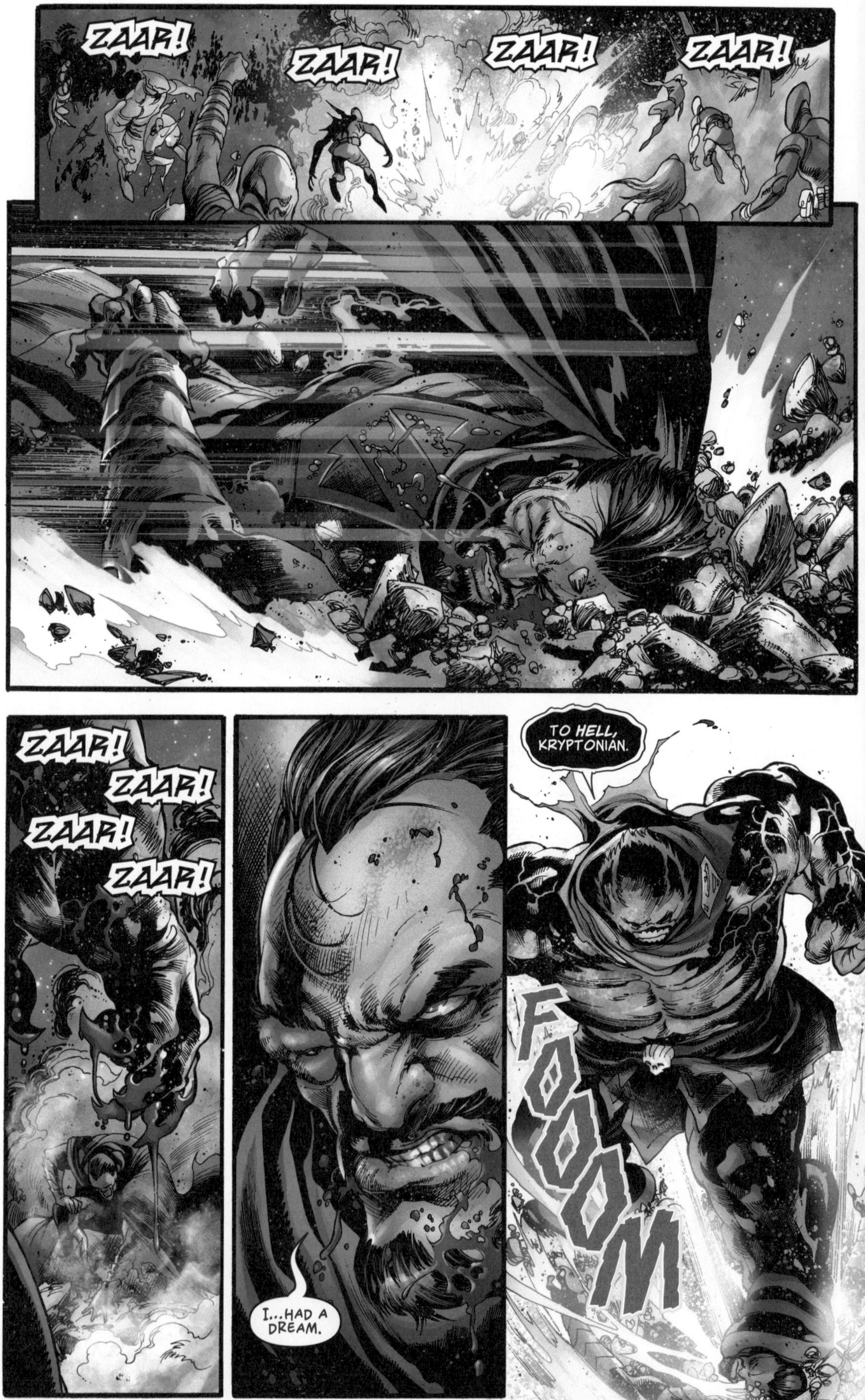
ZAAR!
ZAAR!
ZAAR!
ZAAR!
ZAAR!
ZAAR!
ZAAR!
ZAAR!
I...HAD A DREAM.
TO HELL, KRYPTONIAN.
FOOOM

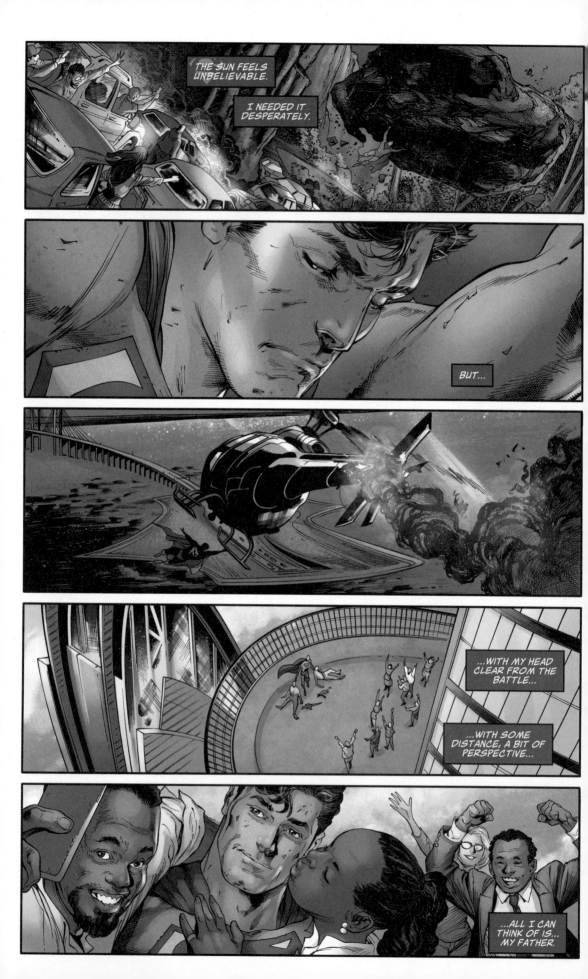

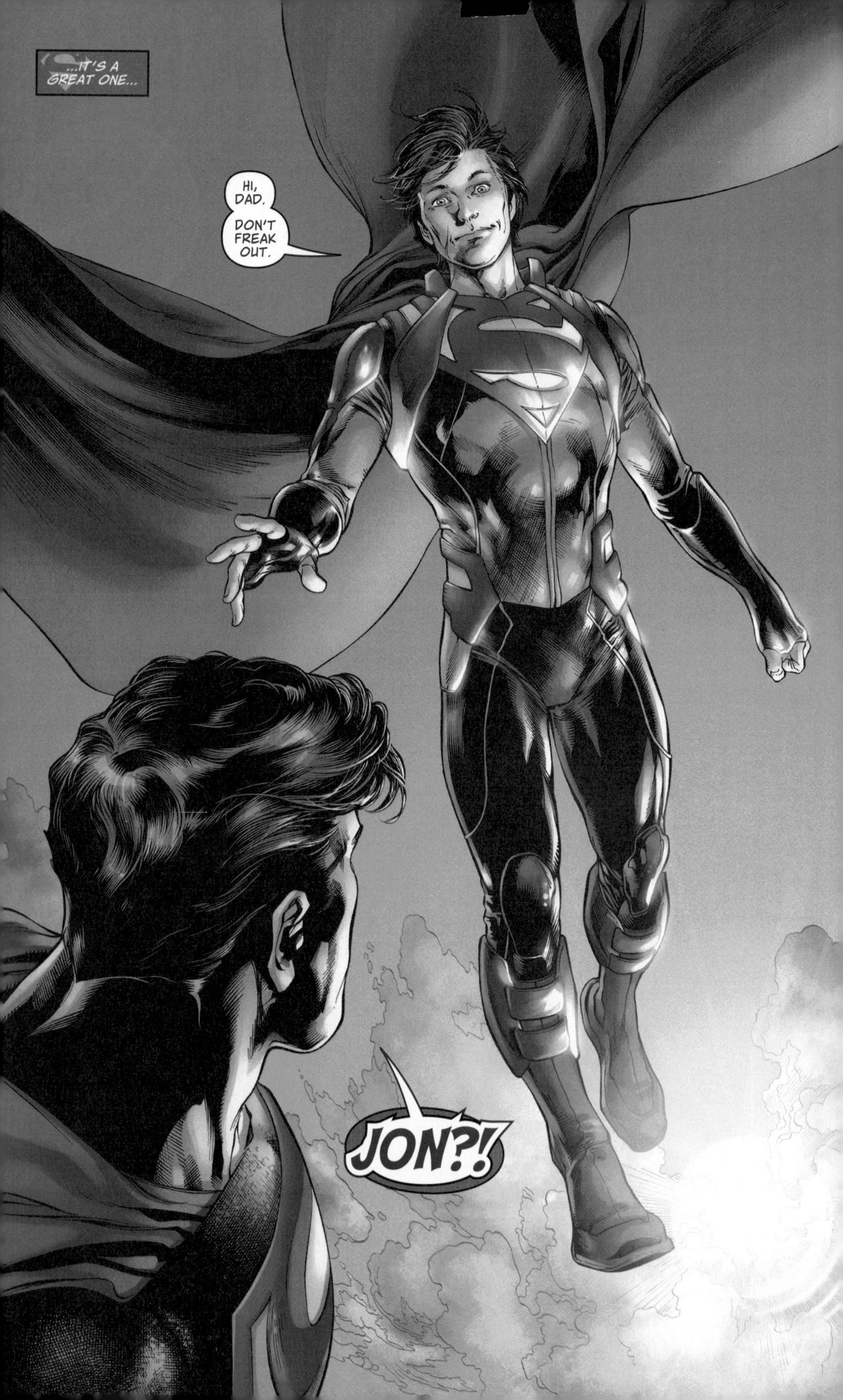
...IT'S A GREAT ONE...
HI, DAD.
DON'T FREAK OUT.
JON?!

VARIANT COVER GALLERY

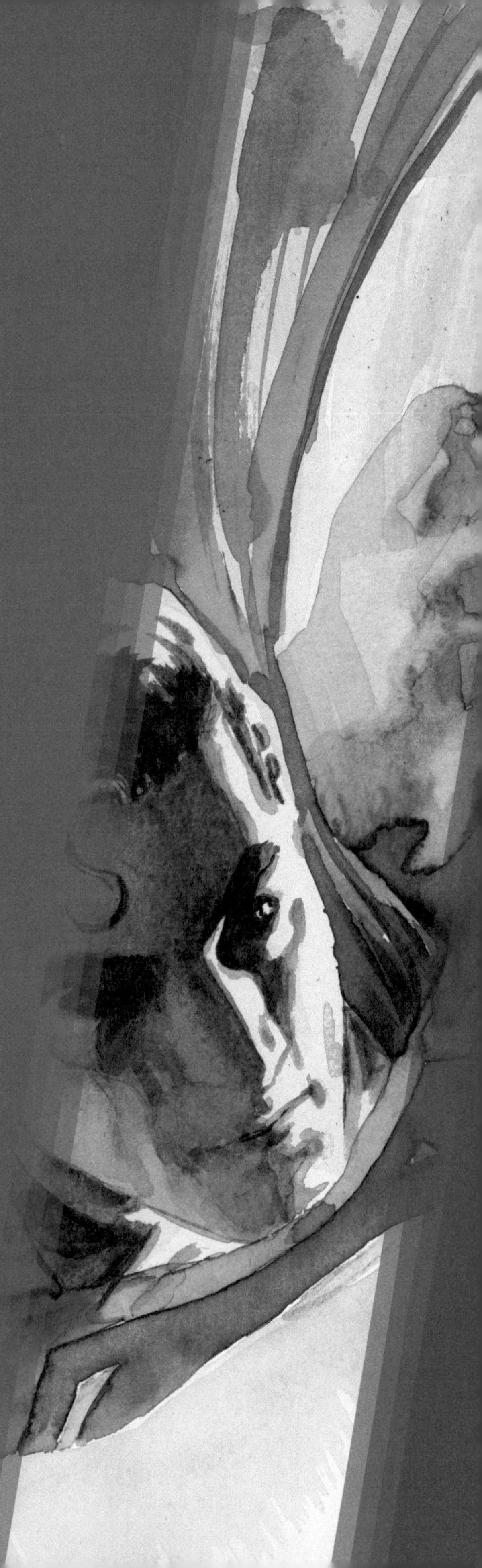

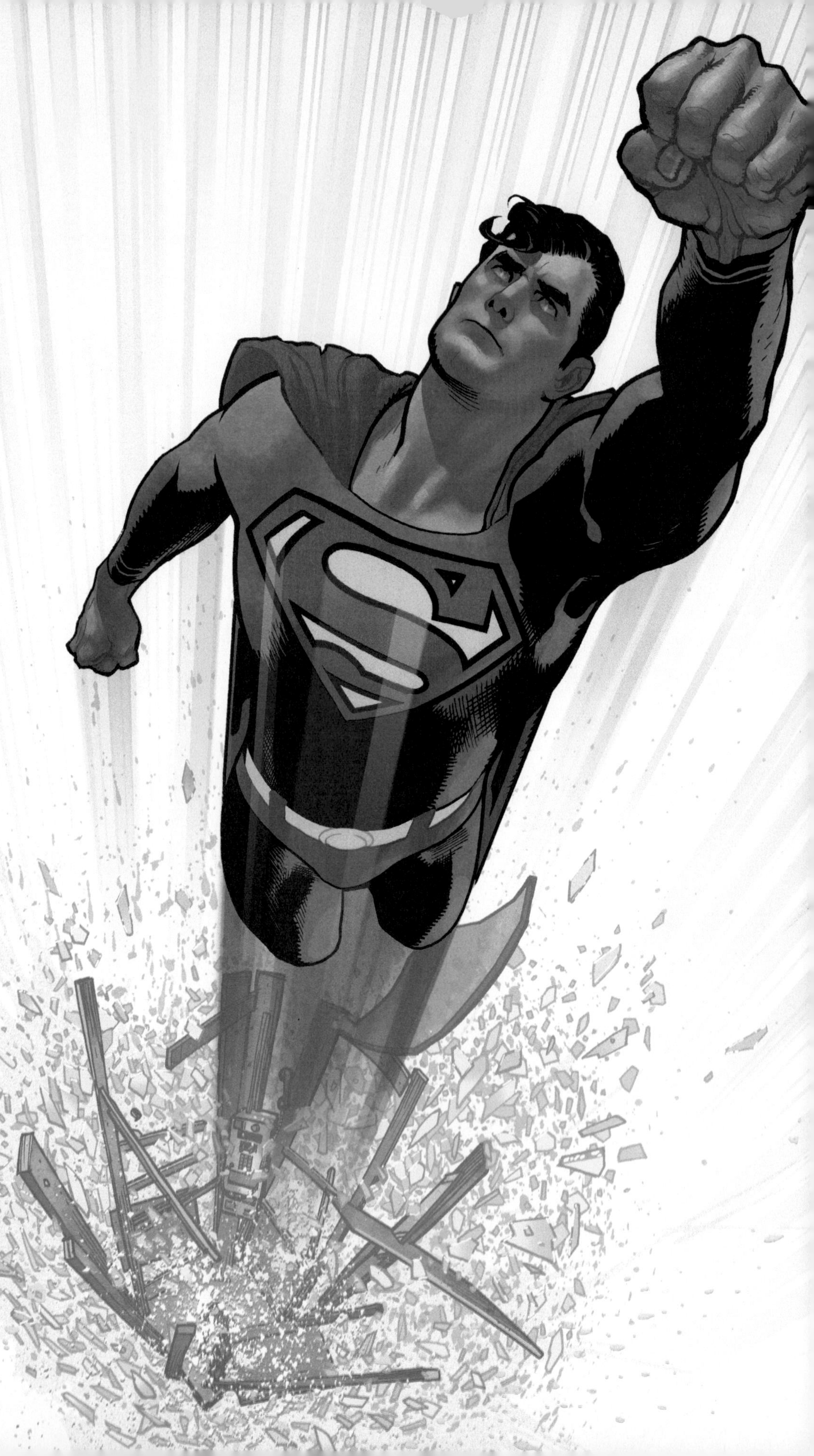

SUPERMAN #1 variant cover by ADAM HUGHES

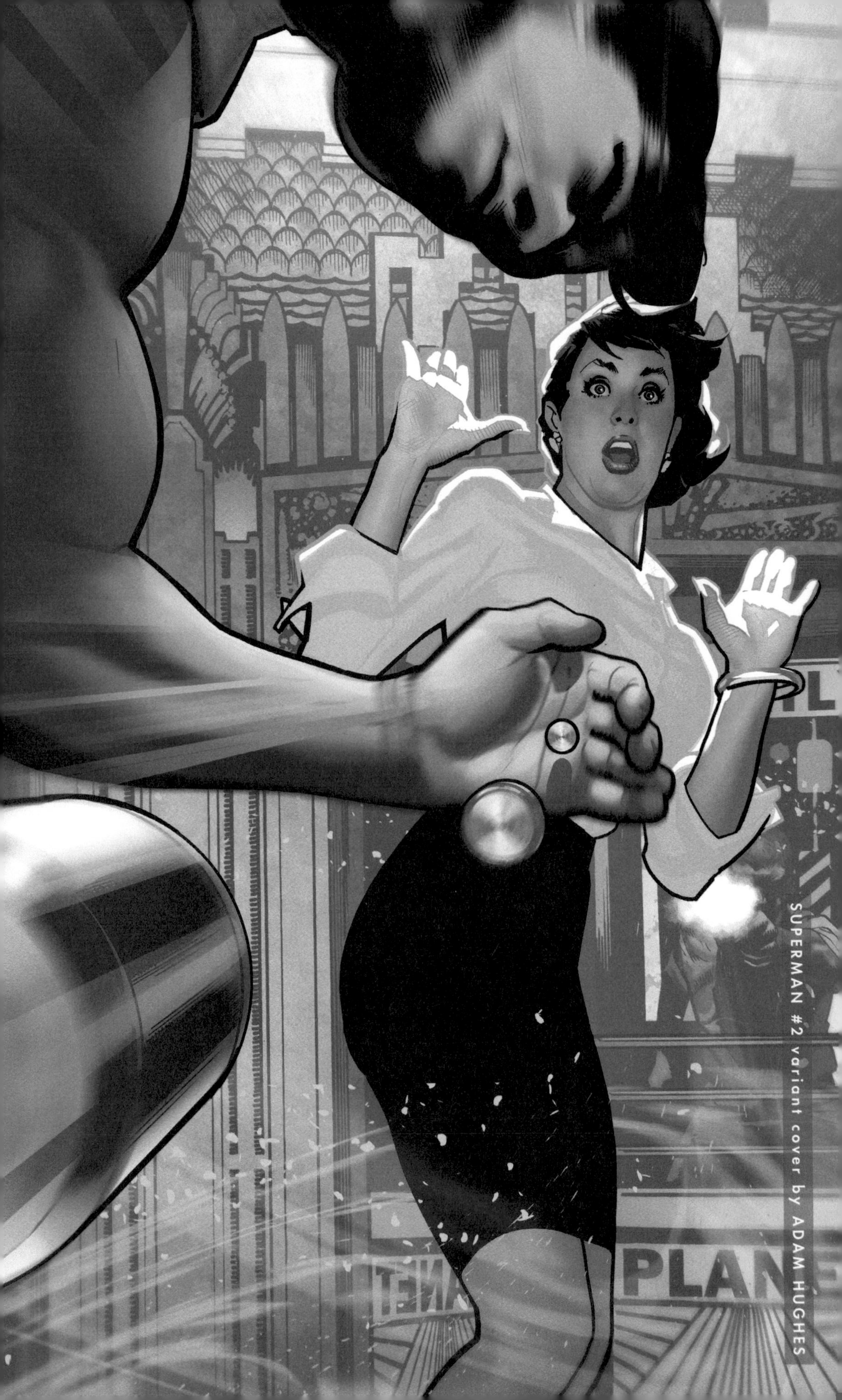

SUPERMAN #2 variant cover by ADAM HUGHES

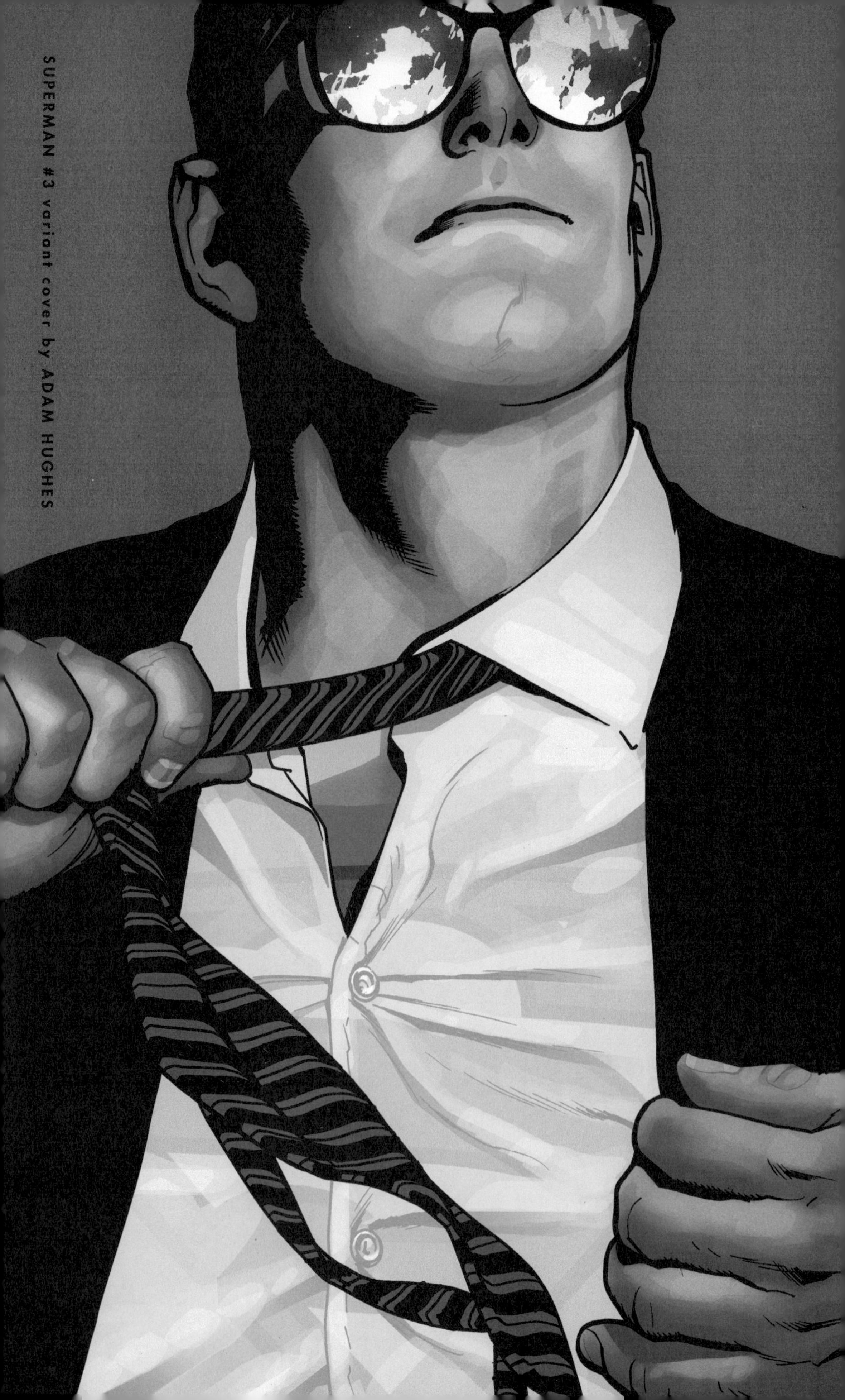

SUPERMAN #3 variant cover by ADAM HUGHES

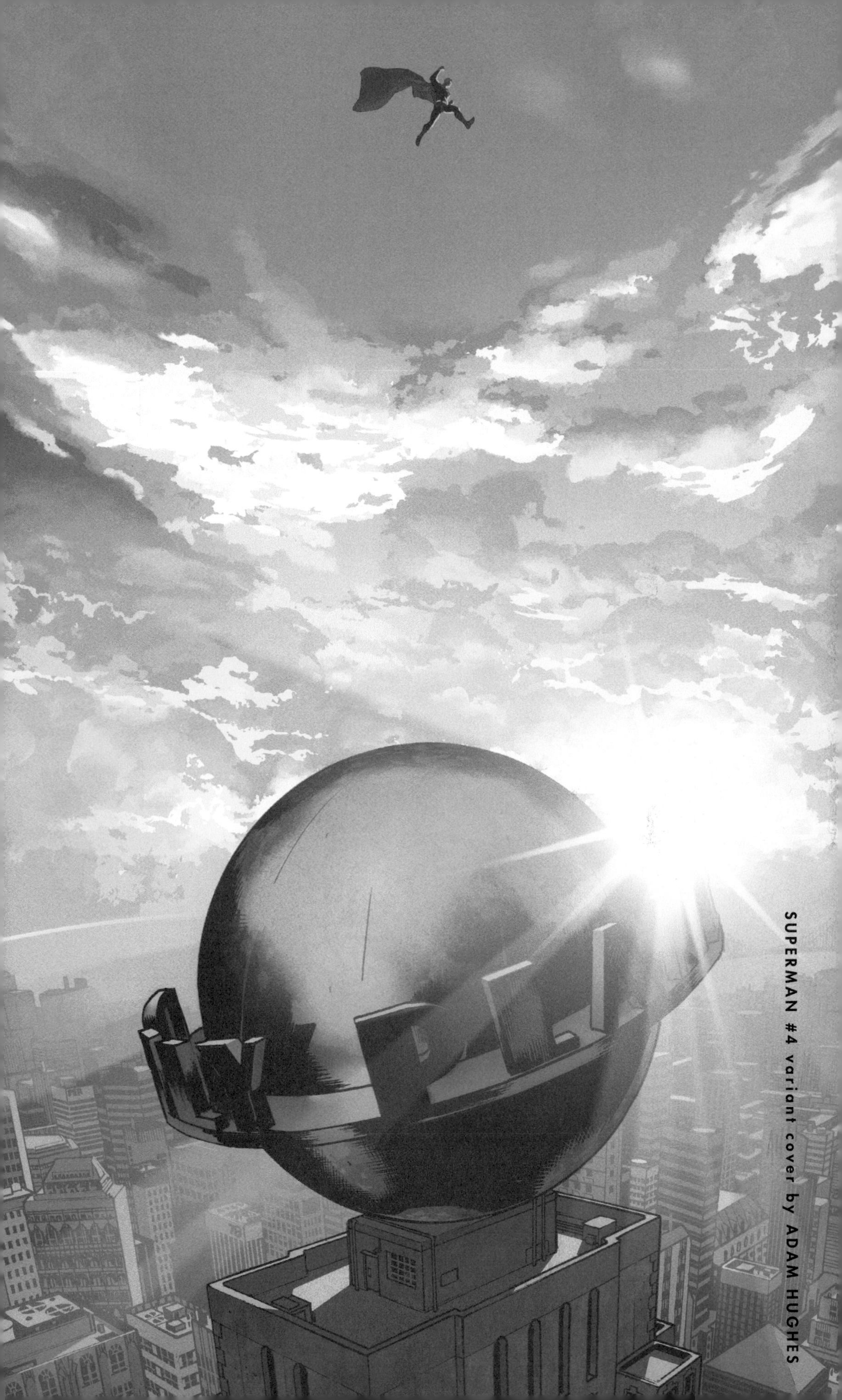

SUPERMAN #4 variant cover by ADAM HUGHES

SUPERMAN #5 *variant cover by* ADAM HUGHES

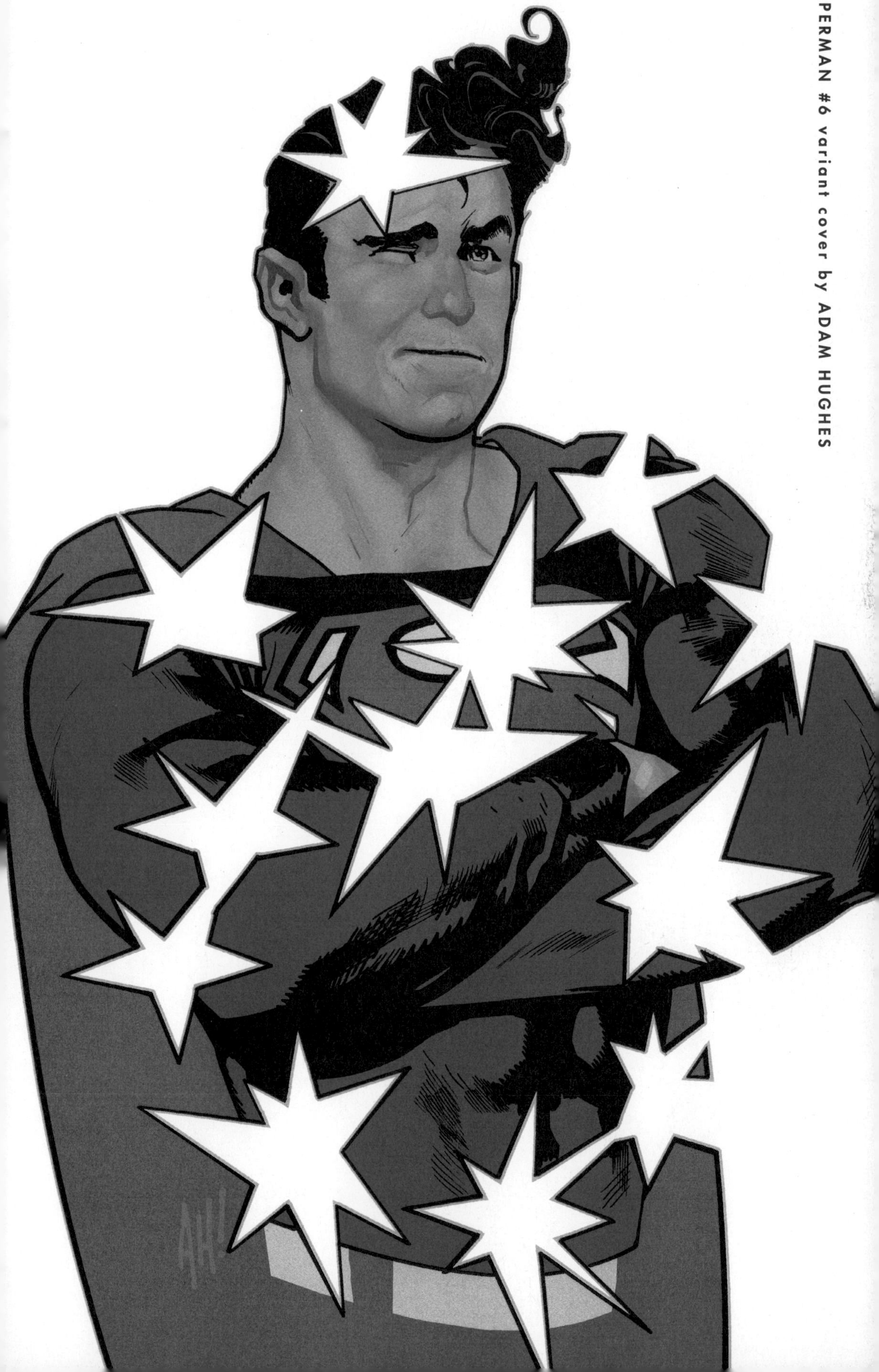

SUPERMAN #6 variant cover by ADAM HUGHES

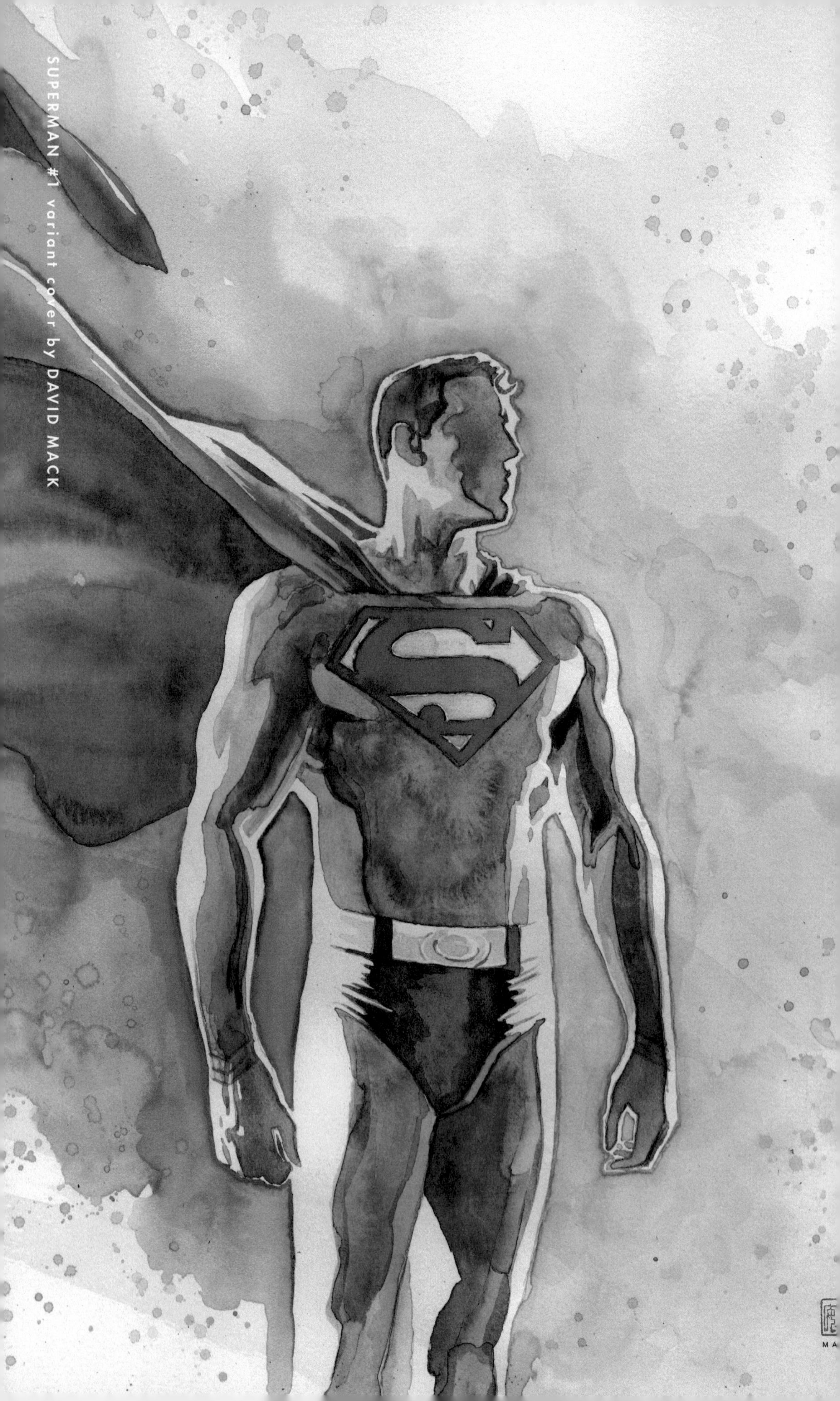

SUPERMAN #1 variant cover by DAVID MACK

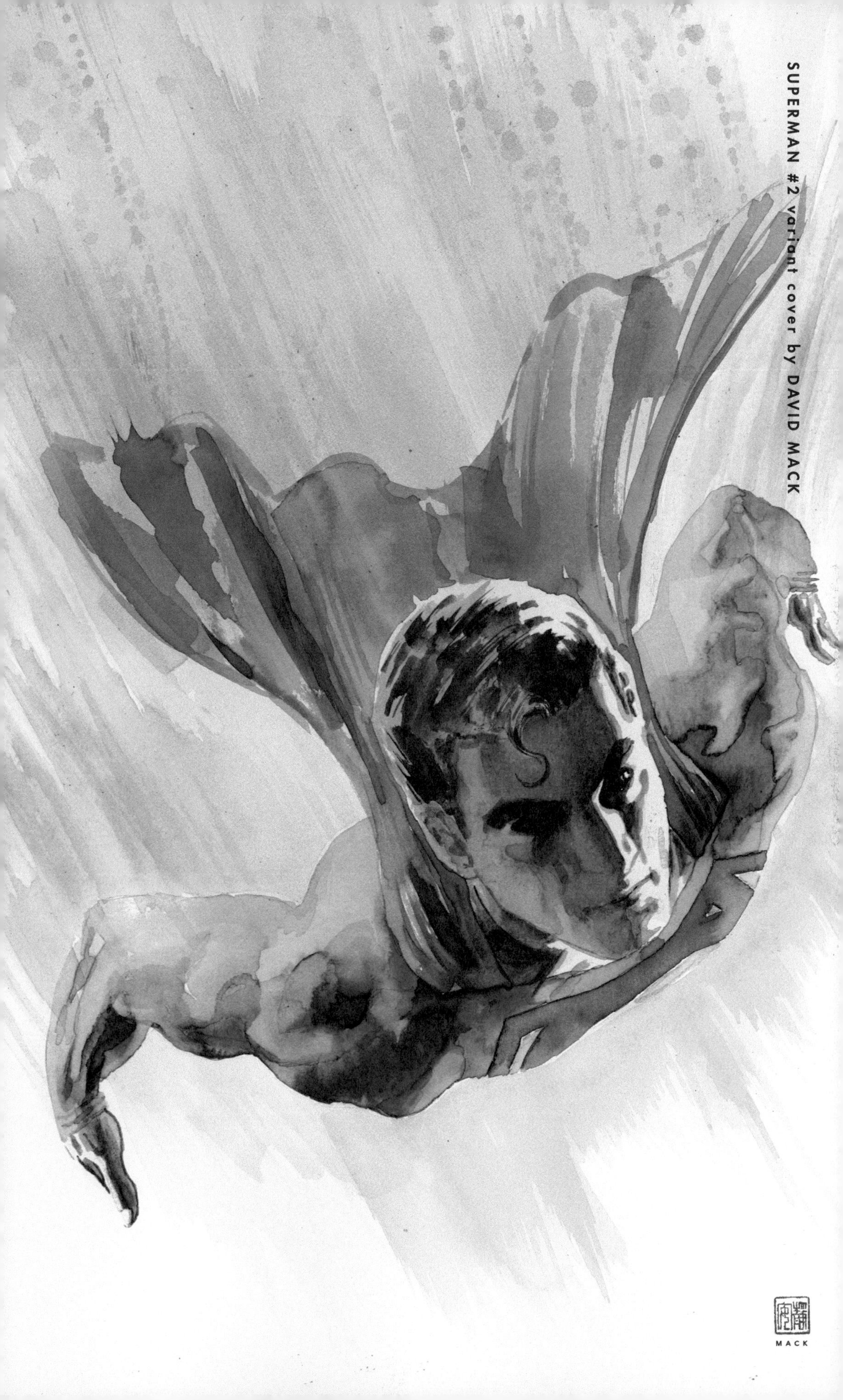
MACK

SUPERMAN #2 variant cover by DAVID MACK

SUPERMAN #3 variant cover by DAVID MACK

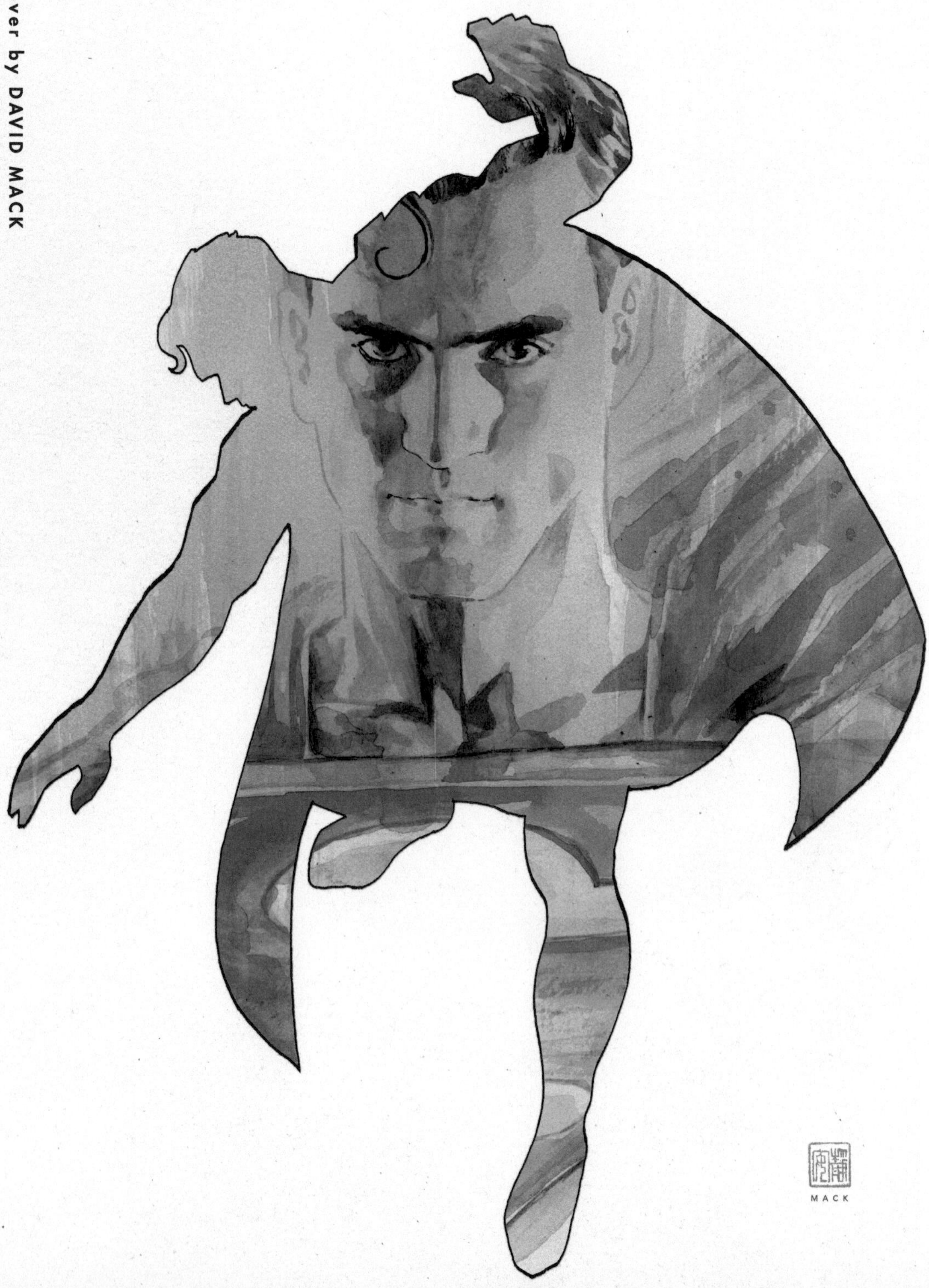
MACK

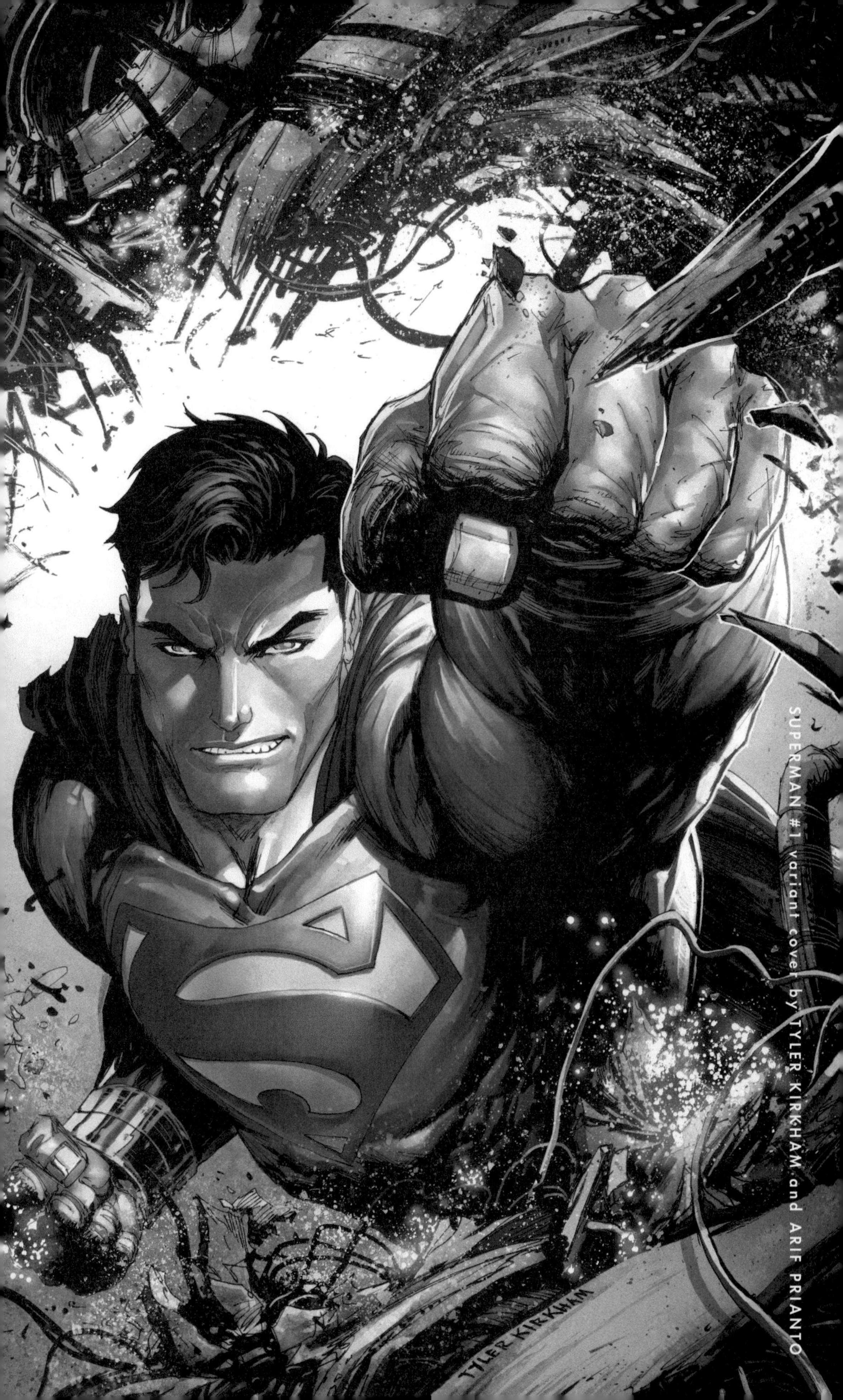
TYLER KIRKHAM
SUPERMAN #1 variant cover by TYLER KIRKHAM and ARIF PRIANTO

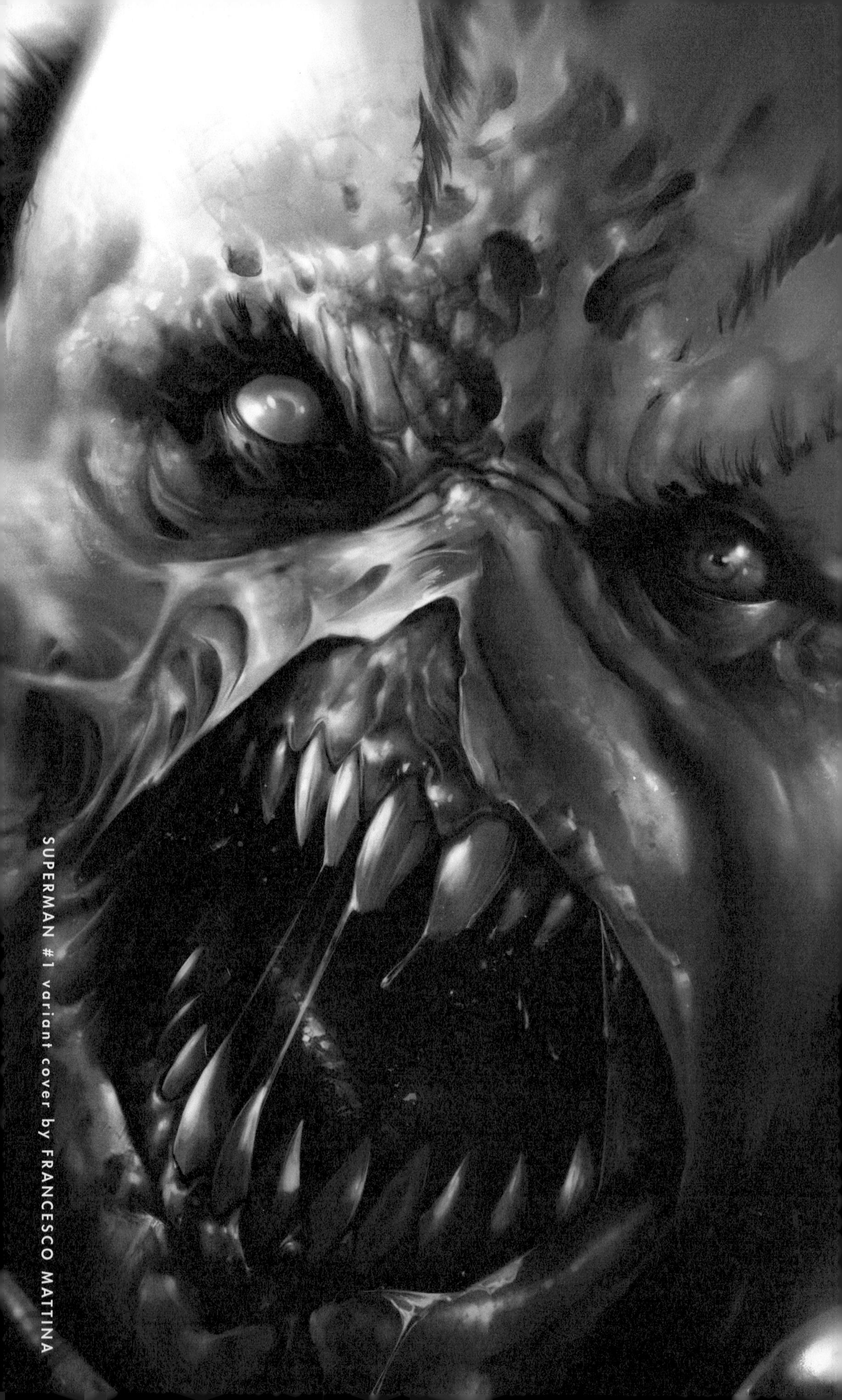

SUPERMAN #1 variant cover by FRANCESCO MATTINA

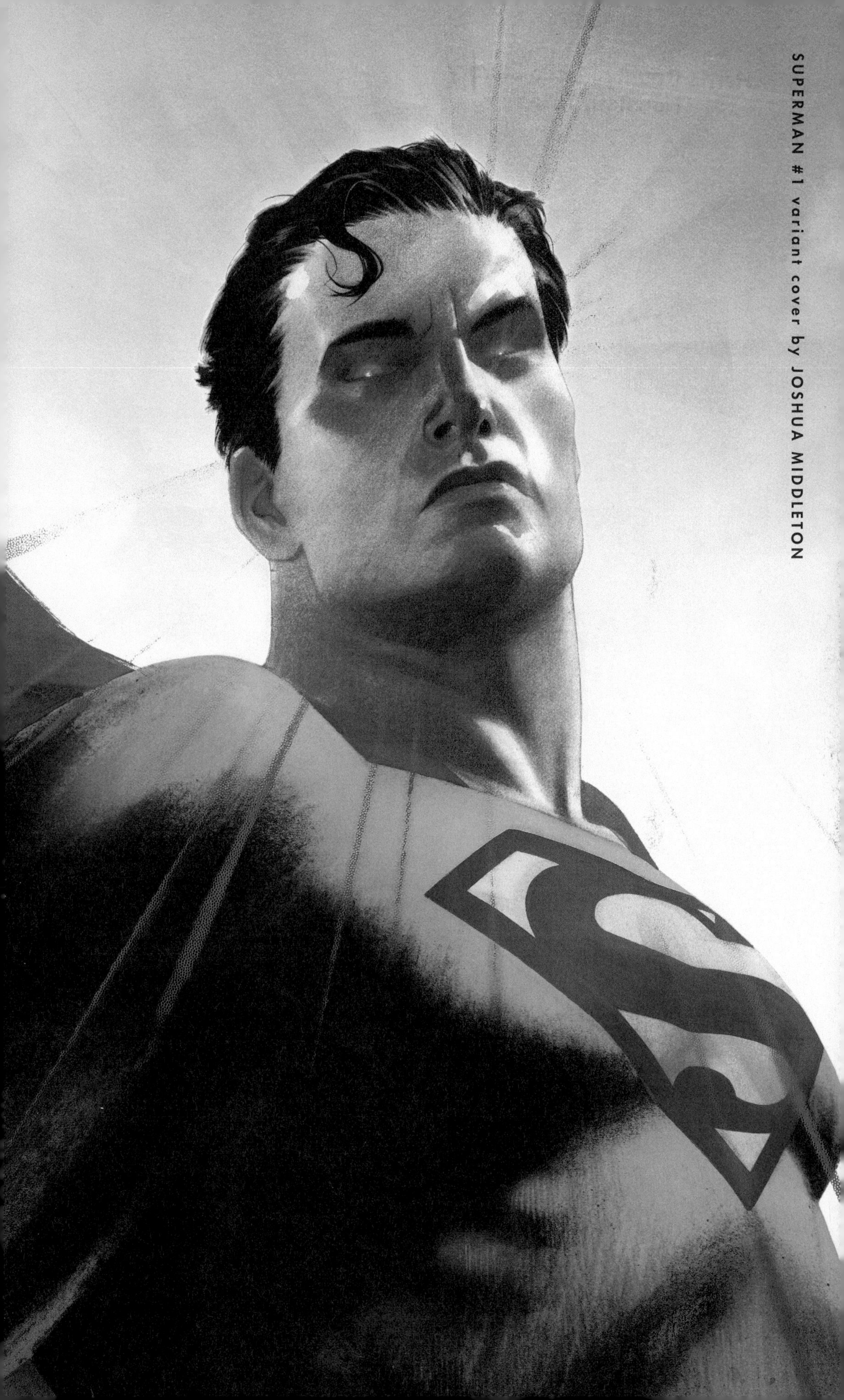

SUPERMAN #1 variant cover by JOSHUA MIDDLETON